The Age
of
Sex Crime

The Age
of
Sex Crime

Jane Caputi

Bowling Green State University Popular Press
Bowling Green, Ohio 43403

Contents

Preface

This book is a feminist analysis of the sexualized serial murder of women by men in modern Western society, a subject that is at once frightening and enraging. There is no sensationalism here; rather, my aim is to provide a political analysis and demythicization of this most extreme form of patriarchal violence.

This work is based upon my American Culture doctoral dissertation, completed at Bowling Green State University, Ohio, August 1982. Particularly helpful during that time were Professors Ray B. Browne, Michael T. Marsden, and Arthur Neal and I thank them. I also express my appreciation to William L. Schurk, Sound Recordings Archivist at the Bowling Green State University Music Library for his inspired assistance.

My research was immeasurably deepened by the interest and contributions of my friends Conée Ornelas, Geoffrey Lealand, Josephine Maplesden, Robbie Goff, Kathleen O'Neill, Steve Hesske, Eileen Barrett, Peggy Holland, and Marla Gibbs. All drew my attention to important materials during the course of this work. I also thank Peggy Holland for her reading of an early version of the manuscript. Above all, I thank Fran Chelland for her close and careful reading of the final draft. Her comments and support were invaluable.

I am also grateful to my friends Benjamin Shapiro, Judi Franzak, Helene Vann, Toria Price, and Barbara Loren for their much needed help during the final stages of proof reading.

Finally, I thank my editor, Ray B. Browne, for his sustained interest and encouragement, a support that was critical throughout the process of completing this book.

Introduction
Sex Crime Comes of Age

Margaret Atwood writes that when she asked a male friend why men felt threatened by women, he replied that, "They are afraid women will laugh at them." When she asked a group of women why women felt threatened by men, they said, "We're afraid of being killed."[1]

When is an act sexed? When do you kill, or die, as a member of your gender, and when as whoever else you are? Are you ever anyone else?

Catharine A. MacKinnon[2]

Most men just hate women. Ted Bundy killed them.

Jimmy McDonough[3]

Lust-murder, rape-murder, serial murder, recreational murder: these are new terms for a relatively new kind of crime. And accompanying these are new names or, more accurately, nicknames for a new kind of criminal. Names like Jack the Ripper, the Düsseldorf Ripper, the Blackout Ripper, Jack the Stripper, the Lipstick Killer, the Boston Strangler, Poland's Red Spider, the Michigan Murderer, the Cape Cod Killer, the Coed Killer, the Strangler of the Andes, the Mad Biter, the Son of Sam, the Hillside Strangler, the Yorkshire Ripper, the Stocking Strangler, the Trashbag Murderer, the Atlanta Child Killer, the Beauty Queen Killer, the Green River Killer, the Night Stalker, the Southside Killer. Why such colorful masks? Why such drama? And why the accelerating procession of such killers marked by territory and remembered by method?

Yet even these most sensational cases only just sight the borders of what law enforcement agencies have lately recognized as a new phenomenon—the rapidly increasing incidence of serial sex killings.* FBI statistics show serial murders to have increased drastically in the last twenty years. There were 644 such murders in 1966 and an estimated

---

*Most criminologists make a distinction between *mass murder* and *serial murder*: *mass murder* refers to a single crime in which a number of persons are killed (e.g. Richard Speck's murders of eight women in Chicago, 1966), while a *serial murder* refers to a number of killings by a single person over a period of months or even years. See Donald T. Lunde, *Murder and Madness* (Stanford, Ca.: Stanford Alumni Association, 1975), p. 47.

1

4,118 in 1982, comprising nearly eighteen per cent of all murders that year. In addition, the Justice Department estimates that there are at the very least thirty-five and possibly as many as one hundred such killers now roaming the country.[4] Justice Department official Robert O. Heck sums up the general situation:

We all talk about Jack the Ripper; he killed five people [sic]. We all talk about the "Boston Strangler" who killed 13, and maybe "Son of Sam," who killed six. But we've got people [sic] out there now killing 20 and 30 people and more, and some of them just don't kill. They torture their victims in terrible ways and mutilate them before they kill them. Something's going on out there. It's an epidemic.[5]

Although Heck's statement is superficially correct, his language works to obscure what actually *is* going on out there, for the "people" who torture, kill, and mutilate in this way are men while their victims are predominantly females—women and girls—and to a lesser extent younger males.[6]

As this hierarchy indicates, these are crimes of sexual/political— essentially *patriarchal*—domination.[7] Nevertheless, that political factor is everywhere erased in mainstream discussion and analysis of serial murder. Law enforcement officials and much of the mass media instead usually refer to this phenomenon as "motiveless crime," as an inexplicable epidemic of "recreational murder," the work of a mysterious new breed of "sexual psychopaths." Consider, for example, the *Albuquerque Tribune's* studied bewilderment over the motivations of Christopher Wilder, sadistic killer of a still unknown number of young women during the summer of 1984:

Wilder's death leaves behind a mystery as to the motives behind the rampage of death and terror. With plenty of money, soft-spoken charm, a background in photography, and a part-time career on the glamorous sports car racing circuit, Wilder, 39, would have had no trouble attracting beautiful women.[8]

It is imperative to remember that this man not only murdered women, but first extensively tortured them. Although the FBI refuses to release all the details of that abuse (fearing that these would spur "copycat attacks"),[9] it was revealed that Wilder had bound, raped, repeatedly stabbed his victims, and tortured them with electric shocks. One woman (who survived the attack) had even had her eyelids glued shut. Obviously, Wilder did not wish to date, "charm," or "attract" women; his desire was to destroy. It is only by seeing through this miasma of man-made mystery[10] that we can grasp and name this phenomenon of "sexual murder" as sexually political murder, as functional phallic terrorism.

That recognition, however, is impeded by longstanding tradition for, as Kate Millett has noted:

We are not accustomed to associate patriarchy with force. So perfect is its system of socialization, so complete the general assent to its values, so long and so universally has it prevailed in human society, that it scarcely seems to require violent implementation....And yet...control in patriarchal society would be imperfect, even inoperable, unless it had the rule of force to rely upon, both in emergencies and as an ever-present instrument of intimidation."[11]

Feminist analysts such as Susan Griffin, Andrea Dworkin, Diana Russell, and Susan Brownmiller have demonstrated that what is perhaps the most paradigmatic expression of such patriarchal force—rape—is not, as the common mythology insists, a crime of desire, passion, frustrated attraction, victim provocation or uncontrollable biological urges. Nor is it one perpetrated only by an aberrant fringe. Rather, rape is a social expression of sexual politics, an institutionalized and ritual enactment of male domination, a form of terror which functions to maintain the same quo.[12]

Likewise, serial sexual murder is not some inexplicable explosion/ epidemic of an extrinsic evil or the domain only of the mysterious psychopath. On the contrary, such murder is an eminently logical step in the procession of patriarchal roles, values, needs, and rule of force. It enacts a primary principle of male supremacy and can be recognized as one of the latest expressions in a tradition of what Mary Daly first named as *gynocide*.[13] As further defined by Andrea Dworkin, gynocide is "the systematic crippling, raping, and/or killing of women by men...the relentless violence perpetrated by the gender class men on the gender class women." She adds that "under patriarchy, gynocide is the ongoing reality of life lived by women."[14]

Extensive studies of many forms of patriarchal force—harassment, incest, rape, battering, etc.—have been completed by others[15] and I will not attempt to cover that same ground here, but will concentrate on male torturing and killing of women at random. Thus, I will not specifically address the fact that forty per cent of all women murdered in this country are killed by their sexual partners—husbands and boyfriends.[16] I will also be unable to approach the full implications of the phenomenon of male sexual killings of young men. Nor will I attempt to offer a comprehensive history of the current incidence of sexual murder. Rather, my perspective and purpose here will be to examine the genre of modern serial sexual murder, not only as a manifestation of gynocide, but as a mythic/ritualistic act in contemporary patriarchy. Therefore, my focus will be upon those most sensationalized killers and their atrocities—the archetypal actors and acts in the Age of Sex Crime.

Just as the inception of another age—the Nuclear Age—was signalled instantly by the Trinity explosion in the New Mexico desert, July 1945, the Age of Sex Crime was first blasted into being in London, 1888, with the unprecedented crimes of Jack the Ripper. That still anonymous killer essentially invented modern sex crime. We might think of him as its "father."

Father to an Age

As a mythmaker, Jack the Ripper has shown himself to be without rival among criminals, from the standpoint of both the number and the potency of the myths he has evoked.

Tom Cullen[17]

Myths tell how, through the deeds of Supernatural Beings, a reality came into existence, be it the whole of reality...a particular kind of human behavior, an institution.

Mircea Eliade[18]

It...remains fundamentally true to say that Jack the Ripper inaugurated the age of sex crime.

Colin Wilson[19]

Historians have largely concurred that the crimes of Jack the Ripper were without precedent[20] and writer Colin Wilson has gone so far as to claim that this episode ushered in a new era of sexual violation, an "age of sex crime." Of course, long before Jack the Ripper, occurrences of sexual mutilation and atrocity were explicit in other forms. There are, for example, the histories (and legends) of Caligula, Gilles de Rais (the original "Bluebeard"), Vlad the Impaler (the prototype for Dracula), and others.[21] Another tradition of "sex crime" can be traced among the intricacies of the christian/occult world view that prevailed in medieval and early modern Europe. Throughout that era, notions of "sex crime" were thoroughly bound up with beliefs about god and nature, witches and devils, werewolves and vampires, sexuality and sin.[22] And certainly, the history of war reveals a consistent tradition of mass rape, murder, and mutilation.[23] Some of these aspects will be amplified in later chapters. The principal point here is that by the late nineteenth and throughout the twentieth centuries, such practices are no longer the actual or legendary provinces of either maniacal aristocrats or the supernaturally/ diabolically monstrous; nor can they be associated principally with periods of war and crisis. Rather, the rippers, stranglers, mutilators and other sex killers have become explicitly common criminals perpetrating an increasingly common crime.

One group of nineteenth century criminals did directly anticipate the modern sexual murderer. In their history of sex crime, R. E. L. Masters and Eduard Lea write that a large number of criminals, termed "rippers" and "stabbers" by the press, plagued European women throughout the

19th century. Such men did not attempt to kill their victims, but endeavored to stab them in the genitals, breast, and buttocks as they walked through the streets. By the end of the century, these ripper types had become lethal. Masters and Lea claim a veritable "infestation" of such killers between the years 1885 and 1895, including London's Jack the Ripper, Vacher, the "French Ripper," a Moscow Ripper in 1885, a Texas ripper who killed and mutilated a number of Black prostitutes in 1887, and a Nicaraguan ripper in 1889.[24] Also, by the close of the century, Krafft-Ebing had begun to track and classify the "sexual pervert." His *Psychopathia Sexualis* (1885) included a section of sadistic crimes and "lust murders," several of which clearly anticipated the dismemberment and mutilation which were to become the trademark of Jack the Ripper.[25] Still, it was not until 1888 in London that this new type of crime entered and transformed mass cultural consciousness.

The crimes of the Ripper occurred in the Whitechapel district of London, one of the worst slums in the city and an area well-known for prostitution. The unknown killer has been credited with as many as twenty murders, although probably only five were the work of the one man; others were imitative or unconnected crimes. The killer made no attempt to cover up his actions. Rather, he left the bodies on display, out on the open street in four instances. Furthermore, he (or someone pretending to be the killer) advertised his crimes by writing letters to police, press, and citizen groups, nicknaming himself in one letter, taunting the police, predicting future crimes, and even mailing in half of a human kidney to the head of a Whitechapel vigilance group (he claimed to have eaten the other half). Although many assume that these killings involved rape, that is not so. The victims were first murdered (their throats were slit from behind) and then the sexual and other organs were severely mutilated.

Historian Judith Walkowitz has noted that, "Unable to find historical precedents for the Whitechapel 'horrors,' commentators resorted to horrifying fictional analogues."[26] Here are the beginnings of the Ripper mythos—the sex killer as immortal monster, master criminal, even subliminal hero. Subsequently, that mythic figure of Jack the Ripper has emerged as a new gynocidal archetype. Succeeding sex killers are not only incessantly compared and even identified with Jack the Ripper, but, now as then, fictional constructs are superimposed upon the events of modern serial murder. Moreover, the pattern laid down during that original siege now functions as a conventionally repeated formula. Its characteristic ingredients include: the single, territorial killer; socially powerless and scapegoated victims; some stereotypic feature ascribed in common to the victims (e.g. all coeds, redheads, prostitutes, etc.); a "signature" style of murder or mutilation; intense media involvement, usually generating a local sense of siege; a complete identification of mutilation, violence, and murder with "sex"; and an accompanying incidence of imitation or "copycat" killings.

That formula has inspired, structured, and been used to structure the careers of numerous sex killers since Jack the Ripper. It is easily revealed, for example, in the cases of the "Boston Strangler," "Coed Killer," "Son of Sam," "Hillside Strangler," "Yorkshire Ripper," "Ted Murderer," and "Green River Killer." So compelling is that mythic formula that perception of the events are frequently ordered to fit into that structure, even when the facts are clearly in contradiction.* Such archetypal patterning bespeaks the mythic force and ritual function of serial sexual murder in contemporary patriarchy.

Ritual Murder

[Jack the Ripper] sought to make these murders as public as possible. Far from trying to cover up his deeds, he signposted them, hung red flags around them, so to speak. Here, if ever, was murder that advertised, that shouted from the rooftops. But what was the Ripper trying to say?

Tom Cullen[27]

Since the crimes of Jack the Ripper in 1888, sexual murder has emerged as a mythicized criminal genre and, concomitantly, as a ritual of male sexual dominance. This ritual hammers home its meaning through the most dire physical symbolism—the displayed, frequently tortured, mutilated, and murdered female body—an image which haunts this culture and this Age.

Contemporary sex crime is obviously ritualistic in its stereotyping of the victims, its structural continuations, signature styles and fetishes, and, most clearly, in its repetitions. Emile Durkheim held that rituals were "symbolic representations of social relationships."[28] Subsequent theorists, including Ruth Benedict, Edmund Leach, Claude Lévi-Strauss and others, have concurred and also stressed the communicative character of ritual. J.S. LaFontaine writes, "ritual expresses cultural values; it 'says' something and therefore has meaning as part of a non-verbal system of communication."[29]

The sexual murder, the actual mutilation and display of a dead female body, is a ritual that manifestly says a great deal about

---

*For example, police and press knew from the beginning that there were *two* men involved in the 1977-78 rape-murder series in Los Angeles; nevertheless, the nightmare figure presented to the terrorized public was that of the mysterious and singular "Hillside Strangler." More seriously, the predominance of the Ripper myth clearly jammed the police investigation of the "Yorkshire Ripper" case, allowing that killer to escape detection for several years (see Chapter Two).

contemporary sexual ideology and relations (something akin to what lynching says about race relations in this country).[30] When such sexual atrocities occur during war, it is somewhat easier to recognize their symbolic, ritualistic, and communicative character. Consider this account taken from the testimony of a Vietnam veteran concerning war crimes he witnessed and participated in in Vietnam. A squad of men have just beaten and shot a woman to death. One of them, a representative of USAID, approaches her body:

He went over there, ripped her clothes off, and took a knife and cut from her vagina almost all the way up, just about to her breast and pulled her organs out, completely out of her cavity, and threw them out. Then he stooped and knelt over and commenced to peel every bit of skin off her body and *left her there as a sign for something or other.*[31] (emphasis mine)

Such an action is indistinguishable from the crimes of Jack the Ripper, but in one case it was the trademark of the most notorious criminal of the modern era while in the other it was the more or less typical action of a man of war.[32] Both cases function equally as "signs"; both are meant to signify the same thing—the utter vanquishment and annihilation of the enemy.

Parallel actions are continually performed as part of the standard repertoire of sexual murder. Compare the war crime with the peacetime sex crime:

On August 29, 1975, the nude mutilated body of a 25-year-old mother of two was found near Columbia, S.C. Both breasts had been removed, the reproductive system had been displaced, numerous cuts and stab wounds were evidenced by the body, and there was evidence of anthropophagy.[33]

Such overt and extensive mutilation is not, however, the only means used to convey the message of female annihilation. Albert DeSalvo, the "Boston Strangler," decorated and posed the bodies of his victims in what has been described as a parody of the gynecological exam. The victims of the "Hillside Strangler" were characteristically dumped on the hills surrounding Los Angeles. One reporter described his reaction upon encountering the body of one of these victims:

She was completely nude and she was sprawled out on the grass almost as if she were about to engage in an act of sex with a man. The knees were up in the air, her legs were spread apart, the hands were at about a forty-five degree angle from her sides, almost in a position of supplication.[34]

Los Angeles artist Suzanne Lacy has written insightfully on the experience of a city under siege by a Ripper-type criminal. As she reports, media stories typically weld the facts to traditional fictional conventions in order to fix the story into the mind of the public, satisfy audience expectations, and communicate ideologies. One such method includes the repetition of familiar concepts and images:

> Variations on a constantly repeated verbal description, "the nude spread-eagled body of a woman was found strangled today on the side of a hill" became the icon, the major image, around which the drama progressed.[35]

This fixed iconography—"the nude spread-eagled body of a woman"— recurs in many cases of contemporary sex crime and, like overt mutilation, functions to communicate female defeat, degradation, and destruction. The original "spread eagle"—the figure of an eagle with wings and legs spread—is, of course, the emblem on the Great Seal of the United States. *Webster's Unabridged* reports that as a verb *spread eagle* means "defeat completely." The *American Heritage* dictionary adds, "to place in a spread-eagle position, esp. as a means of punishment." Just as the icon of the derogated eagle on the Seal of the United States bespeaks this nation's rape of the wilderness, so too does the endemic spread-eagling of women in patriarchal culture—in sexual murder, pornography, gynecology, and obligatory "missionary position" intercourse—point to the persistent and systematic punishment of women.

In an essay on "The Effectiveness of Symbols," Claude Lévi-Strauss cites the work of psychotherapist M.A. Sechahaye who, "aware that speech no matter how symbolic it might be, still could not penetrate beyond the conscious," realized that "she could reach deeply buried complexes only through acts." Thus, she communicated with her patients through symbolic actions, gestures which Lévi-Strauss termed "genuine rites which penetrate the screen of consciousness to carry their message directly to the unconscious."[36] The so-called "unspeakable acts" of the sex criminal are in this sense genuine rites, symbolically loaded actions which communicate their meanings directly into the unconscious of both women and men within this culture. In this case, however, symbolic expression is needed not so much to reach "deeply buried complexes," as to preserve and further embed deeply buried *truths*, i.e. the loathing for women which riddles patriarchal culture, the reality of the ongoing warfare waged by that culture against women in order to continually enforce male dominance. Although masked as a joke or throw-away phrase, that "war between the sexes" (actually systematic male aggression against women) is traceable throughout patriarchal myth, as evidenced in legends of the defeat of Amazon tribes, ritual rapings of ancient Goddesses by newly arrived gods, and in worldwide traditions of male heroes slaying dragons, serpents, and sea monsters.[37]

Most glaring of all is the content of numerous "creation" myths which, from a female perspective, would more accurately be named *destruction* epics. Scholars such as Adolphe Jensen and René Girard have pointed to the coincidence of violence and creation in the originating myths of numerous world cultures.[38] In many such stories, the act of "creation" literally entails a sexual murder as a male god slays and dismembers a primordial female in order that *he* might refashion the cosmos and claim himself as its creator.[39] Noting the ubiquity of such themes, Charles Doria summarizes:

The oldest known versions of this creation story embody the sea as a whale/serpent/fish woman locked in combat/making love with a god of light/sperm, being defeated/ impregnated, cut open/giving birth, to the various orders of the universe.[40]

Here, the archetypal "battle of the sexes" is outlined: "making love" and making war fuse and become identical. Here, too, through an initial act of sexual murder and mutilation/deformation, the male god purportedly gives form to the world.

It is crucial to remember, however, that these "creation" myths are not about the origins of the world at all, but about the origins of patriarchy which has, nonetheless, claimed itself as the world. And myths such as these do not remain mere fixed spectacles in the past, but travel through time, adapting in form and style. Their function is to stitch together the seams of the prevailing reality, bestowing legitimation and credibility upon that order, continually constructing and maintaining that order. Thus, in the patriarchy, myths of male superiority and victory over the female are continuously, if variously, retold, participated in, and internalized.[41] Moreover, new rituals are generated when needed in order to ensure that these myths may be regularly reenacted. As Mary Daly has argued, it is precisely these archetypal myths of female destruction and mutilation that provide legitimation and continuing commandment for such "sado-rituals" as Indian suttee, Chinese footbinding, the burning of witches in the European Witchcraze, African genital mutilation, and many common practices of American gynecology.[42] Serial sex murder, then, is one of the most recent installments in this tradition of sado-ritual, of reenacted Goddess murder.

Thus based in sacred phallic mythos, gynocidal actions themselves, however consciously or unconsciously, are understood as "godlike," ordained, and utterly compelling. As Mircea Eliade has written, a principal function of divine myth is to provide a model for imitative action—actions which take shape in cultural rites. He notes:

One becomes truly a man only by conforming to the teaching of the myths, that is, by imitating the gods....in illo tempore the god had slain the marine monster and dismembered its body in order to create the cosmos. Man repeats this blood sacrifice— sometimes even with human victims.[43]

Jack the Ripper, in ritual emulation of the patriarchal gods, slew the representative of the Goddess/monster (in this case, the prostitute) and dismembered her body. By thus acting out the archetype, he became godlike, mythic, and heroic to his culture. Subsequent sex killers now also ritually imitate him.

Edmund Kemper, the "Coed Killer," has affirmed the importance of the divine role model. As he told *Newsweek*, "I was making life-and-death decisions...playing God in their lives."[44] Such sentiments, moreover, cannot be confined to some rare and aberrant mentality. Rather, they suffuse and characterize the ethics of manhood and godhood which define this culture. One Vietnam veteran recalled his joy of war:

I had a sense of power. A sense of destruction....in the Nam you realized you had the power to take a life. You had the power to rape a woman and nobody could say nothing to you. That godlike feeling you had was in the field. It was like I was god. I could take a life. I could screw a woman.[45]

"Making love" and waging war, taking a life and screwing a woman— sex and violence here, as in those archetypal epics, fuse. If, in the beginning, the male god "gave birth" to the patriarchal world in an act of sexual slaughter, so too do contemporary players attain their sense of immortality through that paradigmatic deed, and sex crime becomes the deed upon which the man, too, is born.[46]

Sex-and-Violence

Other victims of political repression are understood politically; it is a death-right. I mean, when a man is tortured to death anywhere, people see political persecution; when the same thing happens to a woman the same people see sex.

Annie McCombs[47]

Because they were the first of their type, the murders of Jack the Ripper were not immediately recognized as a series of *sex* crimes. There was as yet no ready explanation, no pre-existing category to contain/ explain such actions. The London *Times* exhibited the typical incomprehension:

...they were confronted with a murder of no ordinary character, committed not from jealousy, revenge or robbery, but from motives less adequate than many which still disgraced our civilization, marred our progress, and blotted the pages of our Christianity.[48]

Apparently the conscious merger of "sex" to this new, extreme form of criminal violence had not yet been accomplished. Yet, in just a few years, Krafft-Ebing was able to articulate the soon-to-be common consciousness:

Case 17. Jack the Ripper.... The murderer has never been found. It is probable that he first cut the throats of his victims, then ripped open the abdomen and groped among the intestines. In some instances he cut off the genitals and carried them away; in others he only tore them to pieces and left them behind. He does not seem to have had sexual intercourse with his victims, *but very likely the murderous act and subsequent mutilation of the corpse were equivalents for the sexual act.*[49] (emphasis mine)

The quintessential consciousness of the sex killer, then, is said to be the pure fusion of sex and violence—a factor which continues to be stressed by contemporary psychiatrists. For example, Dr. Donald T. Lunde and Dr. David Abrahamsen (each of whom have worked closely with serial sex killers), both have stressed that such men are marked by a confusion, usually acquired early in life, of sex and violence.[50] Similarly, Dr. Martin Orne identifies a "sexual psychopath" as someone in whom "the sexual impulse becomes twisted and fused with violence so that the individual derives sexual satisfaction from the violence around a murder."[51] But for anyone who has not completely surrendered to doublethink,* it is obvious that the merger of sex and violence is not some bizarre aberration, but is very much the norm in the patriarchal world.

Certainly, that bond is immediately evident in the two most common slang terms for intercourse, *fuck* and *screw*. Just as commonly, sex-and-violence is said to be the staple ingredient of the American mass media; as *Penthouse* magazine put it, "our national pie a la mode."[52] If sexual violence rests at the core of mass and even "family" entertainments, it could also be argued that sex-and-violence is the central dynamic in much of nuclear family life itself.[53] Moreover, that bonded pair is pivotal to the construction of male heroism and emerges as one of the prime motivating factors in men's self-proclaimed love of war.[54] The merger of sex and violence is by no means the exclusive province of the "sexual psychopath," but, rather, serves as a touchstone for the identification of generic patriarchal ideology.

As Andrea Dworkin and others have extensively argued,[55] *sex*, like everything else in a male supremacist culture, is constructed and defined in male supremacist terms, from that precise point of view. Thus, in this culture, modes of oppression are themselves defined and understood as "sex." "Sex" then *is* violence, for "sex" itself is systematically used to subjugate women—in private relations, through pornography, and criminally through harassment, rape, torture, and murder. Patriarchally

---

Doublethink, as developed by George Orwell in *1984*, means "to hold simultaneously two opinions which cancelled out, knowing them to be contradictory, and believing in both of them." See George Orwell, *1984* (c. 1949; New York: New American Library, Signet Classics, 1961), pp. 32-33.

defined and practiced sex, although frequently mystified as love, eroticism, fantasy enactment, and the "natural" expression of dominance and submission, becomes synonymous with and indistinguishable from violence, pain, force, humiliation, and domination. Equally, pain, force, humiliation, slavery, torture and domination (paradigmatically of women, but also of other oppressed groups) are everywhere suffused with sexual drama and meaning.[56] The "sex" in sexual murder is precisely this patriarchal/pornographic, fundamentally political, sex. What is truly unique to the Age of Sex Crime, then, is not its pure equation of sex and violence for, in one form or another, that fusion is endemic to patriarchal culture. Rather, what distinguishes this age is the new mode for such sexual expression—the "lust murder," the mutilation sex killing.[57]

Finally, as I will argue (and as my use of the phrase "Age of..." implies) sex crime can be seen as a paradigmatic phenomenon of the modern period. Jack the Ripper appeared at the end of the nineteenth century, coincident not only with a powerful movement of Western feminism, but also with the rise of the popular press and mass media, the invention of the camera, the mass production and distribution of pornography,[58] the medical inventions of gynecology and psychoanalysis, and the technologizing of weaponry. All such factors linked into the Age of Sex Crime and all remain equally intermeshed today.

Moreover, along with the Age of Sex Crime we can also recognize the companion Ages of Mechanical Reproduction, the Camera, the Computer, Space, Plastic, Fashion, and, of course, the Nuclear. All such "ages" are composite, deeply intertwined and mutually reinforcing. It is particularly the Nuclear Age which is bonded to the Age of Sex Crime, for nuclearism's inevitable goal of the mutilation and devastation of the Earth is the precise macrocosmic parallel to the crimes of Jack the Ripper and his complete mutilation and devastation of the individual female body.

Nearly one hundred years ago, discussing that very killer, the *Southern Guardian* speculated:

Suppose we catch the Whitechapel murderer, can we not before handing him over to the authorities at Broadmoor, make a really decent effort to discover his antecedents, and his parentage, to trace back every step of his career, every hereditary instinct, every acquired taste, every moral slip, every mental idiosyncrasy? Surely the time has come for such an effort as this. We are face to face with some mysterious and awful product of modern civilization.[59]

But of course, all of these things remain mysteries to this day. The identity of the Ripper, his motivations, make-up, antecedents, and fate—all remain unknown. And all have subsequently become the prime stuff of speculation, fiction, legend, essentially comprising a modern myth. Therefore, I will begin this study of the Age of Sex Crime with an examination of its central/father figure, looking at the reality of the Ripper as well as the mystery which has continually, and expediently, surrounded him.

Chapter I
The Ripper Repository

How many murders did Jack the Ripper commit? There is no agreement...as many as fourteen murders have been attributed to the Ripper, including slayings which occurred long after 1888. In fact, the Ripper became a sort of collective for murder, a convenient repository into which all the unsolved crimes against women of a violent or sadistic nature were dumped.

Tom Cullen[1]

The events of 1888 had an immediate and far-ranging effect. In London and elsewhere, then and for years afterwards, a particular sort of crime would invariably be ascribed to Jack the Ripper. From the very beginning, the man and name functioned primarily not as an individual designation, but almost purely as an outline, a repository, a *type*. Now, nearly one hundred years later, that type has set and the Ripper persona functions not only as the primary model for modern sex crime, but also as a mythic reminder of gynocide for women, a nightmare figure who, as Judith Walkowitz has noted:

...has materially contributed to women's sense of vulnerability in modern urban culture. Over the past hundred years, the Ripper murders have achieved the status of a modern myth of male violence against women.[2]

Remarkably ubiquitous, the mythic Ripper functions as a standard point of reference, a gauge for degree of violence, a criminal type, a source of humor, a social type, an intellectual challenge and source of camaraderie for his devotees (so-called "Ripperologists" and "Ripperophiles"), a party game at college, a stock fictional character, an inspiration for song, a hero, monster, and symbol (alternatively) for both nature and culture. In short, the Ripper has assumed the dimensions of a vast cultural metaphor.

Possible cultural contexts for the Ripper are as riddled and wide open as the following selections indicate:

Imagine...a study of feminism from the point of view of Jack the Ripper....a novel that bristles with irony and wit.

—*New York Times* review of
George Stade's *Confessions
of a Lady-Killer* (1979)[3]

Two women cops working twice as hard for half the glory...TONIGHT: Decoys for a Jack the Ripper.

> —*TV Guide* ad (20 March 1982) for the
> premiere episode of *Cagney and Lacey*

Jack The Ripper Loose In New York

> —front page headline in the
> *National Examiner*, 11 May 1982

Jack The Ripper On Television

> —headline for a newspaper
> commentary on Tom Snyder's TV
> interview with Charles Manson[4]

"Prime Suspect" attempts to portray some news personnel as the most vicious creatures since Jack the Ripper.

> —*New York Times* review of a
> made-for-TV movie[5]

The child of two, three, or four, despite, or rather because of its infancy, is truly then a potential Jack the Ripper.

> —Marie Bonaparte (Freudian
> theorist)[6]

I did myself a great deal of damage through reading blood-and-thunder stories, for instance I read the tale of *Jack the Ripper* several times.

> —Peter Kürten, the "Düsseldorf
> Ripper"[7]

A third class of strangers are so utterly beyond the pale that they seem alien not only to the group, but to the human species. I refer to *monsters*, indicated by names like: pervert, degenerate...psychopath...fiend, demon, devil...Jack the Ripper.

> —Orrin Klapp[8]

The Jack I present is the Jack in all of us, of course.

> —Harlan Ellison, science
> fiction writer[9]

The name gives me this feeling of tingling excitement.

> —college student, 1982[10]

[Dedicated] To Colin Wilson, Dan Farson, Tom Cullen, Robin Odell, and "Ripperologists"—not forgetting JACK who brought us together.... My final acknowledgement is once again to my wife who has patiently deciphered my mutilated and mangled manuscripts....

> —Donald Rumbelow, *The Complete
> Jack the Ripper*[11]

—Knock, knock.
  (Husband): Who's there?

—Jack the Ripper.
(Husband): It's for you dear.

—the *Benny Hill Show.* c. 1980

It sure as hell wasn't Jack the Ripper.

—comment after the first shark attack in
Jaws (Steven Spielberg, 1975)

Jack the Ribber

—restaurant in New York City

I need some help here. Some hands. Just send me anybody. Jack the Ripper. I'll take anyone who's good with a knife.

—Hawkeye, on *M*A*S*H* (CBS, c. 1973)

Everyone feels more relieved if told that Jack the Ripper behaved as he did because someone said it was a good way for him to meet girls.

—Robert Bloch, author[12]

Are You Loveable? Test your desirability quotient.... Score 20-45: You're about as loveable as the black plague. After a woman spends an evening with you, she may feel that a date with Jack the Ripper would have been more emotionally fulfilling.

—self-administered personality test in
Penthouse[13]

[Jack the Ripper] that great hero of my youth, that skilled human butcher who did all his work on alcoholic whores.

—Charles McCabe, columnist *San Francisco Chronicle*[14]

Who is this man...
What's he done and where's he live?
How can a man who's a criminal be a hero to the kids?
The old couples say the Ripper's back, they say it's him all right.

"Stranger in Town," Toto, 1984[15]

Lulu...is hunted down, caught and destroyed by *society's henchman*...Jack the Ripper.
—Sal Gittelman on the plays of Frank Wedekind[16](emphasis mine)

And Jezebel the nun, she violently knits,
A bald wig for Jack the Ripper, who sits,
At the head of the Chamber of Commerce.

"Tombstone Blues," Bob Dylan, 1965[17]

The ghost of Jack the Ripper hovered over Washington today.

—ABC Nightly News, 29 Nov. 1984 (in reference to
Federal budget cuts)

The Senate would confirm Jack the Ripper for surgeon general if President Reagan asked them to.

—Senator Patrick J. Leahy (Vermont) in reference to
Senate confirmation hearing on Edwin Meese for Attorney
General, *USA Today*, 14 May 1985.

General Jack D. Ripper

—name of nuclear-crazed General in *Dr. Strangelove*
(Stanley Kubrick, 1963)

For Jack the Ripper is with us now. He prowls the nights, shunning the sun in a search
for the blazing incandescence of an inner reality.... let the Ripper rip you into an awareness
of the urges and forces most of us will neither admit nor submit to.

—Robert Bloch[18]

If not as inclusively within "us" as Bloch and Harlan Ellison insist, the Ripper nevertheless clearly preoccupies this culture in the form of a pervasive and particularly all-embracing metaphor. For while Jack the Ripper can epitomize ultimate horror—the human monster—he can simultaneously be made to seem as domestic and ordinary as Jack Sprat, as playful as Jack in the Box, as familiar a crowd pleaser as Jack and the Beanstalk, as heroic as Jack the Giant Killer and as recurrent as Jack Frost. Such massive mythicization works to ensure that phallic violence will be considered an unavoidable fact of life, an inevitability of nature. Moreover, it serves as a cosmic distraction, deflecting analysis from the actuality of the crimes and their meaning and fixing attention almost solely on the myth. To begin to counter such a mystique, it is logical to turn first to the facts of the case, but these, when found, are themselves starved of reality.

The Reality

The undisputed facts about Jack the Ripper are sparse; even his identity is based on the
modus operandi alone and there is no unanimity about the number of murders.... Successive
commentators promote their pet variant of the myth at each other's expense.

Alexander Kelly[19]

Nobody can stop the "legend" of Jack the Ripper from finally triumphing over these
facts. Indeed, it can be argued that it has already done so. Jack the Ripper, within a
hundred years of his crime, is already part-folk hero, part-myth.

Donald Rumbelow[20]

By grade school, most of us have heard of the Ripper and hold some associations with his name. Visitors to Madame Tussaud's in 1974 ranked him third on a list of most hated and feared (edged out only by Adolph Hitler and Richard Nixon).[21] Still, few of us can fix his actual crimes with any precision—and with good reason, for the facts are not all that obvious. While fiction has overwhelmingly embraced him, most of the standard fact books—encyclopedias—ignore him utterly. Specialized books can be either difficult to locate or often tell only a completely conjectured account as though it were undisputed fact.[22] And, although the story is regularly retold in the popular periodicals, these versions are always subject to the whims, opinions, and motivations of the individual commentator as well as those of the particular audience that is being addressed.[23] One factual, unsensational, concise and accessible source is David Wallechinsky and Irving Wallace's non-traditional *People's Almanac*.[24]

The basic facts of the case are these. Although varying numbers of murders, from five to twenty, have been attributed to the Ripper, it is generally agreed that he was responsible for only five. All took place within an area of one quarter square mile in Whitechapel in the ten weeks between August 31st and November 9, 1888. A list of the victims in order is:

1.   August 31, 1888. Mary Ann Nichols, throat cut and stomach mutilation.

2.   September 8, 1888. Annie Chapman, throat cut and stomach and genitals badly mutilated. Some of the entrails placed around neck. Uterus stolen from the body.

3.   September 30, 1888. Elizabeth Stride, throat cut, no mutilations and on the same date—

4.   Catherine Eddowes, throat cut and very bad mutilation of both face and stomach; kidney taken from body.

5.   November 9, 1888. Mary Jane Kelly, throat cut and whole of body mutilated.[25]

The People's Almanac denotes the following similarities among these murders:

1) all 5 women were prostitutes; 2) all 5 had been grabbed from behind and had their throats slit; 3) there was an attempt to mutilate all the bodies, though one attempt was thwarted; 4) every killing occurred either on the first or the last weekend of the month, in the early hours of the morning; 5) except for the brutal slaying of Mary Jane Kelly, all of the murders took place out-of-doors in the worst section of town; 6) in none of the cases was there evidence of sexual assault; and 7) each murder was increasingly savage as well as more audacious.[26]

Although murder in the East End was by no means rare, the Whitechapel slaughters, because they were serial, random, apparently motiveless and unprecedented in their ferocity, caught and held the imagination of all London, an imagination made all the more vivid by the sensational coverage of the newspapers, "penny dreadfuls," and broadsheets which abounded at that time. Alexander Kelly's bibliography of Ripper literature indicates that there were at least eight daily newspapers which, with varying degrees of intensity, kept all London, and eventually the world, agitated and informed of the events.[27] Magazines such as the *Illustrated Police News Law Courts and Weekly Record* and *The Penny Illustrated Paper and Illustrated Times* (the "penny dreadfuls") provided extensive and graphic coverage. Furthermore, "Ha'penny broadsheets...were hawked about Whitechapel all during the Ripper's reign of terror."[28] The area took on the aspects of a siege.

Walkowitz has characterized the charged atmosphere around these killings as essentially a media event:

> One cannot emphasize too much the role of the popular press, itself a creature of the 1880s, in establishing Jack the Ripper as a media hero, in amplifying the terror of male violence, and in elaborating and interpreting the meaning of the Ripper murders to a "mass" audience.[29]

And the terror, sensationalism and fixed attention immeasurably increased when the killer, already horrific due to his total lack of identity, suddenly acquired a distinct and jeering personality. In late September, either the killer himself, or his unsolicited proxy, engineered a most dramatic reversal. Instead of simply being written about in the newspapers and broadsheets, the apparent killer began to write to them himself (a tactic later imitated by Peter Kürten (the "Düsseldorf Ripper"), Lucien Staniak (Poland's "Red Spider"), and David Berkowitz (the "Son of Sam").

Throughout the crisis, thousands of letters poured into Scotland Yard and the Central News Agency; in one month alone, the Yard received some 14,000 letters.[30] A number of these claimed to be from the killer himself and it was one of these that delivered the historic impact. On September 28th, the Central News Agency received a letter claiming to be from the killer and signed, "Jack the Ripper," marking the first time the nickname was used. Written in red ink, its tone and message were explosive:

Dear Boss,

I keep on hearing the police have caught me, but they won't fix me just yet. I have laughed when they look so clever and talk about being on the right track. The joke about Leather Apron gave me real fits.

I am down on whores and I shan't quit ripping them until I do get buckled. Grand work, the last job was. I gave the lady no time to squeal. How can they catch me now? I love my work and want to start again. You will soon hear of me and my funny little games.

I saved some of the proper red stuff in a ginger beer bottle over the last job, to write with, but it went thick like glue and I can't use it. Red ink is fit enough, I hope. Ha! Ha!

The next job I do I shall clip the lady's ears off and send them to the police, just for jolly, wouldn't you? Keep this letter back until I do a bit more work, then give it out straight. My knife's so nice and sharp, I want to get to work right away if I get a chance. Good luck.

Yours truly,
Jack the Ripper.

Don't mind me giving the trade name. Wasn't good enough to post this before I got all the red ink off my hands; curse it. No luck yet. They say I am a doctor now. Ha! Ha![31]

Two days later, the Ripper murdered again—this time twice in one night. Both Elizabeth Stride and Catherine Eddowes were killed in the early morning of Sunday, September 30th, within one hour's time and ten minutes walking distance of each other. The body of Stride was discovered almost immediately by a passerby, presumably with the Ripper still near, and the mutilation attempt was thwarted in her case. Within an hour, though, Catherine Eddowes had been killed and mutilated; an ear lobe and kidney were removed from her body.

On that same date, September 30th, a postcard addressed to the Central News Agency was dropped into a London letterbox. The handwriting was identical to the first Jack the Ripper letter and the card was stained with blood. It read:

I was not codding dear old Boss when I gave you the tip. You'll hear about Saucy Jack's work tomorrow. Double event this time. Number one squealed a bit. Couldn't finish straight off. Had not time to get ears for police. Thanks for keeping last letter back till I got to work again.

Jack the Ripper[32]

It seemed possible that the writer was the actual murderer for, although news of the murders had spread through the neighborhood, the details were not generally known until the October 1st newspapers. The police tried to trace the writer by publishing a facsimile poster of both the letter and the postcard and circulating it, asking any who recognized the writing to inform them. That effort was fruitless. Portions of both letters were later printed in the October 2nd newspapers.

But the most apparently genuine correspondence of all did not come until October 16th. The recipient was George Lusk, head of the Whitechapel Vigilance Committee. A small parcel was mailed to him, a package that contained not only a note, but part of a human kidney. The note read:

From Hell

Mr. Lusk

Sir I send you half the Kidne I took from one woman prasarved it for you tother piece I fried and ate it was very nise I may send you the bloody knif that took it out

if you only wate a whil longer.
     signed Catch me when you can Mishter Lusk[33]

This was *not* signed, "Jack the Ripper," but a return address was indicated—"From Hell."

The authenticity of any of these letters remains, like so many things surrounding the Ripper, a matter of controversy, dispute, and mystification. Contemporaries of 1888 tended to reject "the Ripper correspondence *in toto* as a series of poison pen hoaxes, a conclusion with which the police were inclined to agree."[34] Donald Rumbelow cites the memoirs of Sir Robert Anderson and Sir Melville Macnaghten, two police officials and contemporaries of the case. Both firmly believed that the letters were the inventions of "some enterprising journalist,"[35] and not communiques from a killer. But most modern commentators argue that at least three of the letters (the ones quoted here) are genuine. Donald McCormick goes even farther and offers the evidence of a Dr. Thomas Dutton who claimed (on the basis of handwriting analysis) that at least thirty-four letters are from the same man, the murderer.[36]

The question of authenticity has significance beyond the academic or historical, for these letters are a primary source for the mythic continuance of the Ripper. McCormick reasonably argues that without the resonant nickname, "in all probability the crimes...would have long ago been forgotten."[37] These letters also originate the image of "irony and wit," still so frequently associated with Jack the Ripper, the mystique that transforms him into a stylish and likeable rogue, his crimes into what *Life* magazine heralded as "splendidly squalid mysteries."[39] Masters and Lea comment:

Horrible as were his crimes, and indubitably most foul, they were not committed without a certain redeeming grace, a saving wit, a mitigating sophistication and savoir faire, or so he seems to have impressed many of those who have since written about him.[39]

The insoluble mystery of the Ripper's identity, coupled with the distinctive personality created by the letters, are thus used by closet rippers to transform their hero into an endless source of intrigue, a "criminal who, in his twisted way, was a genius,"[40] rather than the repulsive and lethal misogynist his actions reveal him to be.

And what if we side with the Victorians and believe none of the letters to have been written by the killer? Then it becomes clear that the enduring cultural image of "Jack the Ripper" is actually the fantasy projection of an armchair criminal(s) who, for some reason, wanted to give his voice to the murderer in the street. Even if one, two, or three of the letters are genuine, some 128 pieces of correspondence were sent to police, press, or individuals, claiming to be from the killer.[41] Obviously, a significant segment of the populace liked to play at being the Ripper. Some of the more stylish of these, and ones that few would defend as authentic, are nevertheless included in Ripper narratives, contributing further to the concocted personality, expanding the myth. This verse, for example, is frequently cited:

I'm not a butcher,
I'm not a Yid,
Nor yet a foreign skipper,
But I'm your own light-hearted friend,
Your's truly, Jack the Ripper.

Or this verse which dispatches women as efficiently as another does Indians:

Eight little whores, with no hope of heaven,
Gladstone may save one, then there'll be seven,
. . .
Two little whores, shivering with fright,
Seek a cosy doorway in the middle of the night.
Jack's knife flashes, then there's but one.
And the last one's the ripest for Jack's idea of fun.[42]

Thus, the Ripper persona almost immediately became a mask anonymous individuals could assume. Moreover, the myth of the Ripper—from its very beginnings—was a *collective* male invention, a product of criminal, press, and public.

The Ripper reality effectively ended on November 9, 1888, with the fifth and last murder. The victim was twenty-five-year-old Mary Jane Kelly and this was the only murder to occur indoors. It is estimated that the killer spent about two hours mutilating the corpse; sixteen newspaper lines were required to describe those extensive mutilations. After this most savage murder, in Colin Wilson's words, "Jack the Ripper left 13 Miller's Court and walked out of history."[43] No other murders occurred which could be definitely ascribed to the Ripper and the word in police circles was that the Ripper had committed suicide and that his body had been fished out of the Thames in December 1888. Interestingly, by 1905 children in England and Scotland were already affirming the Ripper's suicide in a jump rope rhyme:

Jack the Ripper's dead/And lying on his bed.
He cut his throat with Sunlight Soap/Jack the Ripper's dead.[44]

But this was not to be the only or even final word. Stories that the Ripper had been sighted in Liverpool, Paris and New York arose almost immediately. Early rumors had claimed the Ripper to be a doctor, butcher, foreign sailor, a barber-surgeon or insane professor. Such speculation has never really ceased, but continues as a whole group of Ripperologists continue to rehash the mystery and propose identities and possible ends for the Ripper. The latest and by far the most spectacular is Edward, Duke of Clarence, grandson of Queen Victoria and once crown prince of England—a rumor that received worldwide dissemination.[45]

The history of the Ripper, then, is largely talk. Still, we know him well through that talk and perhaps even better through his appearances in vast numbers of fictional accounts. If Jack the Ripper walked out of history on November 9, 1888, he was immediately welcomed into another realm—that of fiction and, as Alexander Kelly remarked, since then "the distinction between fact and fiction has grown increasingly blurred."[46]

The Romance

As other historians have noted, the tabloid press incorporated many of the forms and themes of popular culture, particularly those of sensationalist melodrama, the literary convention that shaped the Ripper narrative in all the London dailies across the political spectrum. Embedded in this convention was a titillating "sexual script," based on the association of sex and violence, male dominance and female passivity, and the crossing of class boundaries in the male pursuit of the female object of desire.

Judith Walkowitz[47]

A broadsheet issued directly after the double murder of September 30th is of particular interest. To scoop his competitors, one printer, instead of getting an original graphic, simply used a stock woodcut picturing a murder scene from a Victorian melodrama. Underneath the gigantic headline, "Two more horrible MURDERS in the East-End," the graphic displayed a man threatening with a knife and about to pounce upon a prostrate woman.

Such lurid visual tactics spurred *Punch* to denounce the news coverage:

Imagine the effect of these gigantic pictures of violence and assasination by knife...on the morbid imaginations of imbalanced minds. These hideous picture-posters are a blot on our civilization and a disgrace to the drama.[48]

But the "drama" that the Ripper so manifestly provided was frankly not all that dissimilar to the most popular forms of Victorian drama and fiction. In his study of popular literature, Victor Neuburg writes that the most popular group of ballads in the 19th century were those dealing with crimes, particularly those "street drolleries" which:

...were in fact fictitious narratives offered to a gullible public as though they were true and topical. The sales patter, shouted through the streets would make much of such words as 'Horrible', 'Dreadful', 'Murder', 'Seduction', 'Blood', and so on. [49]

But the rhythm and patter of that typical sales pitch soon was eerily echoed by that which accompanied the Ripper's very real campaign of murder. Melville Macaghten remembered:

No one who was living in London that autumn will forget the terror created by those murders....I can recall the foggy evenings, and hear again the raucous cries of the newspaper boys: "Another horrible murder, murder, mutilation, Whitechapel." Such was the burden of their ghastly song.[50]

Neuburg further notes that the newspaper reporting of the "Jack the Ripper" crimes fit neatly into the established "preoccupation of nineteenth-century readers with violent crime," and "laid hold of the public imagination in a way that reprints of Shakespeare or Milton never could."[51] Certainly the grip of these crimes on the public mind was far more analogous to another sort of literature, the "bloods," a type of fiction Neuburg describes as a vulgarization of the Gothic novel with an emphasis on terror and melodrama. Indeed, as Cullen reports, on the streets the morning after the murder of Mary Kelly, "vendors brandished crimson covered pamphlets, which they identified as, 'The Whitechapel Blood Book—only a penny!' "[52] Thus, almost from the very beginning, Jack the Ripper was presented as being as fantastic and supernatural a being as Varney the Vampire or other such monsters of Victorian melodrama. Indeed, as recently as 1970, Noel Annan (Provost of University College, London) referred to the Ripper as "the hero of horror in Victorian Times."[53]

This blending of the factual and fictional became literally unnerving for the Victorian populace at one point. In 1886, just two years prior to the crimes of the Ripper, Robert Louis Stevenson completed *Dr. Jekyll and Mr. Hyde*. And at the very time of the killings, a theater production of that novel, starring the American actor, Richard Mansfield, was enjoying a successful run at the Lyceum. That run had an unexpected ending, however, for public opinion compelled Mansfield to withdraw his production. The *Daily Telegraph* commented: "Experience has taught this clever young actor that there is no taste in London just now for horrors on the stage. There is quite sufficient to make us shudder out of doors."[54]

And in the twentieth century, the Ripper continues to occupy the fictional realm, emerging as the subject in a steady stream of novels, short stories, films, plays, television productions, operas, and popular songs. Even to this day, there is no abatement in Ripper literature. In the past few years, for example, there have been at least three widely reviewed novels which explicitly feature "Jack the Ripper"[55] and uncounted others which feature an unmistakably Ripper-type killer.

The Ripper was first incorporated into a work of fiction as early as 1904 when Frank Wedekind used him as the undoing of his archetypal female, Lulu, in his play *Die Busche der Pandora* (Pandora's Box). Wedekind's commentators have described Lulu as the embodiment of Eros, or the mythic life force of Freud's pleasure principle. She thus acts from instinct, victimizing her husbands and lovers until she herself is victimized and destroyed by Jack the Ripper. Those same critics identify the Ripper with Freud's reality principle, as the force or agent of civilization. In his study of Wedekind, Sal Gittelman calls the Ripper "society's henchman."[56] Millions were recently refamiliarized with this modern fable when PBS televised Alban Berg's opera *Lulu*, a work based upon Wedekind's plays.[57]

But the original popularizer of the Ripper was Marie Belloc Lowndes' best-selling novel, *The Lodger* (1913). Originally appearing as a short story in *McClure's* magazine (January 1911), it was expanded into a novel, passed through thirty-one editions, has been translated into eighteen languages and filmed five times. The first film version, a silent, was directed by none other than Alfred Hitchcock (1926). Tom Cullen calls *The Lodger*, "the favorite Ripper myth...a fiendish killer harbored in the bosom of an ordinary family."[58] The landlady suspects; eventually so does her husband, but neither can act.

Throughout this century, the Ripper has continued to star in all forms of fictions. He crosses genres with ease—from the well-crafted short story (Isak Dinesen), to mystery (Ellery Queen and Anthony Boucher), to horror and science fiction (Robert Bloch and Harlan Ellison), and even to farce (Marcel Carne) and opera (Alban Berg and Phyllis Tate).[59] Audiences for American television programs have had the opportunity to observe the character of Jack the Ripper in episodes of shows as diverse as *Night Gallery, Kolchak the Night Stalker, Vegas, Fantasy Island,* and *Star Trek.* Certain motifs in all of these fictions are consistent and revealing. The most striking of all is that the Ripper *does not die*; by some means he attains immortality.

Resurrection

The melodramatic name of Jack the Ripper, that invention of a quick-minded sub-editor, is largely the reason for his immortality, that and the imaginative folk lore which has always surrounded him.

Nigel Morland[60]

The important thing is that Jack the Ripper has never died as far as the average Londoner is concerned.

Tom Cullen[61]

At a more subtle level, traces of the Ripper's presence constantly intrude into urban women's consciousness. Walking down my street in Manhattan recently, I came upon graffiti emblazoning the Ripper's name on a side of a building. That same week the Lesbian Herstory Archives forwarded to me a threatening letter from "Jack the Ripper:" "THE ORIGINAL JACK not a cheap imitation/I've conquered death itself and am still on this earth waiting to strike again."

Judith Walkowitz[62]

The notion of the Ripper's immortality is perhaps the most dominant motif of the entire myth. Most Americans familiar with the idea might have picked it up from an episode of that still syndicated and wildly popular series, *Star Trek*. This particular episode, "A Wolf in the Fold," was written by Robert Bloch, the author of "Your's Truly, Jack the Ripper" and *Psycho*. During one exploration of strange planets and alien life forms, the crew of the Enterprise are astounded to find an all too familiar figure, the very Jack the Ripper who stalked Whitechapel in 1888; and he is still slaying women. The crux of this plot is that the Ripper is not human at all, but is actually an alien and *eternal* entity, a being that derives sustenance from emotion and who literally feeds on fear. The objects of attack are women, according to the logic or ideology of this story, because women are more easily terrified than men, making them inherently a far more satisfying dish. Thus, eons into the future and light years away, Jack the Ripper with his "hunger that never dies" still stalks his "natural" prey.[63]

But to readers of horror fiction, that script was not all that terribly new. For Bloch, one of the key mythographers of sex crime, had first invented that motif in his 1943 short story, "Your's truly, Jack the Ripper," a story whose fame is second only to *The Lodger* in Ripper literature. The time frame here is 1943 and the original Jack is still alive but now practicing psychiatry in Chicago. His continuing murders (there have now been eighty-seven throughout the world) are blood sacrifices "to some dark gods" in exchange for eternal life. Bloch himself marveled at the endless reprintings, translations, anthologizations, and adaptations of this story, noting: "For some reason, the notion of Jack the Ripper's survival in the present day touched a sensitive spot in the audience's psyche."[64]

That spot is still sensitive and the idea of Jack the Ripper among us remains highly charged. Give that theme a science-fiction twist and the Ripper becomes a time traveler. In Nicholas Meyer's 1979 film, *Time After Time* (based upon Karl Alexander's novel), Jack is a respected doctor and friend to H.G. Wells; his true profession, of course, is unknown to his friends. But, about to be exposed and apprehended at Wells' home, he slips into the basement and conveniently vanishes via Wells' time machine. Arriving in San Francisco in 1979, he is ecstatic. "I belong here completely and utterly. I'm home." Gloating, he mocks Wells' dream of a utopian future and tells him, "The future isn't what you thought. It's what I am." Fiction? Far-fetched? Entertaining? Of course, but let's pause here for a news-break.

1977: David Berkowitz, the "Son of Sam," holds New York City in the grip of a year-long panic. He "hunts" at night, shooting and killing six young people; seven survive his attacks. He brags, "I only shoot pretty girls"[65]

In September, the first of the Hillside Stranglings takes place in Los Angeles; by February, 1978, ten women would be dead.

David D. Hill and Patrick W. Kearney are on trial for the "Trashbag Murders"—the killing of twenty-eight young men over a decade. All the victims were found nude, shot in the head, sometimes dismembered and castrated, and dumped in a plastic trash bag.[66]

In Georgia, from September 1977 to April 1978, seven elderly women are killed by a "Stocking Strangler." An eighth victim survived.[67]

1978: Seven Black women have been killed in New Haven; four of them, it is reported, had previous arrests for prostitution. Black residents claim that the police are not pursuing a solution to the killings.[68]

John Wayne Gacy admits to torturing, mutilating, and killing thirty-two boys and then burying them in the basement of his suburban home in Chicago.[69]

1979: Ted Bundy, after two prison escapes from Colorado, is finally on televised trial in Florida for the bludgeon deaths of two sorority women. He is also the prime suspect in thirty-six similar sexual slayings in the Western states.

In Boston, twelve Black women are killed within six months in a small concentrated area of the city. Police deny a connection among the murders, claiming any similarities to be merely "cosmetic." Local newspapers give the view of a building superintendent in the area that the murders are "a fad, like skateboards."[70]

1980: Over in the home country, the "Yorkshire Ripper" claims his thirteenth victim in a five-year siege. *MacLeans* headlines him, "Jack the Ripper's latest disciple."[71]

In South America, Pedro Alonso Lopez confesses to being the killer known variously as the "Strangler of the Andes," and "The Columbian Monster." He is believed to be responsible, over a seven-year period, for the rape and murder of over three hundred preteen girls.[72]

Lawrence Bittaker and Roy Norris are on trial in southern California for the rape, torture, and murder of five teenage girls; pictures were taken of their victims and their screams recorded on cassette tape. Roy Norris says, "The rape wasn't really the important part, it was the dominance."[73]

1981: William Bonin, James Michael Monro and Gregory Matthew Miley go on trial for the "Freeway Killings," murders of young men throughout the 1970s.[74]

1982: Wayne Williams is convicted of two murders in Atlanta; police close the books on twenty-three of the other twenty-eight killings of Black boys and young men in that city, thus sealing the mystery on one of the most controversial convictions and unresolved cases of mass murder.[75]

   Sixteen-year-old Wendy Coffield is found dead in the Green River outside Seattle. By 1985, thirty-four murders have been ascribed to a "Green River Killer" and eleven other women are missing. Police speculate that the same man may be responsible for "similar serial murders of prostitutes in Montana and Georgia."[76]

   Gerald Stano confesses to the murder of thirty-three women in a decade. The *New York Times* quotes him as saying, "I just can't stand a bitchy chick." A Florida law enforcement agent tells us, "He thinks about three things: stereo systems, cars, and killing women."[77]

1983: Henry Lee Lucas is arrested in Texas for the murder of an unidentified hitchhiker. He asserts that he (usually alone but sometimes with Otis Toole) has killed three hundred and sixty people (that number eventually reaches over six hundred), primarily women travelling alone, that he had murdered by every method but poison, that he had "shot, stabbed, burned, beaten, strangled, hung and 'crucified' his victims, and that some had been 'filleted like fish.' "[78]

   A former Illinois state's attorney pleads innocent by reason of insanity to the stabbing death of 39-year old Kathleen Pearson. His goal, according to court testimony, was to become "the world's greatest Jack the Ripper."[79]

   In Ohio, police suspect a pattern in a dozen rape-murders of young women and girls throughout that state between 1975 and 1980. Most of the victims were between 8 and 14 years of age.[80]

   In Alaska, Robert Hansen is arrested for the rape, torture and murder of seventeen women over a period of ten years.[81]

1984: After a six-week rampage of kidnapping, torturing, and killing young women, Christopher Wilder, surrounded by the police in New Hampshire, shoots himself, perhaps accidentally.[82]

   In Connecticut, Michael Ross is arrested in connection with the slayings of six young women during a two-and-a-half year period.[83]

Suspected serial murderer Alton Coleman is arrested in the Midwest; he is a suspect in the murders of six Black women.[84]

1985: Police confess their frustration as they search for a killer whom they have dubbed the "Redhead Killer." Eight women described as having "red or reddish hair" have been found slain in an area from Pennsylvania to Mississippi. None of the bodies have been identified.[85]

California police officials are searching the area around an isolated cabin to find bodies of the victims of torture-murderers Leonard Lake and Charles Ng. Videotapes found in the cabin show the two men sexually torturing a woman as well as Lake asserting that he wanted "women to submit." A sheriff states, "It's like a horror film."[86]

Richard Ramirez is arrested as the California "Night Stalker," a serial killer who broke into homes late at night, indiscriminately assaulting those within. He is charged with sixteen murders.[87]

A so-called "Monster of Florence" has been shooting couples in the countryside surrounding that Italian city since 1968. The murderer then mutilates the dead woman's body. After the last killing in September, the killer mailed a letter to the police along with part of the woman's genitalia. *Time* magazine reports that there are currently three movies being made about these crimes, including one which they term "a pornographic potboiler."[88]

The body of Elizabeth Ann Landcraft is found in Los Angeles on Christmas Eve. Police connect her death with the slayings and mutilations of ten other women in that city since January 1, 1984. All of the victims had prostitution records; all but two of these were Black. Community groups contend that the police are giving the investigation minimal attention. By June, 1986, the deaths of 17 women since 1983 are being attributed to this one "Southside Killer."[89]

Is it any wonder that a time-travelling Jack the Ripper would feel so at home in the present? That listing of sexual murder, extensive enough, is only representative. As we return to the film *Time After Time*, it is to hear this fictional Ripper triumphantly proclaim, "The world has caught up with me and surpassed me. Ninety years ago I was a freak...now I'm an amateur."

Happy in San Francisco, Jack the Ripper embarks on his typical pattern of mutilation/murder. Wells, however, has chased him through time and finally manages to dispatch him, again via the time machine, but this time, "I sent him into *infinity* where he really belongs." And really, where else. For Jack the Ripper has been made timeless. Fiction, rumor and legend claim him far more than fact; the figure of Jack the

Ripper has indeed fled history and been ensconsed instead into phallic folklore and mythology.

This ritual blending of fiction and fact is still continually enacted. When *Time After Time* was released, it coincided with a mass publicity campaign to catch the so-called "Yorkshire Ripper," who had then just killed and mutilated his twelfth victim. Incredibly, the October 30, 1979 issue of *Us* magazine chose to publicize the two events together. On pages 30-31, the headlined story tells us: "A New Jack the Ripper is Terrorizing England." On page 32, the next headline reads: "The Stars Really Fall in Love in a New Jack the Ripper Flick." Such a blithe juxtaposition suggests that there is hardly any worthwhile distinction at all between a "New Jack the Ripper" and a "New Jack the Ripper Flick," as if each were equally fantastic, each equally imaginary, each equally fun.

The puzzle of the Ripper's identity, his melodramatic name, the way the crimes so suddenly and inexplicably ceased, the unprecedented brutality of their execution, the symbolic character of the victims: all these are said to explain what Nigel Morland has called "the imaginative folk lore that has always surrounded him." Yet "imaginative folk lore" sounds so harmless, so innocent, so playful. We might more accurately name this phenomenon to be a legitimating mythicization, in short, *propaganda*, an "imagination" which functions to further the reality of sex crime/gynocide.

First of all, such mythicization naturalizes both the crime and the criminal. In 1888, this phenomenon of sexual murder was incomprehensible, unprecedented. Yet by the end of the 20th century, it is as familiar and accepted as any other "environmental" hazard.[90] Correspondingly, the fictions of the Ripper portray him as eternal, infinite, changeless—an unconquerable force of nature. This process is precisely that which Roland Barthes has identified as "the very principle of myth:"

...it [myth] transforms history into nature....myth has the task of giving an historical intention a natural justification, and making contingency appear eternal.[91]

Thus sex crime is lifted out of the historical tradition of gynocide and represented as some mysterious force of nature, the expression of deeply repressed "human" urges, a fact of life, a supernatural evil, a monstrous aberration—anything but the logical and eminently functional product of the system of male domination. Political analysis, the naming of the causes of male violence, is meant to be silenced before it can even begin, waylaid amidst the melodramatic conundrums of the myth.

Secondly, just as the archetypalization of the Ripper ensures that

A new Jack the Ripper is terrorizing England

West Yorkshire Police Constable Alan Firth patrols a lonely stretch of his beat in the heart of Ripper country. Right, a 19th-century woodcut of the Ripper.

there will be others, made in his image and likeness, to follow in his footsteps, so does the transmutation of the Ripper history into mythic narrative and formula indicate that it will be, quite literally, *easy to follow*. For myth is a partner to ritual; it demands a reenactment, a re-creation of the original event. In his studies of myth, Mircea Eliade has continually stressed the mimetic imperative. Again, according to him,

The stars really fall in love in a new Jack the Ripper flick

Us, Oct. 30, 1979. Reprinted with permission.

all myth derives from some paradigmatic act or primordial event. Moreover, "It is in the myth that the principles and paradigms for all conduct must be sought." In effect, "one becomes truly a man only by conforming to the teachings of the myths, that is, by imitating the gods."

This principle of *imitation* is glued to the phenomenon of the Ripper and indeed to all of modern sex crime. As early as 1889, police in London were puzzled by a number of crimes which bore a distinct similarity to those of the Ripper. Some feared that the original killer was again becoming active, but they finally concluded that these were a series of "imitative crimes."[92] In New York City in 1891, a prostitute was found murdered and mutilated in a Manhattan hotel. The next day the newspapers were screaming that "Jack the Ripper" had arrived in America.[93]

Such imitations—both consciously by the criminal, or more abstractly, as when the media and police frame perceptions of a sex crime through the well-established Ripper formula—have continued throughout the twentieth century. Blithely commenting upon the series of sex murders in Yorkshire in the late 1970s, *Time* magazine called them, "The Ripper's Return."[94] Next, I will turn to an examination of those most celebrated successors of Jack the Ripper—uncovering, again, both the histories and the attendant myths.

Chapter II
The Ripper Repetitions

It seems as if there were no progress in the human race, but only repetition. We can almost hear them, if we listen, singing the same old song...

Virginia Woolf[1]

I am down on whores and I shan't quit ripping them until I do get buckled...

Jack the Ripper[2]

Stacey was a whore....I'd kill her again.
I'd kill them all again.

David Berkowitz, the "Son of Sam"[3]

It wasn't fuckin' wrong. Why is it wrong to get rid of some fuckin' cunts?

Kenneth Bianchi, the "Hillside Strangler"[4]

The women I killed were filth, bastard prostitutes who were just standing round littering the streets. I was just cleaning the place up a bit.

Peter Sutcliffe, the "Yorkshire Ripper"[5]

I was death on women.

Henry Lee Lucas[6]

As previously noted, as many as twenty murders have been attributed to Jack the Ripper. Such distortion indicates not simply hysteria or hyperbole, but another sort of extreme reaction—emulation. Writing in 1945, Alan Hynd told the readers of *Good Housekeeping*:

Other killers may have begun to take a leaf from the Ripper's book by the beginning of 1889, with some success in simulating his technique, so that there arose confusion as to whether specific crimes were those of the Ripper grown careless or the work of imitators who hoped their deeds would be charged to the master murderer.[7]

Basil Thompson in his history of Scotland Yard wrote that a similar murder in 1889 was not actually the work of the Ripper, but "was one of those imitative crimes so often committed after a series of crimes has deeply impressed the public mind."[8] Nearly one hundred years later, the Ripper's profound impression on the cultural mind obviously has not faded and neither has that pattern of imitation.

Actually, such a pattern was discernible as early as 1943 and Robert Bloch saw it and worked it right into his classic horror story, "Your's

33

truly, Jack the Ripper." This story is told in the first person; the narrator is Chicago psychiatrist, John Carmody. The doctor is visited by a self-proclaimed Ripper hunter, Guy Hollis, who proceeds to tell him an utterly fantastic story. He claims to have followed a distinctive trail of similar, Ripper-type murders across continents and over decades, ending finally in Chicago, 1943. His explanation for the trail—the immortality of the one and original Jack the Ripper:

I could show you clippings from the papers of half the world's great cities....The trail is there, the pattern. Unsolved crimes. Slashed throats of women. With the particular disfigurations and removals. Yes, I've followed a trail of blood....Eighty-seven such murders—and to the trained criminologist, all bear the stigma of the Ripper's handiwork.

Recently there were the so-called Cleveland Torso slayings. Remember?[9]

Hollis' theory is, of course, ultimately validated by his own death at the hands of the eternal Ripper, none other than Dr. Carmody himself. Thus, the motif of the Ripper's immortality—itself frequently imitated in popular fictions—functions not only to signify an eternal continuation of male sexual violence but, at the same time, to provide a symbolic mirror for the actual imitative and similar crimes that have regularly recurred, as the media recite, ever *since* Jack the Ripper.

Not since Jack the Ripper terrorized London just 75 years ago had a great metropolis dwelt in such fear of senseless murder.

The *Saturday Evening Post* on
the "Boston Strangler"[10]

Not since Jack the Ripper has a single individual caused so many nightmares.

The *Reader's Digest* on
the "Son of Sam"[11]

Spurred By His Taunts, Police Search For Britain's Bloodiest Ripper Since Jack.

Headline in *People Weekly* on
the "Yorkshire Ripper"[12]

Mass murderers in the mold and mode of Jack the Ripper have appeared at various times and places in the modern world. When they do, reference is invariably made, particularly in the American and British press, to the original Ripper. Concomitantly, the generic identity of such crimes is continually cross-referenced and reaffirmed.

There are some indications that some of the most famous sex killers have been deliberately imitative, consciously projecting themselves into the Ripper frame. For example, Peter Kürten, the "Düsseldorf Ripper" (active 1925-29), averred that he had read the story of Jack the Ripper several times and that it had made a profound impression on him. Kürten also went so far as to write to the press in the supposed manner of the original Ripper.[13] When Albert DeSalvo decided to confess to the crimes that until then no one had remotely connected him to, he announced to his lawyer that he was about to break the biggest story of the century, something "like Jack the Ripper."[14] And when David Berkowitz's apartment was searched, his bookshelves contained not only pornography and a growing collection of "Son of Sam" clippings, but also a volume on Jack the Ripper.[15]

More often, it is the mass media that affirms the link—particularly when prostitutes are the primary victims, when the killer or others send taunting messages to the police and press, and when so-called "signature" mutilations are performed on the dead women's bodies. The press then nicknames the killers with such obvious derivatives as the "Düsseldorf Ripper," the "Blackout Ripper," "Jack the Stripper," and the "Yorkshire Ripper."[16] Moreover, manifold Ripper references are continually evoked. For example, in 1964 when *Newsweek* reported on England's "Jack the Stripper," they chose to frame their story within two of the original reports on Jack the Ripper from the London *Times*, 1888. The *Newsweek* article itself also contained wild inaccuracies (but favorite legends) about the nineteenth century killer, e.g. that he "quite likely killed as many as twenty prostitutes," and that he sent "letters written in blood to the police."[17] And in 1979, after the eleventh mutilation murder in Yorkshire, *Time* magazine headlined their story "Ripper's Return" and used two telling graphics. The first was an illustration from *Punch*, 1888, referring to the Whitechapel crimes; the other was a photograph of the "battered body of Josephine Whitaker," the contemporary victim of the Yorkshire killer. The time-spanning conjunction was thus verbally and visually asserted.[18]

Still, the similarities need not even be that precise in order for the lineage to be traced back to Jack the Ripper. Only those few basic elements are necessary in order to classify the generic sex crime: a single killer around whom a mystique is formed; a series of similar murders; a repeated/ritualistic style of slaughter; an apparently particular type of victim; and a specific region that is terrorized. As soon as such a pattern becomes evident, Jack the Ripper becomes the most dropped name in town. For example, when *Movietone News* made a documentary about the "Boston Strangler," that film opened with "Jack the Ripper" washing his hands in the Thames; only then did it cut to the horror in Boston.[19] And when *Reader's Digest* published an original article on Ted Bundy, the cover blurb announced: "Caught: America's Jack the Ripper."[20] Such continuing references back to Jack the Ripper serve again to fixate attention upon melodrama, mystery, and personality, effectively negating political analysis. Moreover, these conventional references also indicate that the Ripper's crimes are serving as the "divine model" or "paradigmatic act" for modern sex crime, continually suggesting a cycle of ritual imitation, an inevitable reenactment.

Such emulation of the Ripper—whether intended by the criminal or put into that frame by the press—comprises a first circle of imitative crime. Within that ring are the most sensationalized killers. A second ring, however, is then formed when these newer models throw off their own unique and easily imitated patterns, inspiring an often less celebrated but definite ring of "copycats." During the "Boston Strangler" crisis, the Attorney General's office issued a comprehensive report which concluded that in "probability" one man murdered the first five victims, but:

[T]he slayings of the other six were the work of chillingly clever "imitators." The implication was that police would have to continue to deal with "imitators" from time to time.[21]

Even after DeSalvo's confession to thirteen killings, some authorities continued to believe that only the first five murders were committed by one man (not necessarily DeSalvo) and that the others were the work of unknown men who "cashed in on the earlier publicity."[22] Cognizant of such patterns of imitative crime, police officials frequently refuse to divulge all the details of a particular killer's method. For example, police in Yorkshire would not disclose that killer's trademark knife wound (his "signature") "for fear of copycat killings."[23] Such cautions, however, are not necessarily effective. Indeed, after Sutcliffe was caught it turned out that one of the murders it was assumed he had committed, in truth he had not. Thus the inescapable and widely expressed conclusion was that there was still "another lunatic lurking out there."[24]

The phenomenon of imitative crime ensures that in every case of serial sexual murder there will remain some concurrent similar killings that cannot satisfactorily be charged to the "master murderer." The implication is that there is *always* another lunatic out there.* Again we see the structural continuation of the Ripper myth. That killer was never identified, a circumstance that now feeds the notion of the "eternal" Ripper, the never named, could-be-anyone killer. And even when a case of sexual murder seems to be closed, even when the killer is identified, confesses or is convicted, that characteristic mystification still frequently manages to hold sway.

---

*That phenomenon also, of course, promises *future* crimes "inspired" by the sensationalized killer. Commenting on the Christopher Wilder case, FBI Assistant Director, O.B. "Buck" Revell, announced that the bureau would not disclose the most graphic details of his assaults for, as Revell noted: "the more bizarre the acts the more likely you are to find copy cats. And inevitably there are going to be more Wilders out there." See "Journey of Terror," *People Weekly*, 30 April 1984, pp. 38-43.

For example, although Albert DeSalvo confessed to the Boston stranglings, he later retracted that confession. Also, there was no material evidence to substantiate his guilt; thus, he was never actually tried for those crimes, but was imprisoned for a series of burglaries, assaults, and sex offenses. In 1968, one of his cellmates reported that DeSalvo was not the Strangler at all, but had been tutored for the role by another convict. DeSalvo is now dead, stabbed by another inmate at Walpole in 1973. Authorities are still divided concerning his guilt as a serial killer.[25]

The familiar mystification also suffuses the case of another two stranglers, Kenneth Bianchi and Angelo Buono—the "Hillside Strangler." When Bianchi was arrested, he at first professed utter innocence and ignorance of the crimes. As he presented himself, he was the all-American boy who had come to California for the "sun, the girls, the beaches, the dreams." Later, under hypnosis (and as evidence was gathering solidly against him) he suddenly manifested a multiple personality consisting of the good, normal "Ken" and an evil, murderous, foul-mouthed "Steve." The great majority of psychiatrists who examined him were convinced that he was actually suffering from this mental disorder and were willing to testify to that effect. Had events proceeded this way, Bianchi could have been found not guilty by reason of insanity and for that reason would not have been allowed to testify against Buono (whom he had by then implicated as his co-murderer). However, police managed to uncover evidence which demonstrated his fabrication of the split personality; that coupled with the determined skepticism of one psychiatrist toppled Bianchi's scheme and he admitted that he had been faking. Both he and Buono have been found guilty and sentenced to life imprisonment.[26] Buono maintains his innocence.

David Berkowitz, the "Son of Sam," similarly held authorities and the public spellbound with his stories of possession by demons, led by the father figure, Sam, who supposedly commanded him to kill through his barking dog. Later, Berkowitz admitted that he was faking insanity and making up all the melodrama. He then claimed that he had not been acting alone, but had been the "designated trigger man for a 20-member cult dedicated to 'violence, depravity, sex, and murder'." Psychiatric explanation, which may prove ultimately to be as outlandish as Berkowitz's own, blames his murderous rampage on an "unresolved Oedipal conflict" and trauma around both his biological and adoptive mothers.[27]

Although common belief charges Ted Bundy with anywhere from thirty-six to over one hundred sex murders, he has been tried and convicted for just three. Moreover, Bundy, although he speculates endlessly to reporters on the mentality of the man who would commit such murders, speaks only in the third person. He has never admitted his own guilt.[28]

And in the two years since he was first arrested, Henry Lee Lucas has apparently been unable to stop confessing, ultimately claiming a total of over 600 murders throughout the United States and five other countries. In general, law enforcement agencies have believed his stories and, based upon his confessions, have closed the books on over 210 murders throughout 26 states. However, first investigative reporters and now Attorney General Jim Mattox of Texas are claiming that the physical evidence in no way supports these actions, that the police have been using the confessions as an opportunity to tidy up their books, and that Lucas is putting on the show in order to delay his scheduled execution. Most importantly, as Mattox recently noted, "numerous killers are free because the authorities have been fooled or have accepted bogus murder confessions."[29] Most investigators now agree that the great majority of Lucas' confessions were fabricated, and that he was probably responsible for only three murders—not six hundred. Nevertheless, he has been heralded from the *New York Times* through *Life*, *Penthouse*, and *ABC News 20/20* as the most vicious and prolific sex murderer in U.S. history.[30] Therefore, with some collaboration from both press and police,[31] Lucas has been fixed into the public mind as the epitome of a terrifying new breed of sex killer, one who travels across vast territories, killing untold numbers of victims as he happens upon them, randomly, silently, and thereby escaping not only detection, but also *notice* for years.

Thus, just as Jack the Ripper was cast as a mythic master criminal, a veritable archetype and repository for murder, so too are many of his followers. The gynocide itself is all too real, yet when such killings are so willingly charged to one, all powerful, ubiquitous, even supernatural criminal, it is phallic propaganda, not reality, that is being served. Hugh Aynesworth, one of the reporters who exposed the gross inconsistencies in Henry Lee Lucas's confessions, still acts elsewhere as a mythographer for Ted Bundy, finding in him:

...a preternatural ability to manipulate, a capacity whose effect was akin to magic. It was this power that made him such an effective killer and so impossible to track down.[32]

Such assertions only glamorize and mystify the sex killer while distracting from a realistic assessment of the actual conditions of sex crime. Not only does this culture encourage men to be highly manipulative and aggressive, while enforcing acquiescence and submission, hence victimization, in women, but logic suggests that a lone man moving from place to place and killing only strangers would leave few clues to his identity and remain well beyond the scope of traditional detection.*

*Indeed, it has often been when these "preternaturally powerful" killers make glaring slips, calling attention to themselves, that they are captured. Bundy got caught because he was driving around in a stolen car at 4 a.m. through dark alleys. Berkowitz was traced after he parked at a fire hydrant and got a ticket while committing one of his murders.

Furthermore, we might realize that the ease with which random sex killers (like rapists, wife beaters and murders, etc.) escape notice and punishment has far more to say about the climate of acceptance for violence against women in this society than it does about any "preternatural" abilities and powers of individual killers. In truth, this myth of the ubiquitous, magical, omnipotent, recurrent, Ripper-like killer has actually functioned to *shield* sex murderers from capture. In the Lucas case, "numerous killers" went free as the police cleared their books of unsolved murders and, as I will detail later in this chapter, in Yorkshire, the actual "ripper" went free for years as the police assiduously pursued a figment.

This myth of the superhuman killer is promoted not only through evocations of the original Ripper, but also through a more general and pervasive association between the sex killer and the supernaturally monstrous. A key factor in the mystique of Jack the Ripper was his incorporation into the horror genre as a stock character. Concomitantly, subsequent sex killers are promoted throughout the media as manifestations of all the traditional monsters—werewolves, vampires, and phantoms—while in horror fiction itself, a twofold phenomenon has occurred. First, it is now common for the "monster" to be simply a "human" sex killer (as in *Psycho*, Alfred Hitchcock, 1960).[33] Secondly, contemporary horror stories about traditional monsters frequently present these creatures as active serial murderers (e.g. *The Howling*, Joe Dante, 1980). All such trends reflect the continuing accretion of a folklore of monstrosity around contemporary sex crime.

The Monstrous

The Yorkshire Ripper is Britain's most notorious mass murderer and, like Son of Sam, the Boston Strangler, and his Victorian namesake, he has slipped into folklore and become a macabre public bogeyman.[34]

The city was running scared and the police were supposed to restore calm by arresting the monster who was killing over and over again.

> Ted Schwarz on the "Hillside Strangler"[35]

I am deeply hurt by your calling me a wemon [sic] hater. I am not. But I am a monster. I am the "Son of Sam"...I am the "Monster"—"Beelzebub"—the chubby behemouth.

> David Berkowitz, letter to police (1 April 1977),
> printed in the *Daily News*, 5 *June 1977*[36]

One of the components of the Ripper formula is the creation of a felt state of siege, a reign of terror in which the "monster" is felt to be the "master," a state produced by the actions of the sex killer, but unarguably intensified and participated in by the mass media. The situation in the summer of 1977 in New York is exemplary. During his spree as the "Son of Sam," the killer who randomly shot young women who walked alone on the street, or sat in parked cars with other women or men, David Berkowitz wrote highly dramatic and disturbing letters to both police and press, letters which were subsequently printed in the daily papers. One such letter was sent to columnist Jimmy Breslin of the *Daily News*:

> Hello from the cracks in the sidewalks of New York City and from the ants that dwell in these cracks and feed on the dried blood of the dead that has settled into these cracks.

> Hello from the gutters of New York City, which are filled with dog manure, vomit, stale wine, urine and blood.

> Don't think that because you haven't heard from me for a while that I went to sleep. No, rather, I am still here, like a spirit roaming the night. Thirsty, hungry, seldom stopping to rest; anxious to please Sam.[37]

The first day that just a part of that letter was printed, the *Daily News* sold a record-breaking 1,116,000 copies, a record that stood until the day Berkowitz was apprehended in mid-August. Actually, an extraordinary number of newspapers was sold throughout that entire summer as the *Post* and the *News* vied in a circulations war, turning their most sensationalist attention to this story. So intense was their coverage that the *New Yorker* condemned the sensationalist press in an editorial uncannily similar to the one *Punch* had issued ninety years earlier deploring the lurid coverage of the Whitechapel crimes. The *New Yorker* charged the city's tabloids with what we might call "self-fulfilling publicity," of possibly encouraging the killer, or another of like mind, to strike again "by transforming a killer into a celebrity...into a seemingly omnipotent monster stalking the city."[38]

Then mayor, Abraham Beame, summed up the melodramatic fascination of that time:

Son of Sam. I even liked the name and that in itself was terrifying. I knew it would stick...would become his trademark. There had been six attacks, all laid at the feet of a single individual, and you could see it all building, the fears of the people, including my own, and the headlong rush of the press to create a personality, someone they could build a story around....The letter fused everything together [this refers to the first letter Berkowitz wrote to the police in which he named himself "Son of Sam"]. It was one man against an entire city.[39]

Not only that spectacular name, but Berkowitz's self-articulated monstrosity and his style and choice of victims struck a particularly resonant note for the "Son of Sam," the monster who preyed on parked teenage couples, seemed the very embodiment of that most common bogeyman of teenage horror—the stalking maniac of such modern urban legends as "The Hook."[40]

The attention of the people of New York, particularly throughout the summer of 1977, was riveted on that overwhelmingly monstrous killer. The prevailing mood was marked by both fascination and fear. The *New York Times* noted the pervasion of a ".44 Caliber Cloud of Fear," and *Commonweal* declared the killer to have been the "psychological master" of the city.[41] Men wearing T-shirts bearing the police sketch of the killer's supposed face were spotted on the streets. Talk of the "Son of Sam" had become the "staple of conversation." A disco in Queens where two of the victims were shot was referred to as a "national monument." Above all, again in the words of the *Times*, "where the 'Son of Sam' struck, young women walk in fear."[42] For although men had been attacked, the primary targets were clearly the women they were with, particularly, police warned, women with "long, brown hair." Lifestyles changed. The disco and restaurant business suffered, while the haircutting business boomed.[43] Many women cut or dyed their hair, wore wigs, or hid it under hats. Here, it should be noted that the idea that a killer is obsessed with a particular type of woman—be she a coed, redhead, or girl with "long, brown hair"—is a recurring one in cases of serial sex murder. Although this may occasionally have some basis in reality, more frequently such fetishes are the fabrications of the media and/or police and serve primarily to further eroticize the killings. The murderer in actuality picks victims on the basis of availability. Significantly, Stacey Moscowitz, the last woman shot by Berkowitz, had blonde hair.

During the "Son of Sam" siege, many women, whatever their hair length or color, responded to the terrorization by simply staying at home whenever possible during those critical months. And even after Berkowitz was captured in August 1977, reminders of the horror continued to haunt the women of New York—some deliberately planted by big business. Berkowitz had been widely quoted in the press as liking to "shoot pretty girls." Incredibly, just a few months after his arrest, Max Factor introduced a new female face moisturizer called "Self Defense." As the billboards throughout the city threatened: "Warning! A Pretty Face Isn't Safe In This City. Fight Back With Self-Defense." Here the cosmetics firm unabashedly aligned itself with the point of view of the sex killer, frankly trying to cash in on the fear he had generated, and simultaneously slotting all women into the archetypal patriarchal role of the desirable/vulnerable victim.[44]

Nightmare is a word commonly employed to describe the experience of a region terrorized by a Ripper type killer—and that "nightmare" continues to be a recurring one. David Berkowitz was captured on August 10, 1977, on the east coast of the country and on October 17 of that same year, Yolanda Washington was raped and strangled on the other shining sea in Los Angeles. By the end of February, ten women and girls had been found dead under similar circumstances—nude, raped, strangled, and dumped on hillsides around L.A. Their bodies showed evidence of lengthy tortures.[45] The first victims were described by the police as "part-time prostitutes," streetwomen, runaways; Yolanda Washington was Black. There was little public interest or outcry. However, the fifth and sixth victims were two schoolgirls, Dolores Cepeda, 12, and Sonja Johnson, 14. At this juncture, media coverage exploded and public panic along with it. Moreover, certain resonances from the Ripper formula undoubtedly worked to amplify that terror. For example, although police and press knew from the beginning that the killings were the work of two men:

...each new corpse was reported in the press as another victim of the mysterious "Hillside Strangler." There is now no way of knowing whether that expression was coined by the police or the press.[46]

Los Angeles, like New York during the just past summer, was now a disaster area—the staked-out territory of a designated monster and a similar climate prevailed:

At the peak of the murders, thousands of women in the Los Angeles area remained home at night; shopping centers were frequently deserted in the evening; and sales of guns and guard dogs skyrocketed.[47]

By the late 1970s, New York and Los Angeles were just two of the many United States regions that had experienced a siege from a Ripper-style killer. But prior to this spread of serial sex crime in the 1970s, America's exemplary episode of this type had been in Boston in the early 1960s. During that time, the "Boston Strangler" generated widespread panic among the women of that city. Gerold Frank describes the general scene as the terror took hold:

Wild stories began to circulate, whispered by one woman to another, told authoritatively by cabdrivers to curious out-of-town passengers, stories which vaguely approximated the truth: that the bodies were left exhibited in obscene positions, that the killer did not rape his victims—this was frightful enough—but assaulted them with a "foreign object," attacking them in death or as they lay dying....Chilling reports appeared in the press. The Strangler was a man "of animal strength in his hands and arms"...who "scaled the apartment house walls to reach open windows"....Women all but barricaded themselves in their apartments.[48]

Again, the operation of the Ripper myth was evidenced throughout the crisis; paramount was the notion of the single, obsessed and preternaturally powerful killer. As Jack Iams, writing in the *Saturday Evening Post* pointed out, the police themselves always maintained that the "Strangler" as such was a "figment of public imagination," that the murders were almost definitely the work of several individuals. Yet, as he observed, "those same police officials...refer to their quarry as The Strangler—just like everybody else."[49] Again, the mythic force of the formula predominates over the facts. Yet it was in Yorkshire, twenty years later, that mass acquiescence to the Ripper myth, especially on the part of the police, proved to be most efficacious to the killer himself.

For five years the so-called "Yorkshire Ripper" eluded capture, becoming ever more daring in his strikes, and turning from killing only prostitutes to attacking any woman he found alone at night. After the eleventh mutilation-murder in 1979, the police launched an unprecedented publicity campaign which they hoped would lead to the killer's identification. The core of that campaign was an edited version of a tape that had been sent to the police and which they believed to be a genuine transmission from the killer. The voice on the tape called himself "Jack the Ripper," taunted the authorities, and mentioned obscure details of the murders. As part of the campaign, that tape was played daily on radio and television; its recorded message could also be heard regularly in bars and discos. Furthermore, anyone could hear it anytime by dialing a special telephone number. Forty thousand people per day reportedly called in to hear that message.[50] This is part of it:

I'm Jack. I see you are still having no luck catching me....I reckon your boys are letting you down George [Oldfield, police investigator]. Can't be much good can you?...I'm not sure when I will strike again, but it will definitely be some time this year, maybe September or October—even sooner if I get the chance.[51]

Untold numbers of people shared that experience and shared it repeatedly. The presence of the Ripper was insinuated into every atmosphere. As *Time* magazine phrased it, the Ripper became "Britain's best-known unknown man."[52]

Added features of the campaign were special newspapers profiling the murders and providing a transcript of the tape. These also included samples of the handwriting from three "Ripper" letters that had been mailed to the newspapers. In one of these, the writer boasted, "at the rate I'm going I should be in the book of records."[53] News agents gave away 2,000,000 copies of these papers. A Ripper poster replaced the normal transmission card of ITV, then on strike. A Ripper Roadshow barnstormed outside pubs, shopping centers, factories, and in town squares and village greens. Posters and billboards were set up in over six thousand sites. A typical billboard pleaded:

HELP US STOP THE RIPPER FROM KILLING AGAIN. LOOK AT HIS HANDWRITING [photograph]. LISTEN TO HIS VOICE [telephone number]. IF YOU RECOGNIZE EITHER, REPORT IT TO YOUR LOCAL POLICE.[54]

The police admitted that with these tactics they were "igniting a myth" and possibly creating a "superman," but gambled that the overwhelming publicity would break the case.[55] They were wrong. In January 1980, after four fruitless months, the campaign closed down; no relevant information had surfaced. The killer, Peter Sutcliffe, a married truck driver, was not caught until January 1981, and then only by chance. The police were making a routine prostitution arrest of a woman whom Sutcliffe had in his car. But there were false license plates on the car and Sutcliffe had his tools/weapons with him. He was arrested and confessed to thirteen murders, as well as seven attempted murders, and was convicted in May 1981.

The actual man, Sutcliffe, clashed utterly with the image of the Ripper that had been so pervasively and unforgettably projected. He asserted that he was greatly angered with the media for calling him the "Ripper" and denied any sexual motivation for his crimes. But the real shocker was that, although undoubtedly the murderer, Sutcliffe was *not* the man who had made the tape or sent any of the "Jack the Ripper" communications to the police. All such messages were an elaborate hoax, a criminal joke played on the entire country and engineered by some still unknown man, a hoax which disastrously diverted the police from the track of the actual killer as they assiduously searched for someone who matched the distinctive voice, accent and handwriting of the wrong man.[56]

Apparently, there was one piece of actual correspondence from Sutcliffe. It was a poem mailed to the Sheffield daily paper, *The Star*, months after the other "Ripper" letters and tape were received by the police. Entitled "Clueless," it nevertheless contained the most significant clue up to that point, a broad hint that the tape was spurious, a meaning, however, that was not taken. It read in part:

'Clueless'
Poor Old Oldfield
Worked In A Coldfield
  Hobson Has No Choice
  Misled By A Voice*

---

*Hobson and Oldfield were two principal police investigators of the case.

That letter was signed " 'The Streetcleaner' (T.S.)"[57] and was mailed on September 6, 1979, just four days after the eleventh murder and one month before "Project R" (the publicity campaign) was launched around the Ripper tape. Although the hint was ignored, the letter clearly suggested that the tape was not genuine: "Hobson has no choice/misled by a voice."

And that tape was, of course, a consummate fake. It nevertheless rang true to the police and mass of listeners because it so completely resonated with the established formula and so thoroughly satisfied the mythic setting for the mass sex crime. The voice called himself Jack the Ripper, taunted the police and announced future crimes, an utterly clear rendition of the Ripper formula. And it is very likely that it was just that compelling fulfillment of tradition and expectation that so thoroughly decoyed police judgment as to the validity of the tape. Any authenticity resided only in the tradition. And Yorkshire in a sense represents a dual imitative crime as two separate men enacted the Ripper syndrome. One performed the actual murders, but the other provided the public relations, the image, the myth. And it is crucial to remember that it was the messages of the *pseudo*-Ripper that galvanized the publicity blitz and thereby stamped the idea of the perpetual or recurring Ripper, the immortal monster, into collective consciousness. It remains unknown whether any of the 1888 communications came from the actual killer. In the late 1970s, however, the believed messages were indisputably the work of an armchair criminal who enjoyed fantasizing himself as the Ripper. And the identity of that man, someone whose presence haunted Britain for several years, remains a mystery. Although Sutcliffe is locked up, his shadowy counterpart is still "out there." As one Englishwoman commented:

Now Sutcliffe is in prison, can we really feel safe? The campaign to convict this man has uncovered a hornet's nest. What about all the law-abiding citizens who secretly harbour the desire to emulate him and become famous.[58]

Fantasy identification with a Ripper, so clearly compelling in 1888, has lost none of its fascination. The great pretender in Yorkshire carried that mind game to the limit, yet his case is not unique; in every instance of the mass and sensationalized sex crimes, to varying degrees, something similar happens. Scores of men call up the police, write letters to newspapers, tell friends or appear in person at the local precinct to declare that *they* are the killer. Just as police must accept that they will have to deal with "chillingly clever imitators," so too will they have to sort out the equally clever and persistent confessors. The motivations behind these confessional urges are diverse, but might include phallic feelings of envy, guilt, personal insignificance, desire for fame,* and, at root, a powerful identification.

Showing Identification

Male reaction to the murders mirrored...misogynist attitudes and took a variety of forms, from a conscious imitation and impersonation of the Ripper to a more latent identification with the criminal and subtle exploitation of female terror.

Judith Walkowitz[59]

Throughout the city men's jokes, innuendos, and veiled threats (I might be the Strangler, you know) revealed an identification.

Suzanne Lacy[60]

As one woman who lived in Tallahassee during 1978 recalled regarding the Bundy murders, "One of the most disturbing things was the series of jokes and innuendoes that men traded about the murders."[61] Such joking was not atypical. Earlier, Kate Millett had noted two simultaneous male responses to events of sexual atrocity: the first, a "scandalized, possible hypocritical indignation"; the second, "a mass response of titilation...[and] expressions of envy or amusement."[62]

The Bundy case has consistently aroused not only some jocular moments, but also a public display of mourning because here the white, middle-class victims could be characterized as the stereotypic "daughters of men." However, a much different response is met when the women killed are not white, not "family women," and not middle class. During the first six months of 1979, twelve Black women were murdered within a small area of Boston. Barbara Smith points out:

The victims were universally described as runaways, prostitutes, or drug addicts who "deserved" to die because of how they lived. The distorted portrayal of the girls and women could be expected in a city notorious for its racism, but there was a particular sexist turn, because the victims were not only Black, but female.[63]

In Boston in 1979, or in Los Angeles** where, since 1983, at latest count, seventeen women, all but two of whom were Black, have been slain

---

*When two men in a California jail falsely confessed to the "Green River Killings," the *New York Times* headlined its story: "2 Inmates Brag of Killing 11 Women on Coast," 8 Aug. 1984, Sec. 1, p. 10, col. 6.

**In Los Angeles, Black community groups have taken it upon themselves to inform women of the danger, pass out sketches of the suspected killer, etc. As Margaret Prescod, founder of the Black Coalition Fighting Back Serial Murders stated: "There'd be more response from police if these were San Marino housewives....If you're Black and living on the fringe, your life isn't worth much." See "The L.A. Slayer," *Newsweek*, 6 June 1986, p. 28.

by a so-called "Southside Killer," there is little official action and scant "public" outcry—particularly when compared to the uproar raised during the "Hillside Strangler" and "Night Stalker" cases. Still, the pornographic joking remains. A white woman living in Boston during those months in 1979 recalled the following incident:

I had known this man for a few months and dated him—a University professor, very distinguished and all, in his mid-forties—and had just gone to bed with him for the first time. After his climax, he gripped me hard and cracked, "Don't move now or you'll be the twelfth black victim." Although this was supposed to be a "joke," it was absolutely clear that he was getting off on this implied threat to me. We'd just had sex and now all there was was danger. I never wanted to see him again and I never did.[64]

Manifestly, all instances of sexual terror serve as lessons for *all* women. Moreover, it is clear that when men "jokingly" assume the mask of the current Ripper, Strangler, etc., they are correspondingly demanding that women play along by identifying with the sexual victim.

Such sadistic joking may be the most ordinary form of identification with the sex killer, but there are other, far more elaborate, modes as well. A man living in England during the time of the "Yorkshire Ripper" told of one friend's reaction:

During the last eighteen months before Peter Sutcliffe was arrested, a friend of mine, who works at an agency for photo-journalism, was undergoing Freudian psychoanalysis. The analysis encouraged him to "regress" further and further back to his early childhood until he actually experienced some of the feelings of being a baby—and even feelings of being in the womb! One of the aims of the therapy, I think, was to relieve his depression by enabling him to express feelings of anger and to "act out" a lot of his negative emotions. As a journalist he heard the "inside" story (which later proved to be untrue and only a rumor) of the Ripper's "signature"— his method of mutilation which had not been revealed to the public. Apparently, after he had killed his victim, he cut off one breast and then inserted it into the stomach or womb. This made a deep impression on my friend who felt he understood why he did this. I think he associated this act with the omnipotent fantasies of babies he was then "experiencing" and with powerful feelings of anger and hostility against the mother. As the murderer was still free at this time (and the press was full of stories about men who were suspected of being the Ripper), my friend, at times, felt *he* was the Ripper.[65]

This extreme private identification, perhaps facilitated by the Freudian analysis, is not unique. Rather, strains of it can be found in the mass forms of public communication as well—particularly in popular song.

Perhaps because the "Yorkshire Ripper" siege was so lengthy, publicized, and so pervasively paralleled to the original Ripper, the identification it inspired was especially pronounced. In 1980, British rock musician Trevor Rabin released an album called *Face to Face.* It contained a song called simply, "The Ripper." Rabin boasts: "Rats, they'll call

me just the Ripper/ And George would love to know my name." Further
taunting "George" (Oldfield, police inspector), the singer notes that while
the police may be "fast," he is "quicker." Moreover, he has "done it
all before" and it is time for all of us to "open up [our] doors for the
Ripper."[66] Three factors come through here: the Yorkshire Ripper is
made one with Jack the Ripper; the song is basically a singing version
of the pseudo-ripper tape, so widely popularized during the publicity
campaign; and, most remarkably, it is sung in the first person—the
performer identifies himself with the ripper as do all those rockers who
sing along.

   Rabin's song, however, pales by comparison with Thin Lizzy's 1980
tribute to the ripper called "Killer on the Loose." Once again, first person
identification is the mode; the lyrics comprise a fairly elaborate violent
fantasy and carry a most explicit threat:

Some people they call me Jack
. . .
I'm looking for somebody and don't even know her name.
I might be looking for you
. . .
For there is something I've got to do to you honey
And it's between you and me.

The chorus wails about the "killer on the loose again, a ladykiller on
the loose." And this song not only identifies the lead singer with that
killer, but also insists upon the identification of the listening female
with his intended victim. The lyrics pick up with the killer scoffing
at those who believe that he "don't exist" and tells us that "I'm confessing,
I'm a mad sexual rapist." He goes on to threaten that he will be "standing
in the shadows of love":

Waiting for you.
Don't unzip your zipper
Cause you know I'm Jack the Ripper.[67]

This anthem, along with Rabin's "Ripper" actually was released while
the "Yorkshire Ripper" was "on the loose."* The face to face
identification could hardly be more complete. Popular songs such as
these function as one of the many forms of culturally accepted propaganda
for sex crime, rock 'n' roll ballads recounting the exploits of these outlaws/
heroes of the patriarchal state.

---

*Ironically, that same album by Thin Lizzy contains another cut entitled "Genocide:
The Killing of the Buffalo." Thus this band hypocritically mourns the nineteenth century
slaughter of the Indians and the buffalo and the accompanying rape of the wilderness
while simultaneously celebrating twentieth century gynocide as a pornographic fantasy,
a dream drama of male omnipotence, a means to get off on female fear.

A piece in which a rock singer identifies himself so literally with a sex criminal is not without precedent. Ten years earlier, a similar killer provided the inspiration for a similar song. This one was written and recorded by the group commonly nicknamed "the greatest rock 'n' roll band in the world"—the Rolling Stones. That song, "The Midnight Rambler," is their hymn to the "Boston Strangler." Although the recorded version of that song opens with the doublethinking disclaimer that it is *not* about "the Boston," Susan Brownmiller has analyzed the lyrics and discovered that they are taken almost directly from the confessions of Albert DeSalvo, as reported by Gerold Frank in his study of that case. Brownmiller asks us to compare the lyrics with DeSalvo's description of the murder of Beverly Samans. Throughout that song, a chant is repeated. "Oh, don't you do that, oh don't do that," followed by a description of "the Midnight" who tiptoes into a bedroom in order to "hit her head...rape her...hang her." The song ends finally with the lines, "I'll stick my knife right down your throat."[68] Reading the confession of DeSalvo we learn that "Don't do that" was the repeated cry of Samans as she was raped and then murdered. Also, unlike other Strangler victims, the cause of her death was not asphyxiation; it was a knife wound in the throat.[69]

A *New York Times* rock critic describes the atmosphere during a live performance of this song by the Stones:

Keith Richard sways through a long, threateningly erotic guitar introduction as Mick slowly removes a bright gold sash. On the first line, "You've heard about the Boston Strangler," the lights suddenly dim and Jagger is outlined in a deep red floodlight. He slinks around the stage, *a slim-hipped, multisexual reincarnation of Jack the Ripper*.[70](emphasis mine)

Here Mick Jagger merges indistinguishably into the Boston Strangler who then becomes Jack the Ripper—a consummate sex symbol for the Age of Sex Crime.

And by the end of "The Midnight Rambler," Mick is also now singing in the first person.

I'm gonna smash down on your plate glass window,
put a fist through your steel plate door
. . .
I'll stick my knife right down your throat, baby, and that hurts.

Brownmiller comments:

"Midnight Rambler" is Mick Jagger's orgasmic, heightened re-creation on stage of the rape-murder of twenty-three-year-old Beverly Samans, the most viciously mutilated of the

Strangler's victims.... Mick has become the mythic Strangler.[71]

Such a song and such a rock concert are quite literally a *re-creation*, for this is definitive ritual, the dramatization of the paradigmatic event with the performer assuming the persona or mask of the hero. Jagger is sacralizing, glorifying the event and the killer. The ritual of the song and performance invite millions of male listeners over the years to identify with the Strangler/Ripper via their hero, Mick Jagger, and millions of women to identify with the silenced victim. Moreover, the message that surfaces here is one that is usually communicated only subliminally, i.e. the sexual criminal, not only the rapist, but also the mutilation murderer, functions as a *hero* to his culture.

The Heroic

[Jack the Ripper] that great hero of my youth, that skilled human butcher who did all his work on alcoholic whores.

Charles McCabe, *San Francisco Chronicle*, 7 Oct. 1971

So let's salute the mighty Bundy,
Here on Friday, gone on Monday.
All his roads lead out of town.
It's hard to keep a good man down.

An Aspen folksinger[72]

Our heroes and their narratives are an index to
our character and conception of our role in the universe.

Richard Slotkin[73]

The mythos of sex crime plays not only upon the monstrous imagination, but also on the heroic. It was Brownmiller who pointed out, "'Hero' is the surprising word that men employ when they speak of Jack the Ripper." She quotes Noel Annan writing in the *New York Review of Books* who called him, "the hero of horror in Victorian times," as well as Charles McCabe cited above.[74] This bizarre and amused attitude toward atrocity, this movement towards heroization persists into feelings about not only Jack, but also about his followers.

When Ted Bundy was awaiting trial for the murder of Caryn Campbell in Aspen, Colorado (after having been convicted for attempted kidnapping in Utah), he managed to escape twice.* The first time he was caught and returned to custody; the second time he was successful and traveled to Florida where he murdered again. But upon the news of his escapes (particularly the first) a phenomenal reaction occurred.

*And on July 19, 1984, Ted Bundy and another death row inmate were caught in an attempt to break out of Florida State Prison. *New York Times*, 20 July 1984, Sec. A, p. 8, col. 5.

All observers concur: "In Aspen, Bundy had become a folk hero."[75] "Ted achieved the status of Billy the Kid at least";[76] or "Aspen reacted as if Bundy were some sort of Robin Hood instead of a suspected mass murderer. A folklore sprang up out of the thin Rocky Mountain air."[77] T-shirts appeared reading: "Ted Bundy is a One Night Stand." Radio KSNO programmed a Ted Bundy Request Hour, playing songs like "Ain't No Way to Treat a Lady." A local restaurant offered a "Bundyburger" consisting of nothing more than a plain roll. "Open it and see the meat has fled," explained a sign. All this fun and glorification, although after his second escape the FBI took Bundy seriously enough to name him to their 10 Most Wanted List, seeking him "in connection with 36 similar-type sexual slayings throughout several Western states."[78]

Just as Bundy's white, young, generally middle-class victims, were stereotypically portrayed as "anyone's daughters," Bundy himself seemed to be the fatherland's ideal son. He was universally described as good looking, intelligent, personable, attractive to women—in short, the All-American Boy. In 1975, at the height of the "Ted Murders" "Warren Zevon struck a hit with his "Excitable Boy," a song about the stereotypically normal boy who, after taking "little Susie to the Junior Prom...raped her and killed her, then he took her home." But as "they all said," he was "just an excitable boy."[79] And in 1978 when *New Times* published a story on Ted Bundy, its coy title asked if he too were "Just an Excitable Boy?"[80]

Bundy, as all the media stressed, was a former law student, a Young Republican, and once wrote a rape prevention pamphlet for women (and John Wayne Gacy, killer of boys, was a clown). His victims, although they were last seen in public places, in crowds, with friends, just inexplicably vanished. A *Reader's Digest* article likened Bundy to the most famous film monster of the 1970s, "Like a shark patrolling a crowded beach, he stalked, struck and was gone."[81]

Within two months in Florida, Bundy had attacked six women; three died. Two, Margaret Bowman and Lisa Levy, were bludgeoned and mutilated as they slept in their Florida State University sorority house. Just a few days after the killings, NBC had been scheduled to broadcast a TV movie, *A Stranger in the House*, a thriller about a psychopathic killer of sorority sisters; for obvious reasons, the network felt obliged to cancel local showings.[82] A seemingly bizarre coincidence like this is something like a slip of the societal tongue, one of those moments of brief but unintended clarity, here pointing to a connection between the normalcy and frequency of gynocidal "entertainment" to the actual proliferation of gynocide itself.

In 1980, Ted Bundy received his third death penalty in Florida; as of early 1986, appeals are still in progress. While on trial, Bundy was the subject of scores of in-depth articles, from the *New York Times Magazine* through *Rolling Stone, Cosmopolitan,* and the *Reader's Digest.*[83] All types of audiences heard his story. Many also actually saw it, for the Bundy trial was one of the first where television cameras were allowed into the courtroom.[84] After his convictions, at least five non-fiction books have appeared that recite his narrative as well as a made-for-TV mini-series, *Bundy: The Deliberate Stranger* (NBC, 1986). For fiction readers, a 1982 novel, *Missing Persons,* gives a barely disguised rendition.[85]

Bundy is not the only mass sex killer to be so celebrated.* The *New Yorker* accused the tabloids of transforming a killer (Berkowitz) into a celebrity and, just two years after his crimes, letters written from jail by Berkowitz were being auctioned off by art dealer Charles Hamilton in New York.[86] The *New Yorker's* accusation included the idea that the sensational coverage of the criminal might actually be encouraging him to continue killing. And a few years later, Berkowitz indicated that indeed it had. He avowed that after his fourth shooting:

I didn't care much anymore, for I finally had convinced myself that it was good to do it, necessary to do it, and that the public wanted me to do it. The latter part I believe until this day. I believe that many were rooting for me. This was the point at which the papers began to pick up vibes and information that something big was happening out in the street. Real big![87]

The fact of the patriarchal male's identification with the sex killer, would indeed suggest that "the public" was "rooting for" Berkowitz. For, in a patriarchy, the "public" *is* male, i.e. it habitually and systematically (albeit invisibly) reflects the male point of view, normalizing male power.**

---

*In an interview on National Public Radio's "All Things Considered," the late Thomas Thompson, author of the best-selling novel, *Celebrity,* commented on this phenomenon:
A celebrity is someone who is celebrated for some extraordinary accomplishment...but we make, and I'm guilty of this, we have celebrity criminals nowadays. The "Hillside Strangler," a man who murdered several ladies in Los Angeles was captured in Bellingham, Washington and he went into court there one morning about a year ago and copped a plea which made it certain that he would never get the death penalty and got a life imprisonment. And he did all his legal business in the morning and that afternoon the very same day, he wrote me a long and eloquent letter asking me if I would write his autobiography and he thought it would be a terrific movie as well.
Thompson declined that offer. "All Things Considered," 6 May, 1982.

**This argument is developed with great power in Catharine A. MacKinnon, "Feminism, Marxism, Method, and the State: Toward Feminist Jurisprudence," *Signs: Journal of Women in Culture and Society,* 8 (1983), 636-658. One of her basic points is that interpretation from the male standpoint is systemic and hegemonic, that "objectivity" is essentially society's reflection of its own viewpoint, again, the male viewpoint. Such an analysis is reminiscent of de Beauvoir's observation that the relationship of man to

We can also recognize here the action of *public* as a pseudogeneric. As linguist Julia Penelope has argued, words such as *man, professor, doctor, person,* or *people,* usually function to signify *males.*[88] Thus Henry Lee Lucas tells *ABC News 20/20,* "All across the country there's *people* just like me."[89] (emphasis mine)

Whether as monster, master, celebrity, hero, or all of these, the sexual murderer performs both practical and symbolic functions for the culture that has produced him. He not only massively generates the sexual terror which preserves male power, but he also functions to promote male pleasure. In their history of sex crime (1963), Masters and Lea note:

When a ripper or stabber is at large somewhere, especially if he is at large somewhere *else,* the average person [read *man*] is able to experience a certain pleasure in considering his exploits and the efforts of the police to capture him. His crimes may be treated, particularly in magazines and in books (where distance is temporal as well as spatial), with a certain levity, as has been the case especially with Jack the Ripper.[90]

Of course, the simple fact of being an adult male guarantees that "distance" from sexual danger. Not surprisingly then, it is in adult "men's magazines" that the characteristic levity and implicit heroization are most clearly pronounced.

Hustler, for example (at one count the thirty-seventh best-selling magazine in the country),[91] has consistently endorsed Kenneth Bianchi as their kind of guy. In one issue (August 1980), *Hustler* offered a parody of advertising, "Ads We'd Like to See," a semi-regular feature. Here, they used the well-known format for Dewers Scotch as a model, proposing their own "Doer's Lite Label" ad starring Bianchi:

Kenneth Bianchi: Occupation: Hillside Strangler
Latest Accomplishment: Cindy Lee Hudspeth, 20.
Quote: "You gotta treat 'em rough..."
After knocking off a couple of bimbos, the Hillside Strangler likes to kick back and relax with *Doer's Lite Label.*[92]

Thus, the sex killer is a *doer,* a man admired for his accomplishments, a hero who enacts what the readers of *Hustler* presumably only fantasize about or perform on a smaller scale.

This grotesque glorification did not pass unnoticed. A feminist group, "The Preying Mantis Women's Brigade," organized to destroy

woman is not symmetrical as it might first appear, for man occupies both the masculine and the neutral "as is indicated by the common use of *man* to designate human beings in general." Simone de Beauvoir, *The Second Sex,* trans. and ed. by H.M. Parshley (c. 1952; New York, Knopf, 1971), p. xv.

over 550 copies of the magazine on newsstands in the Santa Cruz area, accusing *"Hustler,* Bianchi and other mass murderers of women [of] work[ing] in direct collusion with each other." They further stated:

These magazines were destroyed in memory of Cindy Lee Hudspeth, age 20—a victim of the Hillside Strangler, Kenneth Bianchi. They were destroyed in retaliation against *Hustler's* "joke" which aggrandized Bianchi.[93]

In yet another instance, *Hustler* affirmed its, and its readers, identification with sexual killers, its collusion with sexual torture and murder.[94] In March 1984, "Free Beaver Hunt Caps" were offered to all those who submitted nude photos of themselves to the magazine. Illustrations for that offer showed both Bianchi and Buono wearing the caps. Underneath Bianchi's picture is this: "Ken Bianchi says, 'I was a real eager Beaver Hunter, but with this cap I could have caught some more.' " Underneath Buono's: "Angelo Buono says, 'These caps are neat! I bet if I wore one, the girls would be dying to meet me.' "[95]

The "hunter" reference, so superficially evoked here, actually is a pervasive and crucial one in the mythos of sex crime.* "Coed Killer," Edmund Kemper boasted, "I was the hunter and they were the victims." He further spoke of "admiring my catch, like a fisherman."[96] Speaking in the third person about himself, Ted Bundy related that:

...what really fascinated him was the hunt, the adventure of searching out his victims. And, to a degree, possessing them physically as one would possess a potted plant, a painting, or a Porsche.[97]

David Berkowitz concurred, writing to the press:

I love to hunt. Prowling the streets looking for fair game—tasty meat. The wemon [sic] of Queens are the prettyist [sic] of all. I must be the water they drink. I live for the hunt—my life. Blood for papa....I want to make love to the world.[98]

Here the ideology of sex crime takes on a characteristically American tone. As Richard Slotkin analyzes it in *Regeneration Through Violence: The Mythology of the American Frontier 1600-1860,* in this culture founded upon the violent and rapturously mythicized conquest of the wilderness, the *hunter* has emerged as the "archetypal American hero."

---

*And how different is the patriarchal poet? Consider Alfred Lord Tennyson in "The Princess" Part V, 1, 147):
Man is the hunter; woman is his game.
The sleek and shining creatures of the chase,
We hunt them for the beauty of their skins;
They love us for it and we ride them down.

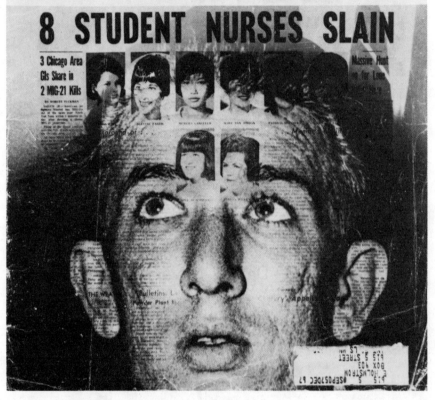

Copyright © 1967 by *Saturday Evening Post.*

SPECIAL FEATURE

TO CATCH A KILLER

BY NATHAN M. ADAMS

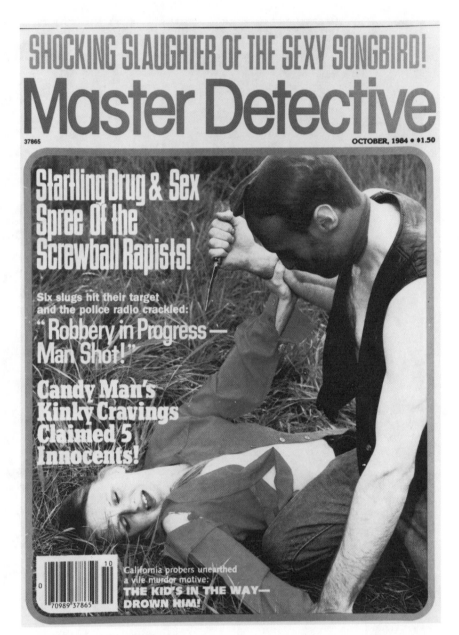

SHOCKING SLAUGHTER OF THE SEXY SONGBIRD!

Master Detective

37865   OCTOBER, 1984 • $1.50

Startling Drug & Sex Spree Of the Screwball Rapists!

Six slugs hit their target and the police radio crackled: "Robbery in Progress — Man Shot!"

Candy Man's Kinky Cravings Claimed 5 Innocents!

0 70989 37865   10

California probers unearthed a vile murder motive: THE KID'S IN THE WAY — DROWN HIM!

Moreover (and not too surprisingly) that hunter's "violence [is] markedly sexual in its character." In many typical myth narratives, the hero must slay a sacred animal, usually a deer, who represents the Goddess of Nature. This hunt is said to represent a "symbolic sexual union which proves the vigor of the hero and restores fertility to the forest." (Here, as in other patriarchal myth, female murder is sexualized while heterosexual union is presented as a rapturous act of violence and bloodshed.) Slotkin comments:

An American hero is the lover of the spirits of the wilderness, and his acts of love and sacred affirmation are acts of violence against that spirit and her avatars.[99]

He further identifies this mythic tradition of "self-justifying acts of violent self-transcendence and regeneration" as one which has provided legitimation for such American atrocities as the genocide against the Native Americans, the slaughter and near or complete extinction of many animal species, and the crusade of obliteration in Vietnam. It is a tradition which, he concludes, has left the American landscape marked with a "pyramid of skulls."

All of this rings true to a great extent. Still, it would be folly to particularize this agenda as only a national circumstance and thereby fail to connect it to the larger patriarchal imperatives. Slotkin continues:

The love we have for the things of the world, the delight we take in them, goes hand in hand with our destruction and conversion of them, perhaps because the act of destruction itself somehow makes us believe in our manhood and godhood....Our heroes and their narratives are an index to our character and conception of our role in the universe....The trophies they are perpetually gathering have no material value; their sanctity derives from their function as visual and concrete proofs of the self-justifying acts of violent self-transcendence and regeneration that produced them.[100]

Gladly extracting ourselves from such *manhood, godhood, we* and *our*, women can recognize that this archetype of the hunter/hero and his rampage of violent self-transcendence underwrites not only American frontier mythology, but also many other myths of patriarchal origins/ "creation." Moreover, this scenario is reflected not only in the devastation of Vietnam, but also in the atrocities of modern sex crime. For in the framework of the patriarchal imagination, women are perpetually identified with the "things of the world," the *objects* of phallic love/ destruction, and "trophies" of the archetypical hunts. We and all the other "others"—Indians, trees, buffalo, the Earth itself—are relentlessly hunted by the man, god, and socially self-affirming heroes of phallocracy. Just as "in the beginning" the primordial Goddess was slain and dismembered, just as in the origins of white America, the "virgin land" was conquered and razed, so too are individual women now stalked and hunted by the modern hunters/heroes of this land of sex-and-violence.

The identification of the sexual killer with the traditional American hero was once again affirmed by *Hustler* in its August 1981 issue. The cover announced an "Exclusive Report" on the "Hillside Strangler." This report is written by Ted Schwarz with the assistance of Bianchi's ex-lover, Kelli Boyd, and attempts a psychological "profile" of the killer.[101] But to get the whole picture, you must realize the article in its context. Beyond the crushing irony of such a subject being analyzed in *Hustler*, it is crucial to look specifically at the placement of the article in the magazine and its relation to the surrounding materials. Raymond Williams has described a central characteristic of the television experience to be that of *flow*—that is TV programs are surrounded by commercials and other programs, an uninterrupted following of one thing by another. The result of this flow is a powerful tendency to blur the contents together, a result encouraged by programmers so that one program leads effortlessly into another.[102] "Flow" is operative in magazine format as well and can be effectively applied to analysis of magazine content.

In *Hustler*, the article on the Strangler is wedged between two highly evocative segments. Directly preceding it is an article entitled, "Orgasm of Death." This refers to a fad among young men of applying a noose to their own necks while masturbating. The idea is to achieve partial asphyxiation while climaxing; this reportedly intensifies the pleasure. However, the accident rate is high and some kill themselves unintentionally. By the end of the article, this stimulation technique starts getting referred to as "strangulation as a means of getting off" and warnings of its dangers are issued.[103] After this setup, the reader turns the page and immediately comes face to face with a large photograph of Kenneth Bianchi, someone who clearly did use "strangulation as a means of getting off." The photo of Bianchi is surrounded by smaller pictures of his victims, or, as *Hustler* a few months earlier had phrased it, his "accomplishments." We immediately get to read a few choice quotes from the Strangler:

When you fuck a broad man, you take full charge....
You gotta treat'em rough....It wasn't fuckin'
wrong. Why is it wrong to get rid of some fuckin' cunts?[104]

Of course, the entire visual point of *Hustler* and all of pornography is that women are "fuckin' cunts" so once again the distinction between the sexual killer and his promoters disappears.

The "intimate" report on Bianchi is interrupted after only a few pages for a nude photo layout called, "Jesse James Rides Again." The female model is shown daydreaming over the book, *The Legend of Jesse*

James, when that outlaw hero himself suddenly appears, all in black and holding a very long rifle. Moreover, "Jesse" himself bears an astonishing resemblance to Kenneth Bianchi; both are very dark, with a pronounced moustache. At first, he appears most threatening, but then settles down for an erotic session with the posed and spread-eagled daydreamer. Once again, pornography completely equates rape and sex, women with willing victims, and rapists, even sexual murderers, with legendary heroes. This sequence over, and the reader properly primed, the article on the "Hillside Strangler" is immediately resumed.

These are not disparate segments but steps in a subliminal flow sequence. The first sets up the connection between sexual pleasure, strangulation, and death. In the second, the "Hillside Strangler" is introduced and profiled. And sandwiched between the pages on the sex killer is the pictorial which figures the legendary outlaw as potent, commanding, raping stud. Finally, the facial similarities underline the connection between the 19th century hero/badman and his 20th century analogue.

Like their counterparts from the past, the 20th century outlaw heroes are also "doers," men of action and record-breaking accomplishments, daring men known by the number they have killed and the territories they have terrorized, role models for both emulation and fantasy identification. Contemporary sex killers are memorialized in countless narratives, ranging in style from the sensationalist press to sober biographical, psychological, and sociological studies. There is also a genre devoted exclusively to the meticulous recounting of their exploits—the "true crime" genre, taking form in magazines such as *Front Page Detective, True Detective,* etc., as well as the pulp books which trace the careers of individual criminals, focusing upon special patterns and proclivities, details of sexual mutilation, etc. How then do such 20th century myth narratives serve as an index to this culture's character? What do they reveal regarding its conceptions of manhood and godhood? Jimmy McDonough, a longtime follower of such subjects and frequent contributor to horror fanzines, gives his expert opinion. First introduced to *True Detective* at the age of eight, he soon found himself "hooked forever." He "had to know more":

Soon I was hunting through old *Look*'s and *Life*'s with dates of atrocities burned in my mind. DEC '57—ED GEIN—Jan '58 - STARKWEATHER—etc. Then came books. Books solely about mass murderers, their crimes, their minds. Some written in strange florid styles published on obscure regional presses. Soon I had 30 or 40 of them.

Strictly an impulse at first, it congealed into something that made much more sense later. It was never a case of getting a boner from the often surgically detailed descriptions of sexual mutilations that seem to be a basic protein to nerds. More like the books pointed to a black destiny I might freak out to if I didn't watch out.

When I was a sociopathic teenage hothead I used my words and actions to burst others into flames. This was a time when I could relate all too well to these books and their detached feelings. *Because Bundy, Gacy, Carr are in a way the ultimate men. Monuments of misogyny, homophobia, and self-hatred. These books are grotesque roadmaps to the Raging Bull boneyard. I'M A MAN, they scream, eMmm, Ayyy, eNnnn....*[105] (emphasis mine)

Surely many men, like McDonough, who traveled that particular patriarchal initiation rite/route, also did not freak out to that particular black destiny. Many simply imbibed the values and went on to become filmmakers, rock stars, gynecologists, surgeons,[106] everyday batterers and rapists, military strategists, weapons manufacturers, war heroes, pornographers, politicians, priests, storybook writers for children,[107] etc. For the sexual killer—no matter how hypocritically reviled by his patriarchal culture—should be recognized, finally, as its "ultimate man," its subliminal hero, the inevitable enactment of phallocracy's most fundamental conceptions of manhood and godhood. This is the underlying premise of all the narratives of sex crime, the punch line behind all the familiar jokes, and the allure of the first person identification: the ordinary patriarchal man found behind the masks of both the prepotent monster and the master criminal/hero.

This situation becomes only more apparent as we move from the narratives of the actual crimes and criminals, to those which mirror them in the vast symbolic world, the fictional fantasies of sex crime which so preoccupy the mass media.

Chapter III
Crime Formulas

What, then, can be said of the cultural functions of formulaic literature? I think we can assume that formulas become collective cultural products because they successfully articulate a pattern of fantasy that is at least acceptable to if not preferred by the cultural groups who enjoy them. Formulas enable the members of a group to share the same fantasies.

John Cawelti[1]

He couldn't help thinking what Bishop would do to her body, those breasts, that abdomen. He shuddered. But was Bishop really so different? He himself had often thought of killing women, especially in his more youthful years, of torturing them and making them suffer. But that was just fantasy. Just typical male fantasizing.
    Wasn't it?

Shane Stevens, *By Reason
of Insanity[2]*

Following closely on the trail of the actual incidents of serial sex murder, a growing number of novels and films throughout the 1970s and 80s have focused upon the sex killer, further articulating the mythos of sex crime. These are largely formulaic works and are generally classified as "thrillers," or, more elaborately and specifically, as "gorenography" or "slasher" products.[3] Here, I will examine a number of such slashing, chopping products, particularly as they articulate the larger ideology of sex crime.

In a 1979 piece in the *New York Times*, Jack Sullivan identified (and not unhappily) a "currently popular species of thriller that attempts to generate excitement by piling up female corpses."[4] He mentions four such books: Jimmy Breslin and Dick Schaap's *.44*; Dan Greenburg's *Love Kills*; Shane Stevens' *By Reason of Insanity*; and Steven Whitney's *Singled Out*. To these I will add: C. Terry Cline's *Missing Persons*; Dave Klein's *Blind Side;* George Stade's *Confessions of a Lady-Killer*; T. Jeff Williams' *Strangler*; and Jonathan Valin's *Final Notice*. Another novel, *The Dead Zone* by best-selling superstar Stephen King, contains a completely developed subplot about a Ripper-type killer of young girls.[5] This is not an inclusive listing but, rather, one which is representative of books about serial sex killers written in the late 1970s. Among these, two explicitly fictionalize the careers of real killers—*.44* for Berkowitz and *Missing Persons* for Ted Bundy. Because one earlier work is similarly focused— William Goldman's *No Way to Treat a Lady*, a 1964

63

novelization of the "Boston Strangler"—I will also include it in the discussion here.[6]

Film portrayals centering on the sex killer have also become common during the late 1970s and early 1980s and I will refer specifically to eight of these: *The Toolbox Murders* (Dennis Donnely, 1978), *Halloween* (John Carpenter, 1979), *10 to Midnight* (J. Lee Thompson, 1980), *Maniac* (William Lustig, 1981), *Pieces* (J.G. Simon, 1983), *Tightrope* (Richard Tuggles, 1984), and *Mean Season* (Philip Borsos, 1985). Again, these works are representative, not inclusive, and here also it is mandatory to include one work from the early 1960s—Alfred Hitchcock's *Psycho* (1960), the paradigmatic film of the Age of Sex Crime.

All of these works, both film and literature, display common motifs and conventions and the following recur noticeably:

1. There is some reference to Jack the Ripper and the established tradition of sex crime.

2. The killer often corresponds with the police or press and adopts or is given a "folk" name.

3. The mother, or occasionally some other female member of the family, is blamed for the criminality of her son because of her psychological or physical abuse of him.

4. The blame or responsibility for their own deaths is given to the female victims both explicitly by the killer himself and, more subtly, through plot construction.

5. The killer claims to love his victims, to be helping or loving them by bringing death to them.

6. The killer perceives himself as waging a holy war against women (a war frequently condoned in the work itself), punishing them for their sexuality, aggression against men, feminism, or what he feels to be women's inherently demonic natures.

7. Male pursuers of the killer experience a strong bond of identity between themselves and their quarry. That bond is underscored when the killer begins to terrorize the girlfriends and/or daughters of a cop or reporter who has been intensely involved in the case.

The first two are obvious components of the Ripper pattern as it structures the actual occurrences of mass sex crime and both have already been discussed in that context. Here I will focus upon the other motifs, particularly as they too are reflected in the actual crimes and criminals. And finally, I will look at the ways in which these fictional formulas, like the conventional narratives of the real criminals, explicitly encourage male readers to identify with the sex murderer, enabling that group to collectively experience an acceptable if not preferred fantasy, to vicariously thrill to the graphic and elaborate depiction of gynocide.

Mother Hatred

If the punishment of the criminal is justified, we must first ask: How did he become a criminal? What was his mother like?

Brockhaus[7]

[H] is [Jack the Ripper's] fantasies were all about cutting bellies. It was the womb itself that fascinated him. Freudians will draw a great many inferences from this...it was the place that bore him about which he felt ambivalent.

Colin Wilson[8]

When a man commits a violent crime, it is invariably founded on his unconscious feeling that he must show his mother that he is not insignificant and is able to take revenge upon her for rejecting him.

Dr. David Abrahamson[9]

If you add the letter *s* to mother, you get smother.

A psychiatrist's suggestion to Kenneth Bianchi[10]

A boy's best friend is his mother.

Norman Bates, in *Psycho*

Patriarchal antipathy for the mother predates both Jack the Ripper and modern psychiatry: fear, loathing and blame for the mother or her representative are rife in the oldest myths and the most familiar fairy tales.[11] Not surprisingly then, that very same pattern is reiterated in the contemporary mythicization of sex crime.

One of the most repulsive novels under discussion is Steven Whitney's *Singled Out*. Like many of the others, this "chopping up women" story is ever so gallantly dedicated to a woman. Its dedication, however, is particularly curious. It reads: "To Eva, Who Was There In The Beginning." This is a most jarring remembrance in a book where a compellingly handsome and charming man picks up women in single's bars, takes them home for sex, and then murders them in an increasingly grotesque parade of tortures. He stabs one in the abdomen when she has an orgasm and disembowels another through her vagina; he cuts another's heart out of her body on Valentine's day and crucifies a christian cult member in a Manhattan cathedral. Amidst such an elaborate display of woman hating, Whitney's dedication might also evoke memories of another "Eva" who was also there "in the beginning"—in the "creation" myth of western patriarchy, the story of Adam and Eve.

Contemporary cigarette ads taunt us: "There's a little Eve in every woman."[12] Translated, this reads *guilt* and *evil*. As Elizabeth Cady Stanton, Karen Horney, Kate Millett, Mary Daly, and many others have pointed out, the myth of Adam and Eve ordains that ontological blame be affixed to the primordial mother/female figure. Moreover, the myth of the Fall not only framed Eve, but also set into motion a pervasive myth of "feminine evil," particularly female *sexual* evil. Daly comments:

Women as a caste, then, are "Eve" and are punished by a cohesive set of laws, customs, and social arrangements that enforce an all-pervasive double standard.[13]

Not only are women set up to be the evil and dangerous sex and thereby deserving of any punishment they get, but blame for the male executors of such punishments—from witchburnings to sexual murder—is expediently dumped back on the women themselves—a consummate "double bind." Such a process is particularly obvious in the all-out tendency to blame the mother of the sex criminal for his unrestrained violences against women.

Finding a motivating and justifiable mother hatred in the sex killer has been a conventional ploy since Jack the Ripper first stole the womb from one of his victims. Indeed, it was that very search which first arrested the official investigation of the "Boston Strangler" case in the 1960s. A medical-psychiatric team of experts was formed to construct a profile of the probable killer. In its majority opinion, the killings were the works of at least two men, one responsible for the older women—the first victims—and another, possibly homosexual, for the younger and later victims. It was believed, however, that there was one point of identity between these two distinct killers; each must harbor an old rage against their mothers or some other dominant woman in their backgrounds. These mothers must have been seductive, yet punishing, while the father of each was probably relatively weak and distant.[14]

Susan Brownmiller has analyzed this "expert" profile and realized that while the committee was purportedly profiling the Strangler, it had actually:

...put together an imaginative profile of the Strangler's mother....The Strangler's mother was probably dead, they agreed, but during his childhood she had walked about "half-exposed in their apartment, but punished him severely for any sexual curiosity." Consumed by mother hatred, the psychiatrists divined, the Strangler had chosen to murder and mutilate old women in a manner "both sadistic and loving."

One wonders who exactly it was that was "consumed by mother hatred," whose fantasy such a scenario depicts. Certainly not that of the confessed Strangler, Albert DeSalvo, for, as Brownmiller continues, DeSalvo was actually nothing at all like this fantastic projection. His mother was still alive and he was genuinely fond of her. Frankly, the entire scenario constituted a dramatic reversal for:

The consuming rage DeSalvo bore was uncompromisingly directed against his drunken, brutalizing father, who had regularly beaten him, his mother and the other children during a wretched youth. DeSalvo's father had engaged in sex acts with prostitutes in front of his children, had taught his sons to shoplift, had broken every finger on his wife's hand and knocked out her teeth, and had gone on periodic rampages where he smashed up all the furniture in the house. As a final act of rejection he abandoned the family when Albert was eight.[15]

Neither DeSalvo nor his mother resembled the profile, but that reality did nothing to squelch the continued promulgation and preference for this mythic explanation of the making of a sex criminal. Writing in *Psychology Today*, Colin Campbell refers to the "fictional men" created by the Strangler expert committee in Boston.[16] Precisely so—and like Jack the Ripper, these men (and their "mothers") slid over almost instantly into the overtly fictional world.

William Goldman's *No Way to Treat a Lady*, although commonly thought to be based upon the actual Boston Strangler, is instead based upon the figments concocted by the Strangler committee. Not surprisingly, the basic structure in this novel forms around the mother-son relationship. Three pairs are presented, three sons bound to three demonic mothers and, hence, intimately bound to each other. These are: the Strangler and his dead, but still overwhelmingly dominant, bitch/ mother; a copycat killer and his still living mother who lies and covers up for him; and, finally, our hero, the detective whose mother is not only herself overbearing and intolerable, but is also responsible for the severe facial disfigurement of her son. All in all, each viciously drawn mother stands out as far more despicable than even the two killer sons.

The Dead Zone, a national bestseller by Stephen King, also figures a sex killer as the pure creation of his monstrous mother. To make this point, the reader is taken back into the past when:

...he hadn't been the killer then, oh no, not an animal...he'd only been a scared little boy with a clothespin on his...his...

The word the killer can't quite summon up is *penis* or its equivalent. His mother, "a big woman, a dominant and overbearing ocean liner of a woman," had caught the little boy masturbating and become enraged, screaming to him that he would get a disease, his thing would turn black and pus would run out of it. To let him know what such a disease would feel like (and to let the reader know how vile and essentially castrating a mother she really was), she made him wear a clothespin on his penis for two hours at a time. This stereotypic "witch" not only caused her son's criminality, but also covered up for him so that he could murder again and again. And, once more, a crucial bond of identity between the killer and the normal men in the story is established. The killer himself is a cop, one whom the chief of police in the small Maine town had known for years and regarded as he would "his own son." Even more telling is the moment when Johnny, the psychic hero of the novel, faces the mother of the killer and immediately feels "that this was his [own] mother standing here."

Physical abuse by the mother is a recurring theme. In *Blind Side*, a mother brutally whips and abuses her son when she finds him masturbating. Later, he kills her and subsequently develops a split personality; "mother" now inhabits his head and commands him to kill, an obvious borrowing from the novel and film *Psycho*.[17]

In the cheap gorenographic film *Pieces*, a mother enters her eight-year-old son's bedroom to find him putting together a puzzle of a naked woman in a posed centerfold style; he is happily reciting "Humpty Dumpty" at the time. The mother becomes enraged, starts to beat him, and screams, "I'll kill you if I ever find stuff like that in the house again." Of course, it is her own little son who kills her then and there with an axe, chopping her body into little puzzle-like pieces. Later he grows up to be the Dean of a college and begins to murder the female students there, dismembering them and stitching together his "ideal" female from the various "pieces" of his victims. As the poster for this movie self-assuredly boasts: *"Pieces—It's exactly what you think it is!"*

In the grim and hideous *Maniac*, motivations for the Berkowitz-like killer are, again, traced to maternal trauma. As he tortures a woman he cries, "Mommy, Mommy," and whimpers:

You were wrong to try and hurt me. You left me alone lots of times. I was scared, real scared. I hid in the closet; did you know that? No, you didn't know that. I was afraid that you wouldn't come back. But I won't cry now....And now you're mine, all mine. So many men—why—because they gave you some dollars? But they didn't love you. I loved you. I'm not going to kill you. I'm going to keep you so you'll never go away. I'm just going to keep you so you'll never go away ever again.

At this juncture, he kills the woman with a knife, crying, "Mommy, Mommy, tonight you stay home with me."

Physical abuse or neglect is by no means the only crime with which the mother is routinely charged. In *The Fear of Women*, Wolfgang Lederer gives a comprehensive listing of various psychological studies since 1950 which denote a multiplicity of ways that the "bad" mother produces the sick son. Among these is Gregory Bateson's famous description of the "double-bind" experience and its role in the development of schizophrenia: "mother causes schizophrenia by issuing contradictory messages, by pushing away and pulling back at the same time."[18] Bateson himself offers this illustration from his clinical data:

A young man who had fairly well recovered from an acute schizophrenic episode was visited in the hospital by his mother. He was glad to see her and impulsively put an arm around her shoulders, whereupon she stiffened. He withdrew his arm and she asked, "Don't you love me any more?" He then blushed, and she said, "Dear, you must not be so easily embarrassed and afraid of your feelings." The patient was able to stay with her only a few minutes more and following her departure he assaulted an aide and was put in the tubs.[19]

As Bateson perceives it, the two principal actors in such family dramas are mother and son; the father is remarked upon mainly as "an absence of...a strong and insightful father."

The father is archetypally absent in T. Jeff Williams' *Strangler*, but here, as elsewhere, the mother's presence is dominant and destructive. Those familiar with Bateson's theory will recognize its almost textbook description in this thriller. The point of view belongs to "Sonny," the not too subtly named strangler:

...Mother insisted. "Come on, Sonny, give Mother a kiss. Kiss and make up and never argue again." I sat next to her on the couch and gave her a peck on the cheek. Her skin was cool and I could feel on my lips the downy hairs that grew there. Even as I touched her she stiffened and withdrew from me.

Thus, the paradigmatic misogynist, the sex killer, can be said to be purely the product and responsibility of a woman.

Psychiatrically colluding with the ideology of sex crime, Karl Menninger has expounded just such an idea, appealing to his readers:

Who can look fairly at the bitterness, the hatefulness, the sadistic cruelty of Adolf Hitler without wondering what Hitler's mother did to him that he now repays to millions of other helpless ones? We must remind ourselves again and again that the men by whom women are frustrated are the grown-up sons of mothers who were chiefly responsible for the personality of those sons.[20]

According to this tortuous reversal, it is *women*, i.e. mothers, who are solely to blame for the mutilations and devastations wreaked upon the bodies of women by men. Because that assertion is so desperately deceptive, Menninger and others of his ilk must indeed incessantly "remind" us to swallow that lie.

Such propagandization is also preeminently the function of the sex crime novels. *By Reason of Insanity*, the novel that Jack Sullivan in his "Chopping Up Women" review found to be the most "artistically ambitious" of the lot is also, easily, the most deliberate in its mythicization of the sex killer. That killer, Thomas Bishop, is a composite of Jack the Ripper, Edmund Kemper (the "Coed Killer"), Ted Bundy, and just about any other serial sex murderer who comes to mind. Moreover, in *By Reason of Insanity*, we don't have to waste one moment wondering what Bishop's mother "did to him"; we are told in unsparing detail. As the story goes, she had always believed that her son was the result of her rape by a man she had further convinced herself was Caryl Chessman, the historical "Red Light Rapist" whose case became a *cause célèbre* before he was finally executed on a kidnapping charge in California in 1960. The mother/monster not only fills her son's head with tales of his father the celebrity rapist, but viciously abuses him, beating him regularly with a whip. "The boy" (the killer is referred to, sympathetically, as "the boy" throughout the novel) finally snaps and both slays and partially devours his mother. Institutionalized for fifteen years, he manages a brilliantly planned escape (in the logic of the sex crime myth, all such killers are "geniuses"); then, by virtue of his innate brilliance and the application of techniques learned from watching television, he manages to become the century's most prolific sex murderer. Bishop also adopts a folk name and becomes "Chess Man," regarding himself as "carrying on his father's work."

As with Jack the Ripper, Bishop's primary impulse is toward female mutilation. His grisly murders and dismemberments are thoroughly detailed (in nearly 600 pages)—a lavish manufacture of gynocidal fantasies for the gynocidal culture. Also like Jack the Ripper, Bishop mails not only letters, but organs of his victims to the police and press. This is not just an obscure thriller, but a work by a fairly well-known popular writer and one intended to reach a large and literate audience. The back cover of the paperback quotes the *Chicago Tribune*: "Stevens creates a 'myth monster' for our times."

If the "little boy" killer, the eternal child who is also a matricide, sounds familiar, we might recall an earlier "myth monster"—Norman Bates in *Psycho*. The story of that classic and frequently revived film is undoubtedly familiar to many people. Norman Bates—the stereotypic "boy next door"—is running the failing Bates Motel and apparently living with his aged mother in the old dark house next to the motel. But Norman has actually killed his mother long ago and stuffed her body which he keeps around. Moreover, Norman is schizoid; he assumes his mother's personality, giving *his* voice and intentions to that long dead body. When single women come to stay at the motel, Norman's "mother" kicks into gear and slaughters them. Thus, it is "mother" who is made responsible for the killings, not Norman. Of course on a surface, logical level, we know Norman himself to be guilty; nevertheless critics and viewers over the years continually accept Norman's story and wonder just what his mother did to him that made Norman so bad. The handy psychiatrist at the end of the film has already told us that she was a "clinging, demanding woman" and hinted broadly at an incestuous relationship; viewers can easily fill in the rest.

The enduring irony and characteristic mindbind of *Psycho* is that while at one level it exposes the actual man behind the drag facade of the indicted "mother," it simultaneously buries that truth and heaps even more dirt on the time-honored tradition of scapegoating and mother-hating. For by the end of the film, again in the words of the psychiatrist, "Norman Bates no longer exists." What he terms "the dominant personality" has won; only "Mother" remains. It is "her" image (Norman's face but with the grinning skull of the dead mother superimposed upon it) that closes the film—an image which is meant to trigger all the other implanted associations of evil, reaching-out-from-the-grave-to-devour-men mothers. We are supposed to forget all about the man in drag—the real killer. It is "she" whom we must remember, "she" who endures as the monster, finally "she" who is left to blame.

Like the paradigmatic Mrs. Bates, the other vicious mothers who populate the fantasies of sex crime are also the long dead victims of matricide, stuffed puppets animated only by the deceptive voices of male authors, filled with messages of male self-absolution, misogyny and scapegoating—messages that are presented as coming from *females*, as if it were women implicating themselves. Here the deceptive and purely mythic flaunts its domination over the real. And, not surprisingly, that same mythic pattern dominates and directs the actual cases of sex crime as well. The legitimated reflex of mother-blaming has figured prominently in the cases not only of the "Boston Strangler," but also in those of David Berkowitz, Peter Sutcliffe, Ted Bundy, Kenneth Bianchi, Edmund Kemper, and Henry Lee Lucas.

For example, Dr. David Abrahamson, the psychiatrist most associated with the "Son of Sam" case has argued in various articles and a book that Berkowitz's murderous rage sprang from repressed antagonisms toward both his natural and adoptive mothers and that his killing spree was actually catalyzed by his location of his natural mother.[21] Yet, in those lurid communications from the killer himself, it is a markedly *patriarchal* figure—"Sam"—whose voice issues from the violence command center. As Berkowitz wrote in one letter to the police:

I am the "Son of Sam." I am a little brat.

When father Sam gets drunk he gets mean. He beats his family. Sometimes he ties me up to the back of the house. Other times he locks me in the garage. Sam loves to drink blood.

"Go out and kill," commands father Sam....

Mr. Borreli, sir, I don't want to kill anymore. No sur [sic], no more but I must, "honour thy father."[22]

While male apologists for sex crime scurry to direct blame at the mother, such scapegoating might best be understood as issuing from the same world view that produces the gynocide itself. Rather than following the dead lines of such logic, we might instead grasp the pervasion of gynocidal commandments issuing forth from the myriad manifestations of the patriarchal godfather and the attendant demands to "honour" those fathers.*

While Kenneth Bianchi was fooling psychiatrists left and right with his Jekyll and Hyde act, he simultaneously implicated his mother as the root cause of his malevolence. She was guilty, he said, of child abuse, obsession with his bed-wetting, and a stereotypical smothering, yet punishing, attitude. And here Bianchi was just as widely believed. Court-appointed psychiatrist Ralph Allison, for example, told PBS *Frontline* that Bianchi had been a "victim of his mother's anger." Thus the victimizer becomes the victim, the adult torturer/executioner is transmogrified into the tormented, put-upon little boy. Commenting upon the tendency to blame the mother, Ted Schwarz writes that Frances Bianchi, the adoptive mother, was frequently cast as "a 'witch' and Ken as her created monster." He further notes:

What hurts Ken's mother the most is the way she is indirectly being charged with his murders...she has been accused of child abuse by her own son...yet the child abuse was never truly documented.[23]

Martin Orne, the psychiatrist who helped expose Bianchi's fabrication of the split personality, noted that Bianchi had seen the movies *Three Faces of Eve* and *Sybil* (films about women with multiple personalities) which, as he noted, were like lessons in how to fake a multiple personality.[24] Apparently, Bianchi had also learned—from a ubiquitous range of sources—how to also fake the most patriarchally plausible explanation for gynocide—tracing the cause directly back to "Mother."

Another such killer, Edmund Kemper (California's "Coed Killer," who terrorized the Santa Cruz area between 1972 and '73) was obviously disturbed as a youth; he tortured animals, cut off the heads of dolls, and took a shot at his sister with a gun. When he was fifteen, he murdered both his grandmother and grandfather with whom he was then living. After a five-year hospitalization in an institution reserved for sex offenders, he was released to the custody of his mother; his natural father had long ago absented himself. Kemper then embarked upon a campaign of murder, necrophilia, cannibalism, and dismemberment. Driving

---

*For an acclaimed media melodramatization of this essential misogynist script, see *Prizzi's Honor* (John Huston, 1985).

around, he would pick up young female hitchhikers, expressing his preference for "coeds." He killed, mutilated and dismembered six women—Anita Luchessa, Mary Ann Pesce, Aiko Koo, Cynthia Schall, Rosalind Thorpe, and Alice Liu—before changing his pattern and slaying first his mother, Clarnell Strandberg, and her best friend, Sara Hallett. After this last atrocity, he turned himself in to the police.

In interviews, Kemper has consistently and insistently blamed his mother for all of his actions:

Interviewer: You were involved in the campus because your mother worked there?

Kemper: Yes. I was also involved in killing coeds because my mother was associated with college work, college coeds, women, and had had a very strong and violently outspoken position on men for much of my upbringing....They [his victims] represented not what my mother was, but what she liked, what she coveted, what was important to her and I was destroying it....

I'm not a lizard. I'm not from under a rock. I came out of her vagina. I came out of my mother and in a rage I went right back in....I cut off her head and I humiliated her corpse. I said there—you know. Six young women dead because of the way she raised her son and the way her son is raised and the way he grows up.[25]

In her study of Kemper, *The Coed Killer,* Margaret Cheney comments:

A journalist asked why Kemper had had to "sacrifice" six beautiful young women before he killed his mother—a question which happened to be on many lips, both among medical doctors and laymen—the clear implication being that Clarnell Strandberg more or less deserved killing because her son claimed she was aggressive and domineering (characteristics unquestioningly accepted by the head doctors who had never met her), and because in our patriarchal society mothers traditionally have been blamed for the irresponsibility of their sons, and because, as a woman in her fifties in a youth-oriented society, she no longer commanded much sexual value.[26]

Thus the word of the rapist, cannibal, necrophile, and matricide is accepted unquestioningly by representatives of the patriarchate because he is also a man mouthing patriarchal truisms and perhaps, as well, because they share his feelings. In the same interview quoted above, Kemper was asked where he had learned how to outwit the police. He replied, "From watching television." Perhaps Kemper also had easily assimilated the formulaic messages of mother hatred and scapegoating so embedded in the public mindset, so pervasive and so persuasive in the Age of Sex Crime.

One other case illustrates the extraordinary tenacity and virulence of this most sacred phallocratic lie. If Kemper's word can be taken as gospel, why not that of Henry Lee Lucas as well—another matricide and the boastful confessor to the murders of over 600 people, mostly women, beings he didn't feel "needed to exist." Lucas was interviewed by Sylvia Chase in July 1984 on *ABC News 20/20.* Chase prefaced part of that interview with this:

How did he come to be this way? As we already said, serial murderers in childhood forge an obsessive link between aggression and sex. In the Lucas case, the mother was a prostitute. And like mothers of other serial killers, she was not only hostile to her son she was sexually provocative too.

No documentation or other illustrations are given for that last, outrageous statement. The interview ensues:

Lucas: That's the way I grew up when I was a child.

Chase: How?

Lucas: Watching my mom have sexual acts. She wouldn't go into different rooms. She'd make sure I was in the room before she started anything. And she would do it deliberately to make me watch her you know. And I got so I hated it. I'd even leave the house and go out and hide in the woods and wouldn't even go home. And when I'd go home, I'd get beat for not coming home. And I can't say that, you know, I don't blame mom for what she done. I don't blame her for that. It's the idea of the way she done it. I don't think any child out there should be brought up in that type of environment. And in the past, I've hated it. It's just inside hate and I can't get away from it.[27]

After sharing that moving moment with Henry Lee Lucas, viewers might find themselves warming to his generosity in *not* blaming his mother, monstrous woman that she was. Of course, this is quite a reversal for that is precisely what Lucas was doing. Moreover, after having been tossed the culturally approved scapegoat—Mom—viewers might find themselves now not even blaming Lucas himself for his self-proclaimed mutilations, crucifixions, his filleting of his victims "like fish." Unbelievably, it is never even suggested that this murderer (like Kemper) could also be capable of lying. Although investigators are now doubting Lucas' confessions to the hundreds of murders, no one seems to doubt his veracity concerning his "terrible mother." In another case, police in Yorkshire treated the tapes and letters from the pseudo-ripper as infallible documents because they coincided so precisely with the well-known mythic pattern. So too, all a killer has to do is to imitate the archetypal pattern of mother-blaming and he is instantly and almost universally believed. Both Lucas' and Kemper's mothers are dead, silenced by those very sons,* unable now or then to defend themselves. Only the self-absolving refrains of male voices and versions are heard. The *New York Times* has just reported that John Wayne Gacy as a newborn was given daily enemas by his mother.[28] Norman Bates' "mother" must indeed be smiling.

---

*Lucas killed his mother in 1960 and was sent to prison until his release in 1975.

Blaming the mother for the criminality of her son and further implying that her murder was deserved is part of a larger complex that shifts the blame from the sexual murderer to his victim, the attacker to the attacked, the man to the woman. This exemplifies a phenomenon that Mary Daly has named as characteristic of patriarchal myth, i.e. *reversal*.[29] And *reversal* is also a key factor in the next fictional motif in which the victims themselves are made ultimately responsible for their own deaths.

A Complex of Guilt

He gets ready to leave. He puts away his knife and...is just about to go to the door when he hears her moan. He turns around.

"Sharon?"

She moans again and opens her eyes.

"Sharon, darling, you all right?"

She looks up at him, looks down at her clothes which are slashed to pieces, and begins to scream.

"Sharon, darling, ssshhh!"....

She keeps on screaming. He lunges toward her and puts his hands around her throat and begins to squeeze.

Dan Greenburg, *Love Kills*

As Barbara Smith pointed out concerning the series of murders of Black women in Boston 1979, in nearly all instances of media coverage it was implied that the women were somehow responsible for their own deaths. This pattern is ubiquitous throughout the phenomenon of modern sex crime—again, in both the fictional and the factual narratives.

In his best-selling study of the "Boston Strangler," Gerold Frank briefly discusses the roles of Sandra Irizarry and Jane Downey, research assistant and secretary for the Attorney General's "Strangler Bureau." The entire committee, including these two women, medical experts, and police, had probed into every detail of the slain women's private lives, hoping to find some connection that would lead them to the killer. They all talked often, and with great familiarity, about the victims and Frank tells us that "Sandra and Jane" usually had to defend the dead girls "in spirited discussions with detectives (who were inclined to agree with the psychiatrists that the younger victims might have brought their fate on themselves)."[30] Such official and officious attitudes reflect the basic phallic line that victims of all types of sex crime somehow desired or provoked the sexual assault.[31]

In the more recent case of the "Hillside Strangler," Suzanne Lacy has observed a similar tendency:

Overlooking the obvious connection—each victim was a female in a sex-violent culture—reporters ransacked the pasts of the dead women, searching with the police for clues as to why *these* particular women had been singled out. Mistaking causation for the similarities in each killing, reporters inadvertently upheld the common myth that victims of sex violence are somehow culpable, if only in their choice of action.[32]

It is unclear exactly how any of these victims could have been culpable. Even Gerold Frank, in an otherwise highly detailed study, gives little information on how it was supposed by police and psychiatrists that the younger victims of the "Boston Strangler" had "brought their fate on themselves." That task, it seems, has been left largely to the enthusiasms of the fiction writers who embrace it with as much invective as invention.

In *Love Kills*, the killer is one who weeps over the bodies of his dead, " 'I love you,' he whispers, and means it." He selects his victims and then secretly watches them for weeks, learning everything about them; eventually he comes to their apartments for a "date." By pretending to be a delivery boy or a cop, he gets them to let him in. Then, in nearly every instance, the plot is constructed so that the woman somehow—either through inept or grotesque efforts to defend herself or through misfortune—triggers his violence and thus engineers her own death.

In the opening murder the killer flashes a knife and makes his intended victim dance with him. She goes along with him, but soon makes a grab for the knife, slashing his hand. But he, of course, retrieves it and becomes enraged, so enraged that he makes her strip while he holds the knife to her throat. Just as she is about to remove her "panties," the telephone rings, startling him into stabbing her inadvertently: " 'Linda,' he says softly. 'Oh Linda, I'm sorry. I never meant for this to happen.' "

The next time around, the woman whose apartment he has invaded decides to handle the "psycho" by coming on to him sexually, figuring that she will soon get the upper hand. This male-authored mockery of a woman begins a slow strip and soon:

She has practically pinned him against the fireplace wall, "It's perfect," she thinks. "He's in the middle of the best wet dream he's ever had, and I have totally regained control. I can toy with him as long as I like before I let him off the hook. I might even let him think he's going to fuck me before I'm done with him."

Of course, the killer is by no means enjoying himself but is panicking under her "aggression." She is blissfully oblivious to all such signals though and, given such a setup, few readers are likely to sympathize with her. More likely, they will think "stupid bitch," particularly when she is dead within two minutes of her sexual arrogance. For while she is gloating, her murderer is whimpering:

"I...like to be in charge...I really like to be in charge," he whispers, finding it difficult to breathe.

Trapped by this "suffocating" woman, he "reaches for something to fend her off with," killing her with a brass poker to the head.

We can observe here the complete reversal of attacker and victim. Suddenly it is *he* who is trapped, he who must "fend her off." Most readers must realize the manipulation and know that this is actually the scene of a sex murder by a man who has lied his way into an apartment, intending to kill the woman within. But neither this realization, nor even an "explanation" of Greenburg's deliberate use of irony, really interferes much with the reader's internalization of the underlying myth/ message. For in the archetypal plot of sex crime, it always is the dominant, bitch, tease, whore, castrating woman who is just asking for it and therefore gets it and deserves it. Consciously this is hatefully absurd, as is Greenburg's characterization and plotting. But is any of it more ridiculous (or less effective) than the culturally sacred reversal which ordains that it was Adam who gave birth to Eve?

Greenburg's killer is obviously an old master of such conventional reversal:

He stands there stupidly, watching the blood gush out of her scalp and realizes that he has done it again.

No, it wasn't he who has done it again, it was *they* who have done it again. Women. Treacherous, deceitful women. First it was Linda, pretending to be attracted to him and then trying to get his knife. Now it was Beverly, seducing him and trying to make a fool out of him....All he'd wanted was to love her.

Overall, the scene represents quite a conjuring act. By having his sex killer "attacked" by a woman and by then putting what could be fairly ordinary and common sounding male complaints into his mouth, Greenburg deliberately links those "typical male fantasies" and fears to the extraordinary and sensational violences of the sex criminal; it seems, after all, that they are just boys too.

Strangler, by T. Jeff Williams, is a particularly well-informed thriller. It draws not only upon Bateson's double-bind theory to explain its subject's mental state, but also works into the plot a short story by Ernest Hemingway, "The Short Happy Life of Francis Macomber," as fodder for his killer's delusions. Sonny's career as a strangler (a Kemper-cloned character) begins after he storms out of the house following a terrible argument with his mother. He goes cruising and picks up a young hitchhiker. She introduces the topic of the story and they begin to remember and discuss it; the narrator is the killer:

"Francis Macomber," I mused aloud and tried to place the story. Something clicked in my mind. "Oh, yeah, wasn't he a rich guy who goes on a safari with his wife?"
    "Right, and—"   "and Francis Macomber is a coward because he runs from a lion he's supposed to shoot and—"
    "—and in the end his wife can't stand him because he is a coward and so she shoots him and—"
    "—and claims she was shooting at the lion. Right!
Now I remember."

The two then begin to argue about who was to blame in this story, who really deserved to die—Macomber or his wife. The killer is firm in his opinion:

"Maybe it was Mrs. Macomber who was the real evil," I countered. "She was like a lioness on two legs, always stalking Francis. Ever think that Macomber was only doing his best, but got cut down from behind just when he was about to succeed...And remember what happened to Hemingway? He got sicker and sicker in his mind. Nothing helped him. Maybe he knew all the time that some lioness would cut him down, just like the lioness did to Macomber." Just like my mother did to my father I wanted to add.

The atmosphere in the car has by now gotten quite tense; the conversation shifts to astrology and numerology, but it gets only worse as Sonny continually finds portents which doom the woman in his mind. Finally, he pulls off the road and carries out his attack on the girl he now can see only as a "lioness" about to attack him:

I caught her arms and threw the lioness on her back.
    "You goddamned man-eater," *I yelled, "you will never again kill man."*...[after killing her] "I had won! I had defeated the lioness, something that Francis Macomber and Ernest never had been able to do."

In *Strangler*, the killer is at least nominally insane. His delusions that women are lionesses who attack him are just that—delusions. What, however, do we suppose was Ernest Hemingway's excuse?

As we ponder such elite equivalencies of the sex crime mentality, it is appropriate to turn to a discussion of Columbia University professor George Stade's sex crime novel, *Confessions of a Lady-Killer*. Here Stade presents a political rationalization—anti-feminism—for the serial/sexual murders of women by his hero. According to his logic, women in the form of feminists (as well as female sexuality itself) constitute an attack on men which must be *avenged*. And Stade's hero assumes the role of serial sex killer in order to undertake what, in the context of this very serious novel, becomes a necessary and ennobling ritual.

This is the novel that a *New York Times* critic called, "a study of feminism from the point of view of Jack the Ripper."[33] Its protagonist introduces himself to us immediately, "My name is Victor Grant. I am the hero or villain of the narrative to follow, depending on whether you are a feminist or a human being." Denying humanity to one's enemy is the first and time-honored rationalization for mass murder and that is precisely what Grant has in mind. For his wife, Samantha, has left him, run off to work on a feminist magazine, *"Ms. Chief,"* and establish her own identity. Presenting himself as the injured party, the real villain according to Victor is their neighbor (and wife of his best friend), Jude Karnofsky, professor at Columbia (although Stade presents her as a fraud who got her job only through political pressure), as well as a feminist author and theorist. She too has decided to leave her husband and work on *"Ms. Chief."* Her husband accepts this somewhat passively, but Victor vows vengeance, quits his job and begins a regimen of nearly all-meat diets, exercise and mental conditioning in order to be born again as an heroic slayer of prominent New York feminists, or, as he sees it, to enter upon his chosen "career as a Lady-Killer."

Grant does eventually murder three women before regaining his wife; he then impregnates her and ensconces her in patriarchal pastoralism on his father's self-sufficient enclave in upstate New York. Not only is there no retribution for his crimes, but the novel presents him as perfectly justified, indeed heroic. At first it seems as if this might be only as absurdist parody, but it is, instead, deadly serious in its hates and violences. As John Leonard commented, "What begins in farce ends in cruelty, with no accounting."[34] Victor, self-appointed knight against the dragon of women's liberation, finds himself and is reborn quite literally over the bodies of three dead women who, as another reviewer noted, "haven't done anything more *outré* than being women."[35] *Nation* critic, Keith Opdahl, while hailing this as a "rich and funny novel," still feels a bit uneasy for:

What disturbs me about this novel is the way Victor's voice makes us accept murders that are filled with a feverish hatred of women. How it comes pouring out, this hatred, and how it works as fiction![36]

But the farcical bewilderment of reviewers aside, it is not at all surprising that woman-hating works so well in fiction (we might again recall Ernest Hemingway, D.H. Lawrence, Henry Miller, Norman Mailer, etc.).[37] Moreover, it is fictions such as these which provide the precise symbolic counterpoints to the contemporary reality of mass gynocide and Stade, finally, is a mythographer and propagandist of sexual murder.

This novel also employs that motif so popular with the more formulaic writers; a key theme throughout this entire book is that the women provoke, solicit, and are ultimately responsible for their own deaths. A similar structure operates in each of the murders. Grant invades the hotel room or dwelling of the woman intending to kill, engages in struggle, and then, for some reason, decides to call off the murder. But the woman, usually in some attempt to defend herself, offers some form of sex to him, a sex that soon turns into an attack, i.e. a fist or bite to the testicles. Only then, does the enraged "Avenger" kill them off. Thus the narrator/hero/villain/killer reduces his role to that of the injured party, or, as Opdahl noted, he "makes homicide self-defense." The language of the last murder scene exemplifies Stade's use of this structure:

She was trying to use my strength against me. If I had been thrusting with my knife, it would have passed harmlessly by her. If I had been pushing against her spear hand, I would have hastened its progress toward my neck. But I was not pushing or thrusting. I had simply locked my muscles, when I made my pitch for a truce. I hardly moved at all, therefore. But she moved far too much. She impaled herself on my knife, a good six inches' worth.

Such language is outrageous not only for the sexual imagery—pushing, thrusting, six inches, etc.—to detail a death struggle, but even more so for the reflexive use of the verb *impale*. All responsibility is absolved; she did it to herself and Grant, the lady-killer, assumes the pose of the innocent bystander or mere functionary of fate.

Stade, like Greenburg, robs his victims of any humanity or sympathy, making them ludicrous, despicable and deserving of death. Perhaps the most vicious enactment of this, as well as an equally virulent anti-feminism, takes place, however, in *Singled Out*, a single-mindedly gruesome book. This killer's style is to pick up women in single's bars and take them home for sex, mutilation and murder. He picks up Diann Tinsley, a feminist lecturer who has just come from delivering a speech on "Vaginal Politics," during which:

In the introductory ten minutes of her oration, Diann extolled the virtues of the vagina. Now, a ten-minute oration on the spiritual qualities of the vagina is not what a layman might call an easy trick, but Diann was up to the task. Her sisters were deeply moved by Diann's validation of their private parts. Moving upward, she thoroughly covered both breasts, beginning with the mammary glands and lacteal ducts, while saving, in the fashion of all good public speakers, the more exciting but technically less complex nipples to cap her well-rounded tribute.

Only then did she reach the long-awaited climax—the clitoris—pointing out, for openers, that the word came from the Greek klei-toris, meaning "a small hill." Her sermon on this tiny mount was filled with metaphorical illumination.

> She ended with the two loveliest words she had ever known: Vaginal Power!

Here we have completely entered a world of sex crime. That passage does not purport to represent the perception of the killer; it is the "objective," third person point of view of the writer. That loathing and contempt for women, femaleness, and feminism, is taken as normative, particularly when it can be focused on the (male-created) target of such ridicule and hate, the fictional female and feminist, Diann Tinsley. Male readers are invited to indulge in some normally muted loathing for women and, later, to vicariously groove to her particularly torturous death; female readers are invited to internalize the loathing for their sex that drives gynocide and, later, to imagine themselves in the position of victim. Such are the "shared fantasies" of sex crime.

After her speech, Diann goes out looking for a man to pick up, for:

> After all the words, the anger, the self-expression and disappointment, Diann wanted a happy and sexually fulfilling relationship, perhaps even marriage. She even wanted these things with a man.

> But Diann did so many things wrong that she knew that any man who would put up with her couldn't be much of a man.

Thus "feminism," represented by this character, is trumped up as entirely phoney, the province of failed, frustrated women who deep down are yearning for marriage to "real men."

In the single's bar, Diann, of course, picks up not "Love" but "Death" in the form of the killer (as an L.A. headline screamed during the strangler crisis, "She Looked for Love, Found Strangler.")[38] They go back to his place and later in bed he asks Diann to suggest a particularly cruel way that a man might murder a woman. At first resistant, she finally complies and suggests (and this is absolutely beyond the bounds of belief) that he could disembowel her through the vagina with an ice pick. The killer, of course, does exactly that to her. In the logic of the fiction, that hideous death is made to be of the woman's own devise. But this "woman," like the "mother" in *Psycho*, is a man in drag—in this case, Stephen Whitney, the author of the book. It is his voice through the fabricated feminist Diann Tinsley which belittles and denounces women, which fantasizes the grotesque death. Furthermore, the setup itself, and the extensive contempt for feminism, suggests that feminism itself is the true crime here and the punishment devised is only fitting for that aberration/abomination.

If a frankly stated anti-feminism provides ideological motivation for the killers (and the authors) of several of these books, Shane Stevens gives his killer, Thomas Bishop, a metaphysics of female destruction. He writes in *By Reason of Insanity*:

Women were in constant and perpetual agony, suffering perhaps because of a God given curse. They painfully brought life into the world, knowing that the only result of that life would be death. Such knowledge, visceral and inescapable, maddened them beyond endurance. In their horrifying torment they lashed out at men, those who gave them the seed of life and thereby brought them death. Using every wile at their command they enticed, enslaved and destroyed any man within their grasp.... Ultimately Bishop realized that the demons of his dreams were not only women monsters who had to be destroyed because they were evil, but women who suffered terribly and who desired to have their unspeakable torments ended by the final welcome release of death. That both the incarnate evil and the incalculable suffering should be lodged within the same body seemed to him as reasonable as a woman having two breasts.

This novel is everywhere marked by such an outpouring of words, by a frenzied devotion to every detail of the sex crime myth, exposing not only the vast entertainment value of sex crime (this is, after all, a "popular" novel), but also the role of entertainment in that continuing mythicization. As Stevens continues, the killer is further mystified as being an inevitable "part of nature":

Bishop too could be seen as part of nature's design; weeding out the weak, snaring the strays. Much as the chameleon at the approach of an enemy, he blended into his surroundings to the point of invisibility. And like the beautiful Venus's-flytrap, he was made by nature in the form most desirable to his prey.

All such plottings are meant to conjure the mythic tradition into which this killer is so deliberately cast. Not only is he the one with the "heroic" father (the legendary rapist Caryl Chessman) and the "demonic," earthly mother, but this background provides him with a logic or mechanism for his actions—actions which in this book are imbued with the timeless qualities and functions of ritual:

Now the two things are feeding each other. He survives by killing women who are his mother, and he kills women in celebration of his father.... What we're up against, don't you see, is an incredibly brilliant psychopath with the emotions of a terrified child and the animal instinct to live, *caught in an eternal moment in the mind but where the deed is endlessly repeated in the real world.* (emphasis mine)

Perhaps Shane Stevens has read Eliade; the mythic model is the same— the paradigmatic act (or, as with Freud, trauma) in the "original time," the mythic duration of that eternal moment, and the ritual, compulsive repetition of that act in the real world.

That last reference to Bishop's "brilliance" is one of many similar designations. The killer is variously described as a "genius," a "collectible"; he is at one point compared to Christ, his story to "epic Greek Tragedy," his lineage to a "line of warrior kings, a noble and savage breed." Bishop is the one who is nominally a lunatic, but it is the normal, sane men in the story who offer up sentiments such as these:

"Don't you think he has magic? His hideous desires, his sexual sadism, his sheer invisibility. All are far beyond the normal range. What is magic but a supernatural power over natural forces? Bishop's absolute madness gives him this kind of absolute power. And if that isn't real magic what is?"

Nobody answered him.

"God forgive us," intoned Kenton slowly, "but the Thomas Bishops have become the true magicians of our tribe."

That tribe is apparently an all-male collective; in this world, females exist only as: 1) sacrificial victims for the magical rites; 2) mythic causal mothers/bitches; or 3) peripheral annoyances.

A crucial note for mythicization is sounded at the very end when Bishop dies. When his body is examined, it is discovered that he had never been circumcised. But medical records proved that Sara Bishop's biological son had been; a baby switch had occurred in the hospital. Furthermore, it was shown that Caryl Chessman could never have raped Sara Bishop because he was in jail when the rape occurred. Thus, the entire motivating story behind "Chess Man" had no basis in reality. The killer was then definitely and eternally an *unknown* and the novel ends with characters agonizing over the question, "Who was he?" Who was that masked man indeed? Such mystery surrounding the origins or identity of the hero is a characteristic signpost of patriarchal myth. For when the birth origins are obscured, this can be used to provide an aura of intrigue and ever evocative mystery—similar to that surrounding Jack the Ripper. When identity is unknown, legends can be fertilized which present the boy or man as anyone—a crown prince, the incarnation of a magical or eternal force, a son of the devil or a son of god. And in *By Reason of Insanity*, there is one further function of the killer's nebulous identity, for this killer is clearly intended to perform as a secret identity or *alter ego* not only for the other, nominally normal, men within the book itself, but also for those on the outside—reading.

The Inside Story

All stories involve some kind of identification, for unless we are able to relate our feelings and experiences to those of the characters in fiction, much of the emotional effect will be lost.

John Cawelti[39]

Eastwood plays a louse....We watch in fascination and are taken inside of him and do think about what it is really like to abuse women....

Gene Siskel giving a rave review to *Tightrope*[40]

The structural tendency of popular culture is inevitably toward audience identification with protagonists—heroes and villains, especially when the hero and the villain are more or less the same guy. Of course, *audience* primarily functions (as does Siskel's *we*) to denote a male audience. Whatever derivative fantasy identification women have with male heroes, we must first identify with the glut of female victims, get "inside" those naked, posed, and frequently dead female bodies strewn everywhere throughout the male media.

Both Francois Truffaut and Raymond Durgnat have pointed to the sympathy and identification Hitchcock deliberately evokes for Norman Bates, the killer in *Psycho*.[41] That tradition is continued in the overwhelmingly popular and critically acclaimed *Halloween*. In that film a uniquely technical means is used to encourage audience identification with the sex murderer: the *point of view shot,* also called the *first person* or *subjective* camera.* In this style, all action is viewed from the precise eye-view of one character. In *Halloween*, the sex killer is first introduced as a five-year-old boy who is, nevertheless, man enough to slaughter his teenage sister for having sex with her boyfriend while their parents are out. It is Halloween night and the boy is wearing a clown costume and mask. The murder scene is shot *through* the mask; members of the audience see the action through two eyeholes, as if they were behind the mask too. Via camera style, all viewers are placed inside the perspective of the killer, seeing things, as it were, from his point of view. Since *Halloween*, the use of that style has become conventional in the "slasher" film.

*The characteristic use of this technique in the slasher film was first pointed out by Roger Ebert and Gene Siskel (Oct. 23, 1980) on PBS *Sneak Previews* (see also Roger Ebert, "Why Movie Audiences Aren't Safe Any More," *American Film*, March 1981, pp. 54-56). Ebert and Siskel devoted an entire show to denouncing what they termed "women in danger" films and related this trend to an anti-feminist backlash. While deploring such deliberately exploitative films as *I Spit On Your Grave* (although they neglect to tell the ending of that film where the raped woman enacts a deadly vengeance against each of her attackers), these reviewers nevertheless redeem movies such as *Halloween* and *Dressed to Kill* for their "artistry" and "inventive directorial point of view" (see Ebert, *American Film*). Moreover, just a few years later Siskel completely doublethinks himself by hailing *Tightrope*, particularly in that Eastwood makes "us" really know how "it feels to abuse women and you don't get that much in the movies." As he especially should know, sometimes that is about all you do get in the movies.

Other modes of encouraging identification with the killer are somewhat more subtle. In the novel *By Reason of Insanity*, the killer is recurrently paralleled to the normal men in the book, all of whom, at one point or another, express key components of the mind and make up of the killer: a contempt for women here, a violent impulse there, and everywhere the "typical male fantasies" of sexual annihilation. For example, a police lieutenant investigating the case ponders:

Lots of men kill women. Always been like that, probably always will be. Almost like a sport at times. That was the way men looked at women, wasn't it? As sport? To be plundered one way or another. And then dumped.

But the underlying bond between the killer and the normal men is most explicitly developed in the character of Adam Kenton, the reporter who becomes obsessed with the case, a man who prides himself on his "detachment from women," the man who, when he is in bed with his girlfriend, finds his thoughts roaming to sexual torture and wonders what Bishop the mutilator would do to "those breasts, that abdomen." Formulaic thrillers such as this one blithely offer up a collective fantasy of sex murder to their readers, even providing them with an ostensibly normal man through whom they can more safely and blamelessly identify with the monstrous killer. Indeed, it is just this sacred bond between the archetypal "Adam" and the mad killer which climactically leads to the latter's ultimate capture. For Adam Kenton has followed the case so closely, so obsessively, that he finds:

I can think like him....A month ago I came to New York, the same as Chess Man....I became Bishop. In my mind I moved through the city as he would do it, where he would go, whom he would see.

Kenton finally does find and confront his murderous mirror image. He comes carrying the whip that Bishop's mother had used years ago to beat him with, thereby merging himself into Bishop's "eternal moment," materially enacting his continually relived past. To escape, Bishop plunges out a window in a high-story building. Kenton grabs him:

Now Kenton looked into Bishop's pleading eyes and saw the incalculable pain and fright and madness and as Thomas Bishop's bloodied hand meshed with his, Adam Kenton slowly opened his fingers one by one and released the dying boy.

This notion of Bishop as the eternal "boy" not only engenders sympathy for the killer, but also provides the necessary complement to the myth of the dominant, causal mother. In the patriarchal vocabulary, all sex killers are frightened, abused and terrorized little boys, "victims" of their mothers or some other awful woman. That structure carries the compulsion of the archetype and, again, it is pure deception and reversal. Do any of those who so wholly subscribe to this logic ever pause to wonder why little girls—overwhelmingly the actual victims of abuse by fathers and father figures—do not grow up to enact wholesale slaughters against men?

This conventional linking of the mad killer to the normal hero also figures prominently in a Clint Eastwood vehicle, and predictably a huge hit of 1984, *Tightrope*. Here the normal man is none other than Eastwood himself, generally hailed as the most popular movie star in the world, as well as "Hollywood's major male icon—Mr. America incarnate."[42] Yet, to fully understand this film, we must first refer back to an earlier Eastwood role, that of "Dirty Harry" in the film of that title (Don Siegal, 1971).*

It was in the immensely popular *Dirty Harry* that Eastwood's star persona as cop was forever fixed. In that film, Eastwood played the true urban cowboy—the policeman—the pure, lone, silent and violent Avenger, the totally tough individual who is called upon to save Society from the Bad Man—in this case a mad sniper named Scorpio. To do this he naturally must take the law into his own hands; indeed, for those schooled in the ways of westerners, hard-boiled detectives and rugged capitalists, this is but a formulaic given.

If his disregard for the letter of the law is one feature that makes Harry "dirty," his sexuality is also somewhat muddied. Harry's wife, we learn, has been "tragically," i.e. expediently, killed off in an automobile crash; the embittered Harry is chaste throughout the film— a true knight. But at the same time, he is noticeably voyeuristic (which causes his partner to remark that he knows why they call him "dirty") and obsessively livid against the sexual underground ("I'd like to throw a net over the whole bunch.") In *Dirty Harry*, women figure only as symbols, particularly symbolic *victims* such as Ann Mary Deacon, the child victim of torture, rape and murder whom we see only as a dead, utterly white, exposed and naked corpse as she is lifted by the police from her temporary grave.[43] And finally, although Harry is clearly meant to be the force of "good," the ultimate hero, he is simultaneously bonded to and identified with his quarry, the depraved and manic Scorpio. Nowhere is this more evident than in the exchange where Harry confidently

---

*So popular is this character, that three sequels were made featuring him. So mythic is this character to traditional America that Gene Siskel, waxing wildly over the superb propaganda appeal of the Ronald Reagan presidential campaign film, declared the president to be projecting an image just like "Dirty Harry." *ABC News Nightline*, August 22, 1984.

tells his superiors that the killer will strike again. How, they inquire, can he be so sure? "Because he likes it," Harry replies. And, as Robert Mazzocco noted, "Of course Dirty Harry likes it too."[44]

This shared vein between the cop and his quarry, the hero and the killer, surfaces again as the primary theme of *Tightrope*, thirteen years later. Here, Eastwood's wife is also gone, not merely dead, but this time she has left him for a richer man. This wife is shown only once or twice—as a photograph or as a frozen, speechless and unspeakable bitch whom even her daughters despise. The noble abandoned father is now raising these two young daughters alone (the oldest of whom is played by Eastwood's own daughter). Here Eastwood has also gotten a lot more intimate with the sexual underground. He regularly goes to prostitutes and has a marked penchant for bondage and domination type sex. Moreover, in *Tightrope*, the Eastwood cop now shares some distinctive proclivities, not with a mad sniper, but with a masked serial strangler who is terrorizing the prostitutes of New Orleans. Indeed, this killer strangles two prostitutes directly after Eastwood has been to them. Moreover, both Eastwood and the sex murderer use handcuffs on women— for a sense of "control" as our hero puts it at one point. These and other similarities between Eastwood and the killer become so pronounced that his fellow officers begin to remark upon it. Eastwood even vividly dreams that *he* is the strangler,* dream strangling his newly acquired girlfriend (Genevieve Bujold), a Hollywood rendition of a feminist rape counselor.

As it turns out, the actual killer is an ex-cop, one whom Eastwood sent to jail eleven years earlier on a rape charge. The strangler, then, is waging a personal vendetta against Eastwood himself via his sexual slaughters of Eastwood's women. Growing bored with slaying the prostitutes whom Eastwood has had, the killer goes after first his young daughters and then his girlfriend. This motif—evidenced also in *10 to Midnight, The Mean Season*, and *Final Notice*—again bespeaks the fundamental identity between the killer and his legitimated counterparts. Both "desire" the same women. Moreover, this convention allows the identifying viewer to gratifyingly fantasize himself in the two, mutually reinforcing, male roles at once. He is both the lover and the violator, the protector and the menace.[45]

Our hero, of course, manages to rescue the stereotypic "good girls" (but only after they have been sufficiently terrorized); the prostitutes never

---

*The strangler is masked and hence unidentifiable throughout all of the film until the final sequence. Even there, we barely see his face. Such a plot device underscores not only his archetypal role as the could-be-anyone killer, but facilitates his special role as *doppelganger* to Eastwood.

had any such hopes of salvation. And finally, the inevitable confrontation occurs. Eastwood gets to fight and face the strangler, unmasking and then slaying him in a gore confrontation worthy of *Friday the Thirteenth*. After this melodramatic dispelling of the "bad" cop, Eastwood's *alter ego*, the audience is supposed to believe that Eastwood has also managed to purge himself of his own unwholesome desires, even that urge to rape and murder his own daughters and lover. This is revealed to us in the last scene when he is at last able to accept Bujold's womanly caress (macho-like, he had held himself more aloof previously). The beast presumably vanquished, woman now can get down to her traditional role of civilizing man. This is indeed a message and movie worthy of the Reagan era.

This motif of the "secret sharer"—the underlying unity between lawman and criminal—is not new. Still, it holds a particularly critical place in the ideology of sex crime. What *Tightrope* and its brother products reveal is the all-encompassing network, the closed circle of the world of phallic violence. It is useful here to recall Herbert Marcuse's description of the "unification of opposites" which characterizes the "one-dimensional society."[46] That unification functions not only to contain social change, but to veritably *stop* it at the level of thought by enclosing consciousness in a blocked one-dimensionality. While Marcuse referred mostly to an overt fusion of contradictions (a current example would be the designation of "Peacekeeper" for the MX missile), in sex crime ideology we frequently see the inverse—a false opposition of underlying unities—the lover and the rapist, the cop and the killer.

Speaking of formulaic literature, John Cawelti also ventured into this realm of false opposites. He theorized that the function of the formulaic villain was to enable:

... the audience to explore in fantasy the boundary between the permitted and the forbidden and to experience in a carefully controlled way the possibility of stepping across this boundary.[47]

Yet what we might realize is that the supposed "boundaries" or "opposites" that phallocracy recognizes are definitively deceptive. For what is *genuinely* forbidden or taboo (e.g. women defeating male attackers, regularly and with great force and style, female bonding, etc.) does remain socially unspoken, tacitly censored in the imagineered mass media in order to ensure that it will remain unimaginable and, hence, largely unactualized. On the other hand, the vastly articulated fantasy of sex crime works, not only to stimulate the pseudoforbidden contemplation of gynocide, but, through its ritual reiteration of false boundaries, actually functions to profoundly *delimit* the world.

The axis of that closely watched world is located in what Andrea

Dworkin has called "men's commitment to do violence." If the Scorpio villain likes to kill, so (and equally well) does Dirty Harry; if the strangler in *Tightrope* likes to handcuff women and sexually dominate them, so does his pursuer. The poles are delineated and they are at root identical. We are meant to conclude that there simply is no other world than the one of male violence. As Dworkin has written:

In male culture, police are heroic and so are outlaws; males who enforce standards are heroic and so are those who violate them. The conflicts between these groups embody the male commitment to violence: conflict is action: action is masculine. It is a mistake to view the warring factions of male culture as genuinely distinct from one another: in fact, these warring factions operate in near-perfect harmony to keep women at their mercy, one way or another.[48]

Thus, in the *one* dimension of sex crime, women are graciously allowed to live as girlfriends or daughters, but are routinely slaughtered as prostitutes. Typically then, *Tightrope* functions not only as a gorenographic story of sexual slaughter, but simultaneously as a "love" story. Film critic Roger Ebert tells us that, "It's really about a man learning to be able to love a woman."[49] But he has this precisely backwards, for this film is actually about the teaching of women—through the role model of Genevieve Bujold—to love a man who throughout the entire movie has been unequivocally and deliberately identified with a vicious sex murderer. In the acceptable and moralistic ending, the overt sex killer has been silenced, the evil Mr. Hyde seemingly banished. Now it is time for the good girl to also be sacrificed, not in murder but in marriage to the remaining personality—Dr. Jekyll we presume. The last image of the film—Bujold and Eastwood together—calls female viewers to their archetypal patriarchal vocation, *love*, a love to be freely given to that final unification of male "opposites"—the lover/rapist, husband/batterer, boyfriend/murderer—the normal man with whom she lives and whom she loves, but a man who nevertheless harbors the secret self, the desires and fantasies of the sexual murderer.

Women might also be persuaded/intimidated into believing that we have no choice. The evidence is right there before our eyes. The *bad* woman: the woman alone, the woman outside of patriarchal protection/control is unsafe; she ends up horribly dead. Moreover, her dead, provocatively posed body fills the screen repeatedly. Clearly, the overt necrophilia of the sex killer is matched by the subliminal necrophilia of the film itself. If *Psycho* gave us, according to Raymond Durgnat, a murder "too erotic not to enjoy," veritably a "pornographic murder,"[50] *Tightrope* similarly obliges with close-up and frequent inspection of its victims of pornographic murder.*

*The key murder scene in *Psycho*—the shower slashing death of Janet Leigh—is further discussed in Chapter Six.

These picturesque murders provide both voyeuristic and vicarious thrills for "audiences" in the Age of Sex Crime. Although, nominally, the fantasy of gynocide should be despised, horrific, and rarely portrayed, it is instead widely available—and depicted in great detail and variety. If Hitchcock made sexual murder into cinematic "art" in *Psycho*, the entire formulaic progression of such "trash" films as *The Toolbox Murders* and *Pieces* is to provide a veritable *Kama Sutra* of possible gynocidal styles and techniques: different tools, different settings, different victims, and different fetishes to appeal to the imaginations of as many viewers as possible.* These formulaic products, subspecies of the "thriller" and "horror" entertainment genres, form part of an incessant propagandization of patriarchal dominance. And, like other formulas, they "articulate a pattern of fantasy that is at least acceptable to if not preferred by the cultural groups who enjoy them," enabling those groups "to share the same fantasy." In this case, the group fantasy is the pure fusion of sex and violence, the endless repetition of acts of sexual murder.

Of course, just that fantasy is also shared by the killers themselves. Psychological discussions of sexual murderers consistently stress the primary importance of the killer's fantasies, both for personal entertainment and motivational value. Donald T. Lunde, Stanford psychiatrist, tells us that such men ritually replay fantasies of their own murders:

They can satisfy their urges and sexual needs and so on by thinking about the killings they just did. But after a period of time, usually measured in weeks, the effect of the previous killing starts to wear off and there is a need for a new victim.[51]

In an article on Ted Bundy, Jon Nordheimer characterizes sexual murderers as having "strong and repeated fantasies of revenge and power."

*While many films, particularly the cheaper ones, are quite overt in presenting the gynocidal scene, a mainstream film such as *Tightrope* will occasionally be more subtle. In that film, the audience's visualizations of gynocide are elicited through suggestion, again by using Eastwood as a locus of identification. For example, in the first murder a smashed clock reveals the time of a struggle between the victim and her killer, yet her death did not occur until three hours later. One of the other cops, basically playing straight man to Eastwood, asks, "Why didn't he kill her until later?" Eastwood cracks, "Maybe he wanted three hours with her first." In a subsequent murder, it is revealed that the killer made coffee and got a brownie to eat during his torture of the woman. Again some stooge wonders why he would have done something like that. Eastwood remains the man with the answers, "Maybe he was starting to enjoy himself." The male viewer is clearly being invited to start enjoying himself as well, to use his own imagination to fill in those tantalizing blanks—of the three hour torture session or coffee break contemplation—with his own favorite fantasies. The female viewer is invited into sheer terror.

He adds, "For reasons that are not easily explained, notions of virility are expressed through violence."[52] But such inexplicability is itself suspect, for, obviously, the conjunction of virility to violence, with the companion coupling of femininity to victimization, is one of the most regularly reiterated messages of this culture. Similarly, Dr. Martin Orne, classifying Kenneth Bianchi as a "sexual psychopath," explains the disorder in this way:

What is wrong is that the sexual impulse becomes twisted and fused with violence so that the individual derives sexual satisfaction from the violence around a murder.[53]

Yet "sexual satisfaction from the violence around a murder"—from *Psycho* to *Snuff*,* in *Pieces* or in *Prizzi's Honor*—is the distinctive feature of mass mediated "gorenography" from its most masked, i.e. elite, respected, celebrated, and ordinary products, to its self-proclaimedly trashy and cult manifestations.

One of the filmmaking elite, Brian De Palma (a director who genuflects to Hitchcock in nearly every film he makes and reverently revisions *Psycho* itself in *Dressed to Kill*), is not only a mythographer, but also a spokesman and apologist for sex crime. He whines:

I'm always attacked for having an erotic, sexist approach—chopping up women, putting women in peril. I'm making suspense movies! What else is going to happen to them?[54]

Things can only "happen to" women in the patriarchal grammar. We can also note with extreme irony just who DePalma claims is being "attacked."

And a decade before De Palma, the overtly trashy Herschell Gordon Lewis, the so-called "Wizard," or "Grandaddy of Gore," was making "chopping up women" films for the exploitation market. He has now achieved the status of a cult figure for films such as *Blood Feast* (1963), *Two Thousand Maniacs* (1964), and *The Gruesome Twosome* (1967) to name only a few. In these, vast catalogues of violences and mutilations happen to women, including disembowelment and the fondling of internal organs. Lewis has registered his contempt for those, particularly feminists, who deplore his output:

Snuff is the name of a 1976 film shown in this country, as well as the generic label for a category of pornographic film which depicts (or purports to depict) the actual torture, mutilation and murder of an actress. See Beverly LaBelle, "*Snuff*—the Ultimate in Woman-Hating," in *Take Back the Night: Women on Pornography*, ed. Laura Lederer (New York: Morrow, 1980), pp. 272-78. See also Dorchen Leidholdt, "Coalition Stops 'Snuff,' " *Women Against Pornography Newsreport*, Vol. 5, No. 2, Fall/Winter, 1983. WAP's address is 358 West 47th St. New York, N.Y. 10036.

Our films were designed to entertain in a true Aristotelian fashion....Yes, we mutilated women, but we didn't degrade them. Nor was there any applause for the people who did it. I mutilated women in our pictures because I felt it was better box office. If that group of fanatics [Women Against Pornography] would promise to go see a movie if I disemboweled a man, I'd do it.[55]

But of course, a woman routinely and ritually disembowelling a man would be bad box office, not inherently erotic, exciting or energizing to the "audience"; it would constitute grossly incorrect usage in the Age of Sex Crime, for in the grammar of that age, as Catharine MacKinnon puts it, "Man fucks woman; subject verb object."[56]

Ultimately then, what the sex killers fantasize, enact, and then privately recreate, is graphically paralleled in the normal media projections and largely accepted as entertainment and fun—particularly the star products of men such as Hitchcock, Eastwood, and De Palma. It was Hitchcock himself who told us that we "have to remember that *Psycho* is a film made with quite a sense of amusement on my part. To me it's a *fun* picture."[57] Once again, the point of view of phallic normalcy merges into that of the sex killer. Moreover, as Raymond Durgnat pointed out:

In *Psycho* nothing that isn't disturbing or tainted ever happens, and to enjoy it (as most people do) is to stand convicted and consciously convicted, of a lurking nostalgia for evil (i.e. of thoroughly enjoying it in fantasy)....One does not so much watch as participate in it, as one might in a religious ritual.[58]

Of course, he has named it exactly; *Psycho* is a religious ritual, the necessary symbolic accompaniment to the actual enactments of gynocide. That film, as well as countless other such books, songs, and films, narrate the myth, dramatize the rules of sexual power, imbue their participants with renewed faith or renewed terror, and celebrate that most fundamental patriarchal practice—female sacrifice. Historically, that practice took shape as an explicitly religious ritual in the European Witchcraze (1450-1750). As I will discuss in the next chapter, gynocide then was not mystified as illegal and incomprehensible "sexual murder"; rather, it was the legitimate activity of church and state, the god-mandated hunting, torturing, and killing of *witches*, i.e. women.

Chapter IV
Professional Victims

...given the ambiguous identification of men with "their own" women, who are kept in a state of powerlessness, the myth of feminine evil cannot be lived out to its completely logical conclusion which would be total destruction....complete destruction is reserved for a segment of the female population.

Mary Daly[1]

In the original "Jack the Ripper" letter, the writer set down these memorable lines, "I am down on whores and I shan't quit ripping them until I do get buckled....I love my work and want to start again." Jack the Ripper has become the original role model for the career sex killer in the Age of Sex Crime and his "work"—the slaughter of prostitutes—remains a paradigmatic activity of those killers. Ripperophile Donald Rumbelow has noted that in all "genuine Ripper-style murders...all the victims are prostitutes." He adds, "There have been many prostitute killers especially in continental Europe where the Ripper has become something of a cult figure."[2]

Seemingly just such a killer was active in Yorkshire in the late 1970s—the so-called "Yorkshire Ripper." In the wake of controversy over police handling of that case, the British press has reiterated that the major problem that the police faced in the early years of that investigation was "apathy over the killing of prostitutes." Police work, it was declared, depends upon public interest, cooperation, and support, and, as the *Times* noted, "Such was the apathy at the time that it was virtually nil."[3] It was only later when the "Ripper" began to attack young women who were not prostitutes that there arose public expressions of concern. Ironically, such attitudes were encountered not only in the public, but were openly proclaimed by members of the police force as well.

Four years after the first mutilation/murder, West Yorkshire's Acting Assistant Police Chief Constable, Jim Hobson, issued this extraordinary statement as an "anniversary plea" to the killer:

He has made it clear that he hates prostitutes. Many people do. We, as a police force, will continue to arrest prostitutes.

Here, Hobson matter-of-factly aligns "Ripper" motives and actions to larger social interests as well as police goals. He goes on, shifting voice to a direct appeal to the killer:

93

But the Ripper is now killing innocent girls. That indicates your mental state and that
you are in urgent need of medical attention. You have made your point. Give yourself
up before another innocent woman dies.[4]

From such official statements we learn that it is normal to hate prostitutes.
The killer is even assured of solidarity in this emotion. His deeds, it
seems, only become socially problematic when he turns to "innocent
girls." The logical inference is that the prostitutes are already guilty
and thus deserving of the punishments meted out to them by self-
appointed avengers, or "streetcleaners" as the convicted murderer Peter
Sutcliffe later referred to himself. If police chief Hobson's attitude seems
stereotypically Victorian, so too was Sutcliffe's. As his sister described
his feelings toward women, "He was outwardly old-fashioned, and
virtuously correct....He was not a prude, he just had moral standards."[5]
    Over in the Americas, similar standards of phallic morality prevail.
A member of the task force on the "Green River Killer" (and former
head of the Bundy investigation) told *Newsweek*:

There was wide public attention in the Ted [Bundy] case...because the victims resembled
everyone's daughter....But not everybody relates to prostitution on the Pacific Highway.*[6]

Another expert consultant on the Green River case, psychiatrist John
Liebert, informs us that serial murderers either idealize women or degrade
them, seeing women as " 'angels or whores' with no sensible middle
ground."[7] Yet here again we are at a loss in distinguishing the typical
point of view of the sex killer from that of his society, for that same
dichotomy riddles the patriarchal world view. In the United States, for
example, that attitude is by no means confined to criminals; actually,
it has been identified as a common prejudice motivating judges and
juries to side with the accused in rape cases, disbelieving the victim if
she can in any way be construed as a "bad woman."[8] Moreover, that
identical dualism fundamentally underlies American racism and its
deliberately split vision of Black and White women.[9] And finally, that
stereotypic dichotomy imbues the traditional fictions of this culture,
providing a stock convention in any number of classic novels, westerns,
romances, and soap operas.[10]
    Some of the ramifications of this pervasive ideology as it pertains
to sex crime are manifested in a 1981 *Esquire* article reporting on the
then still uncaptured "Yorkshire Ripper." The author, Guy Martin,
displays "moral standards" similar to Sutcliffe's own when he comments:

*Here, "everyone" and "everybody" clearly refer to the white middle-class.

It is the main grief work for the families of Jack's *non-professional victims* to try to understand how their girls came under this man's hand. By having the same killer as the prostitutes, their daughters have somehow been tainted.[11] (emphasis mine)

Although Martin undoubtedly had no intention of being so illuminating, let us consider the prostitute literally as a *professional victim*, stigmatized and targeted as a member of a sacrificial sex/class.

Actually, it is precisely through the characteristic subdivision of the female sex into patriarchally constructed "good" and "bad" women that a "professional victim" class of women can be produced. In *Beyond God the Father*, Mary Daly argues that although patriarchy has cast the female sex into the role of the primordial "Other," it nevertheless cannot wage its characteristic campaign of complete annihilation against that scapegoat/other because of the close biological, emotional, social, and economic ties that men maintain with some women. Therefore, women are split into two groups: those who are "rewarded" with an impossibly unreal definition of "goodness" and those who are reviled as originally "evil" and punished with the ritual destruction traditionally meted out to "Others." As Daly notes, the most striking historical example of this selective destruction of women was the torture and burning of those designated as witches by the church in early modern Europe—a period now known as the European Witchcraze (approximately 1450-1750).[12]

In the contemporary Age of Sex Crime, it is another traditional female scapegoat, the prostitute, who is the paradigmatic target of gynocide. Like the "witch," the prostitute is an archetypal projection of the patriarchal *bad* woman. The symbolic meanings of each are similar—female carnality, deception, manipulation, and evil. Gordon Rattray Taylor has commented, "Prostitutes were to the Victorians what the witches were to the medievals." He continues, "The Victorians [read Victorian *men*] needed prostitutes as objects on whom to project all the negative part of their feelings for women."[13] Within such a world view (one still firmly in place today), it is inevitable that some type of Ripper figure ("society's henchman") would emerge to enact that ideology, to annihilate that "evil" fetishized in the prostitute. And although differences do mark the gynocidal movements of the Witchcraze and the contemporary period, many similarities in both ideology and practice can be traced. Before exploring that link in detail, I will first offer a survey of that earlier campaign of scapegoating and destruction.

Witch-crazed

Hideous as are the details of the persecution of witch-craft which we have been considering up to the fifteenth century, they were but the prelude to the blind and senseless orgies of destruction which disgraced the next century and half.... Witches were burned no longer in ones and twos, but in scores and hundreds. A bishop of Geneva is said to have burned five hundred within three months, a bishop of Bamberg six hundred, a bishop of Wurzburg, nine hundred. Eight hundred were condemned, apparently in one body, by the Senate of Savoy.

Henry Charles Lea[14]

This period was the age of supreme despair for woman.... When for "witches" we read "women," we gain fuller comprehension of the cruelties inflicted by the church on this portion of humanity.

Matilda Joslyn Gage (1893)[15]

From the early decades of the 14th century until the mid-18th, with the most disastrous period running from about 1450-1650, Europe was in the throes of what modern scholars have termed a "witchcraze." Although estimates range up to nine million, most researchers more conservatively conclude that somewhere between 200,000 and 500,000 witches were executed;[16] at the very least, some eighty-five per cent of these were women.[17] The Witchcraze was not simply an intensification of prior witch beliefs and attitudes, but, rather, it resulted from the construction of a new and systematic demonological world view which radically redefined the witch and insisted upon the existence of an organized cult and conspiracy under the dominion of Satan.

Joseph Hansen visualized the development of the craze as occurring in essentially three phases.[18] During the medieval period, until about 1230, there was a general acceptance of the validity of magic, both good and bad. Both Church and State fought against bad magic, maleficia, in its older and simpler form which included a general array of evil intents and actions which harmed another's person or possessions. There was furthermore a traditional belief in incubi and sucubi, demons who engaged in sexual intercourse with humans. The growth of witchcraft theory between the 11th and 13th centuries was markedly slow because the Church still condemned as superstitious the belief in night-riding groups of female witches who worshipped the pagan Goddess, Diana.[19] There was as yet no concept of the witch as the devotee of the devil, but simply the scattered beliefs about magic which are recurrent in time and place. As Hugh Trevor-Roper has noted, a necessary distinction must be made between these miscellaneous witch beliefs and the organized, systematic demonology which the church meticulously constructed out of them.[20]

After 1230, the scholastic community began to abstractly probe the possibility of a connection between humans and demons; then, the newly founded Inquisition gave credence to these possibilities by designating magical acts as heretical. This brought together the previously disparate concept of the sorceress/sorcerer with the Inquisitorial definition of heretics—people who habitually met after dark in secret groups, reputedly to engage in orgies and to worship the devil. An ideological process was set in motion which combined not only these traditions, but others such as that of night-riding females, thus creating "the disastrous collective term 'witchcraft'...from originally scattered features."[21] By 1430, this assimilation was completed; it was also at this time that women, who had previously been given predominance in only some of the conceptions, were now designated as the primary adherents of witchcraft. The term *witch* now conjured up images of:

Depraved human beings, chiefly women, who made a covenant with the Devil for the purpose of inflicting...all sorts of injuries to their fellow men's body, life, possessions...human beings who participated in the nocturnal Sabbat presided over by the Devil, who appeared in the flesh and to whom they paid homage; who...flew swiftly through the air to this Sabbat and to the places of their harmful activities and who committed sexual excesses of the worst kind among themselves and with the Devil; who formed a huge sect of heretics....[22]

After 1430, spurred by this new image, Europe entered into a "virtual obsession" with witchcraft.[23] In 1486, the *Malleus Maleficarum* (The Hammer of Witches) was released, marking the culmination of the newly invented witchcraft ideology. That tract, printed on Gutenberg's newly invented printing press, included as its preface the papal bull *Summis desiderantes affectibus* (1484) in which Pope Innocent VIII linked the "foulest abominations" and "filthiest excesses" of witches with "heretical pravities" and authorized his "dear sons Henry Kramer and James Sprenger" (the authors) to act as Inquisitors against these witches and, essentially, to clean up or purge the filth. He further condemned, under pain of excommunication, all opposition to witchcraft persecutions.[24] Sociologist, Nachman Ben-Yehuda has commented:

The importance of the *Malleus* cannot be overestimated. Its enormous influence was practically guaranteed, owing not only to its authoritative appearance, but also to its extremely wide distribution....It became the textbook of the Inquisition....The moral backing had been provided for a horrible, endless march of suffering, torture, and human [sic] disgrace inflicted on thousands of women.[25]

It was this "textbook" that explicitly and irrevocably linked demonological witchcraft to the female sex (even the word *maleficarum*, "witches," is given in the Latin form meaning *female* witches) and the *Malleus* stands to this day as a definitive textbook for misogynists. For example, the first part, question six, ponders, "Why is it that Women are chiefly addicted to Evil Superstitions?" Answering their own question, Kramer and Sprenger tell us far more about the "Evil Superstitions" of men. Women, they inform us, are:

....more credulous....more impressionable [than men]....they have slippery tongues....and are weak....more carnal than a man, as is clear from her many carnal abominations....nearly all the kingdoms of the world have been overthrown by women....a woman is beautiful to look upon, contaminating to the touch, and deadly to keep...she is a liar by nature....More bitter than death, again, because bodily death is an open and terrible enemy, but woman is a wheedling and secret enemy.... more perilous than a snare....her heart is a net.... inscrutable malice....reigns in their hearts. And her hands are as bands for binding...[26]

Finally, as the priestly inquisitors hammered it out, "All witchcraft comes from carnal lust, which is in women insatiable." Moreover, so immense is that carnality that "wherefore for the sake of fulfilling their lusts they consort even with devils."[27]

Clearly *sex* itself, as well as the female sex, was at the very root of the witch ideology. Actually, the crime of witchcraft itself in the context of that time was understood as a form of "sex crime." For prior to the contemporary connotation and experience of *sex crime* as male sexual violence, the meaning of that term was quite different. It did not necessarily involve violators and victims, but instead referred to individual behaviors that were judged to be unnatural, hence immoral/criminal. Thus, *sex crime* embraced fornication, homosexuality, cunnilingus, fellatio, masturbation, etc. (acts often collectively lumped under the term *sodomy*).*

Throughout the European Witchcraze, theological dogma ordained the existence of witches and their continuous and sexually criminal relations with the devil, other demons, and among themselves; each witch, for example, was presumed to have fornicated with Satan at the alleged Sabbats.[28] Thus, according to the ideology of that era, it was the witches who were were guilty of committing "sex crimes." But, of course, it was instead they who were the actual victims of sex crime, i.e. torture (explicitly recommended by the *Malleus*), mutilation, and murder. For three centuries, confessions were routinely extracted through elaborate tortures, the methods of which often took explicitly sexual forms. These included stripping, shaving all body hair, routine rape, and "pricking." "Pricking" is especially relevant to the modern understanding of sex crime. Each witch was said to have a "devil's mark" on her body, a spot insensitive to pain. A professional class of men, "common all over Europe" and called literally "witch prickers," armed themselves with long needles and bodkins and roamed about hunting witches. They legally

---

*Some such acts are, of course, still on the books as illegal in many states. Moreover, Dutch scholar F.E. Frenkel, has traced the special abhorrence with which such "sex crimes" are usually regarded by the modern public as directly traceable to christian Europe's centuries-long obsession with witches and devils. See F. E. Frenkel, "Sex-Crime and Its Socio-Historical Background," *Journal of the History of Ideas*, 24 (1964), 333-52.

and professionally stripped, shaved, and stabbed women's bodies all over, ostensibly looking for this spot—actions which clearly anticipated the characteristic methods of the rippers and stabbers who emerged to plague Western women in the 19th century. Finally, after such extensive sexual tortures, the women would be executed—burned or strangled. Obviously, it was not the witches, but rather their persecutors who were consumed with "lust"—not only blood lust, but also that normative phallocentric fusion of sex and violence, the combined "obsession and aggression" that Daly has named "phallic lust."[30] The patriarchs' further obsessions become ever more apparent as we continue to examine the ideology of the Witchcraze.

Glamour and the Male Member

Here is declared the truth about diabolic operations with regard to the male organ. And to make plain the facts in this matter, it is asked whether witches can with the help of devils really and actually remove the member, or whether they only do so apparently by some glamour or illusion.

Kramer and Sprenger, *Malleus Maleficarum*[31]

For those unfamiliar with the history of the Witch Hunts or to first-time readers of the *Malleus*, the most extraordinary feature is the outrageous fixation on sex. It was not only the "filthy lusts" of those "adulterous drabs and whores" who were the chief addicts of witchcraft, nor only their carnal and obscene copulations with devils that so fascinated their persecutors. But another equally vast area of concern was the criminal effect of witches upon male sexuality. As H.C. Erik Midelfort has noted, "impotence" was the "symptom so dear" to the authors of the *Malleus*.[32]

Kramer and Sprenger argued that witches were able to magically obstruct the sexual act through various means; chief among these was the creation of male impotence:

First, when they directly prevent the erection of the member which is accommodated to fructification....Secondly, when they prevent the flow of the vital essences...so that it cannot be ejaculated, or is fruitlessly spilled.

To convince any skeptics that witches can wield so much power over such a personal function, the authors explain that, "God allows them more power over this act, by which the first sin was disseminated, than any other human actions."[33] Thus, once again the hoary story of Adam and Eve is dragged in to legitimate what was, in this instance, perhaps the most disastrous campaign of blame ever erected against women.

Impotence was not the only such concern; these priests pondered long and hard over questions such as how witches can "impede and prevent the power of generation," how they "by some Glamour change Men into Beasts," and, finally, "how as it were, they Deprive Man of his Virile Member." A recurring conviction in the contemporary fantasies of sex crime—both the nominal fictions as well as the ultra-serious ideologies—is that women's sexuality constitutes a direct attack, indeed a veritable castration attempt, upon men. Centuries earlier, two Dominican priests were expressing similar figments and fears about dangerous female carnality, but in their fantasies the female attack constituted a bizarre vanishing act.

Various testimonies and eye-witness accounts are related in the *Malleus* to verify the existence of an epidemic of misplaced members. One young man reportedly "lost his member, that is to say, some glamour was cast over it so that he could see or touch nothing but his smooth body." In a feeble attempt to soothe the castration anxiety they also so obviously thrived on, Kramer and Sprenger continually reassure their readers that when such actions are performed by witches, "it is only a matter of glamour; although it is no illusion in the opinion of the sufferer." This entire subject is then grandiloquently summed up:

> We have already shown that they can take away the male organ, not indeed by actually despoiling the human body of it, but by concealing it with some glamour....And what, then, is to be thought of those witches who in this way sometimes collect male organs in great numbers, as many as twenty or thirty members together, and put them in a bird's nest, or shut them up in a box, where they move themselves like living members, and eat oats and corn, as has been seen by many and is a matter of common report? It is to be said that it is all done by devil's work and illusion, for the senses of those who see them are deluded in the way we have said.[34]

Before dismissing such writings as impossibly absurd, it is crucial to remember that the "importance of the *Malleus* cannot be overestimated" (Ben-Yehuda) and that this work has been cited as an example of the remarkable "extent to which books influence, or have influenced both individual and collective action."[35] Henry Charles Lea makes one further point, "no book did more in its time to promote belief in a superstition it was allegedly fighting."[36]

Accusations of female-caused impotence, symbolic or actual castration intentions ("bull-busting," "man-eating") or female desire to possess a penis ("penis envy") are all too familiar. But what strikes the modern reader of the *Malleus* as newly strange—accustomed as we are to *Glamour* magazine, the "glamour girl" and the "glamour puss"—is the use of that word in the demonological context. Such usage, however, is correct. *Webster's Unabridged* defines *glamour* as "a magic spell: BEWITCHMENT." *Funk and Wagnalls* (1970) adds:

Some charm or enchantment operating on the vision and causing things to seem different from what they really are, as for example, a haze or other softening effect; a magic spell; witchcraft

Glamour, then, once used to describe a particularly dread power of witches, has only recently acquired its meaning of sexual attractiveness. It has, however, retained its haze, for *glamour* is one of those words that many use, but few can define with any precision. Calvin Klein, one of America's premier fashion designers, tried, declaring that, "Glamour is an inner spirit and fire."[37] Ironically, that very definition would have been bizarrely appropriate in the 16th century, only then the "spirit" within was dogmatically Satan and the fire was that of the executioner's stake.* And today, along with *glamorous*, women are continually exhorted to be *fascinating, bewitching, entrancing, enchanting, charming.*[38] Such are the components of modern feminine appeal, yet *all* of these words originally referred to some form of witchcraft and were in common parlance during the craze. Women are now expected to embody these qualities and to accept them, when spoken, as compliments. Yet a few centuries back, those very same words made up accusations leading to death sentences for women; correspondingly, today, they are frequently trotted out as excuses, as "irresistible provocations" for rape. This cluster of fashionable witch words has migrated through time, changing in overt meaning and usage, but still clinging to the female and constituting just one of the many ways that women are still culturally dressed, however subtly, in the costume of the patriarchally-defined witch.[39] And finally, in retrospect, an extraordinary reversal becomes apparent. *Glamour*, defined by the witch-crazed as the demonic ability to confuse reality and distort the senses, was, as such, not a destructive power of the witch, but, rather, was the principal method of her persecutors—the ideology makers who produced the craze itself, who fabricated a myth of demonic witchcraft that proved to be the most fantastic illusion of all.

Rossell Hope Robbins has characterized the witch belief as an "intellectual aberration." Jeffrey Burton Russell has agreed that the "intellectuals were more responsible than the ignoramuses for the witch hysteria." Hugh Trevor-Roper has arrived at essentially the same conclusion:

---

*The composition of a woman surrounded by flame and smoke is a disturbingly familiar one in fashion and advertising imagery, particularly in so-called "glamorous" products. See, for example, a 1973 ad for Yardley of London perfume—"You're the Fire," *Mademoiselle*, May 1974, p. 47.

It [the craze] was forwarded by the cultivated popes of the Renaissance, by the great Protestant reformers, by the saints of the Counter-Reformation, by the scholars, lawyers and churchmen of the age of Scaliger and Lipsius, Bacon and Grotius, Berulle and Pascal.[40]

The utter *learning* of these men suggests again the patriarchal glamour. The etymological root of *glamour* is the word *grammar*. It developed in the middle ages as a mere verbal alteration of *grammar* (as *Webster's* explains) due to "the popular association of erudition with occult practices." Unquestionably, it was the erudite and the elite who imposed the most persuasive and insidious glamour of all—the belief in a vast world of witches and devils who, when they could be torn away from their obscene orgies and filthy lusts, stood ready to overthrow all of christendom. That myth or ideology held near total sway for over three centuries. It was "reality." Indeed, after the 1484 papal bull of Innocent VIII, to disbelieve in that projection was itself heresy, a crime punishable by execution.

Nachman Ben-Yehuda has argued that what made the demonological theory so popular and attractive was that "it had all the characteristics of what could be considered an effective ideology."[41] It is in breaking down and understanding the ideological character of the Witchcraze that much of its relation to contemporary sex crime becomes evident.

Setting Up a Target

Target: why were women the major victims of the craze?...Women had an inferior status to begin with, and their lack of power and organization rendered them ready targets for widespread persecutions.

Nachman Ben-Yehuda[42]

The targets of attack in the witchcraze were...women whose physical, intellectual, moral, and spiritual activity profoundly threatened the male monopoly in every sphere.

Mary Daly[43]

Clearly, any critique of the ideology of the Witchcraze (including my own) will be filtered through the author's own experiences and beliefs. That relativity, always operative in cultural analysis, is most significant here for, after decades of historical neglect, a recent and marked revival of interest in the Witchcraze (and not only by feminists) suggests that this era has an uncanny resonance for the contemporary period. Writing its history can even become a masked method for describing the current culture.

Some indications of this are discernible in a weighty article in the 1980 *American Journal of Sociology*. In this piece, Nachman Ben-Yehuda specifically addresses three questions concerning the craze: 1) why it started when it did, 2) why it was a *witch* craze and not something else, and 3) why women were the primary targets of the craze. Drawing upon

Clifford Geertz' concept of ideology as a result of strain on traditional structures and thought patterns, Ben-Yehuda argues that the Witchcraze was an ideological response to a deep need for redefinition of moral boundaries in a medieval social order that was being shaken to its roots by profound social changes. These included severe socio-economic stress, major climatological changes, new geographical discoveries, demographic revolutions, and the disruption of family and communal life. Moreover, he notes that such upheavals left individuals with pervasive feelings of "powerlessness and anomie," a:

deep confusion...a feeling that society had lost its norms and boundaries and that the uncontrollable forces of change were destroying all order and moral tradition.

Ben-Yeduda further argues that all such disruptions:

...created a feeling of impending doom, thus paving the way for the widespread popularity of the craze. The dissolution of the medieval cognitive map of the world also gave rise to utopian expectations, magical beliefs, and bold scientific explorations. These conditions created the need for a redefinition of moral boundaries as an attempt to restore the previous social order.

Massive redefinition is needed because such upheavals create a "disturbing discrepancy between what is believed and reality." The function of a new ideology then becomes manifest. It is created in order to act as a cognitive glue-all for the unhinging social reality. Ideally, it will enter into chaos and establish order, draw lines, provide answers in the form of dogma, introduce security and realign reality:

The function of ideology is to provide authoritative concepts capable of rendering the situation meaningful and "suasive images" by which the meaning can be "sensibly grasped" and which can arouse emotions and direct mass action toward objectives which promise to resolve existing strain.[44]

Ben-Yehuda's explicit purpose is to discover why women particularly were selected as targets during the craze. He concludes that most of the social upheavals, and hence most of the resulting strain, emanated from the social position of women. Thus, the female witch became the most effective symbol/scapegoat for the new ideology, its most "suasive image."

Going into more detail, Ben-Yehuda delineates five key areas in which the changes and resulting tensions proved most decisive—concerns and tensions that startlingly echo many of the current period:

1.   One of the most severe demographic changes Europe had ever experienced...[was] the large increase in the number of unmarried women...[citing E.A. Wrigley] "between two-fifths and three-fifths of the women of childbearing age, 15-44, were unmarried."

2.   The change in women's traditional role hinged on the fact that she entered a competitive market characterized by lack of manpower. The resulting entrance of women into this competitive job market produced a virulent misogynic ideology.

3.   Deep changes in women's role as mothers...a widespread use of contraception and infanticide, which the church strongly and fiercely denounced as evil.

4.   Among the large numbers of unmarried men and women, there was apparently much sexual license, including religiously sinful contraception and even such capital crime as infanticide. Under such circumstances the relationship between the sexes must have been frequently one of mutual exploitation and fraught with deep feelings of guilt and resentment.

5.   The ideology of the witch-hunt made use of these emotions—it allowed men who indulged in sex that proved unhealthy for them to accuse women of taking away their generative powers....The fantasies about the unlimited sexual powers and depravity of women may have been a reflection of the fear engendered by the large number of unmarried women not subject to the authority of fathers or husbands, as, according to prevailing views, they ought to have been.[45]

At this juncture, the reader might start to wonder if the author is describing the 15th or the late 20th century. Ben-Yehuda's schema and arguments are very persuasive, but I suggest that at least part of this persuasive power stems from the resemblance and resonance of his account to contemporary experience and consciousness.

For example, to update those last five statements, we could leave absolutely intact the points about the competitive job market and changing role of mothers.[46] Then, we could insert "sexual revolution," an unprecedented divorce rate, common cohabitation and the singles' life-style alongside the 15th century categories of "demographic change" and the "sexual license of unmarried men and women."[47] Next can be substituted birth control pills and abortion for "religiously sinful contraception and infanticide."[48] Then a "new impotence" induced by the "sexually liberated woman" can simply be loaded on to the male-perceived mutually exploitative, guilty and resentful relationship between the sexes.[49] Finally, the ideology of contemporary sex crime, like the ideology of the Witchcraze, just may be a "reflection of the fear engendered by the large number of unmarried women not subject to the authority of fathers or husbands, as, according to prevailing views, they ought to have been." In other words, the contemporary manifestation of gynocide—peaking in serial sexual murder, but including the entire range of sexual violence against women (a manifestation which has unmistakeably accelerated throughout the 1970s and 80s), is the violent, systematic response of phallocracy to contemporary feminism.

Other correspondencies abound as well. Today, as in the time of the original witch persecutions, utopian expectations (for technological "miracles") as well as "bold scientific explorations" (into space, biomedicine, genetics, nuclearism, etc.) are everywhere. Yet, they are shadowed by prevailing moods of pessimism, confusion, symbolic emptiness, guilt, alienation, a feeling that society has "lost its norms and boundaries," that things are "coming apart," evidenced by such catchwords as *dehumanization, mass, one-dimensional, narcissistic.*[50] Both the Space Age and the Nuclear Age have done their share in dissolving the cognitive map of the world and the latter has ordained the general fear that there might not be a future at all.* After all, since 1947 we have lived with the "bulletin clock" of the atomic scientists registering each month how close we are to nuclear doomsday; as of this writing that clock stands poised at three minutes to midnight.

Apocalyptic tremors and rumors continue to shake this Bad News Society. As Alvin Toffler writes in *The Third Wave*:

Thus, large numbers of people—fed on a steady diet of bad news, disaster movies, apocalyptic Bible stories, and nightmare scenarios issued by prestigious think tanks—have apparently concluded that today's society cannot be projected into the future because there is no future.[51]

By the end of the 1970s, *Time* magazine noted what it termed a "deluge of Disastermania," a glut of best sellers, popular films, science and religion predicting and describing in loving detail a coming Armageddon.[52] Indeed, the man whom the *New York Times* named as the best-selling author of the 1970s is the born-again preacher, Hal Lindsey. His morbidly entitled book, *The Late Great Planet Earth* (over fifteen million copies sold and also made into a movie narrated by Orson Welles), was the first of his many highly successful prophecy books which drew upon biblical sources to announce that rapturous and eagerly anticipated end.[53]**

*Robert Jay Lifton has written extensively on the "psychic numbing" effects of the nuclear age, the feelings of overwhelming helplessness and alienation that can form as a response to the threat of nuclear annihilation. Equally disturbing is the parallel, but very different, reaction that Lifton terms "nuclearism"—"the embrace of the bomb as a new "fundamental," as a source of "salvation" and a way of restoring our lost sense of immortality." Robert Jay Lifton and Richard Falk, *Indefensible Weapons: The Political and Psychological Case Against Nuclearism* (New York: Basic Books, 1982).

**Many fundamentalists claim that seven years before the "final battle" and the end of the world as we know it, a period known as the "Tribulation" will begin, a period marked by the appearance of the antichrist and a reign of unmitigated disaster. However, true believers will be spared living through this time because right at its opening they will all be taken up bodily by god into heaven. This "taking up" is known as "the Rapture."

Not surprisingly, as disaster consciousness has climbed, so has belief in the devil.[54] And accompanying that belief, sometimes probably triggering that belief, is a noticeable increase in the devil's popular exposure. The publication of Ira Levin's novel *Rosemary's Baby* in 1967 (made into a film by Roman Polanski in 1968) signalled the opening of a period of fashionableness for what the *New York Times* later termed "satanophany."[55] Another best seller, William Blatty's *The Exorcist* (1971) was also soon followed by a hugely popular film (William Friedkin, 1973). While audiences across the country thrilled to the depiction of a pubescent girl possessed by the devil, many also picked up the latest Hal Lindsey babbler—*Satan Is Alive & Well in the United States* (1974). Two years later, precisely that point was graphically made in the hit film *The Omen*, (Richard Donner, 1976), a bloody story of the birth of the antichrist into a politically elite American family. Like the Lindsey books, this film drew overtly upon the biblical prophecies of the book of Revelations, and its tone also was unarguably apocalyptic. Film critic Robin Wood, after noting that satanism was one of five dominant motifs in the horror genre over the past two decades, went on to comment: *"The Omen* would make no sense in a society that was not prepared to enjoy and surreptitiously condone the working out of its own destruction."[56]

In the world of rock music, the Rolling Stones was one of the first bands to pick up on the demonic theme, first with an album, *Their Satanic Majesties Request* (1967), then with the hit song, "Sympathy for the Devil."[57] And throughout the 1970s and 80s, the subspecies of rock known as "heavy metal" has consistently pushed demonic as well as sexually sadistic imagery in their lyrics and visual presentations. Iron Maiden, for example, in black leather and chains, scream out explicitly satanic lyrics on their album, *The Number of the Beast*, while Judas Priest (similarly clad) include a piece called "Eat Me Alive" on their album *Defender of the Faith*.[58] Here they sing of forcing a woman to perform oral sex on a man at gunpoint. Soon this genre with its characteristically twinned imagery of satanism and sadism was explicitly linked to serial sex murder. Richard Ramirez, the man arrested as the California "Night Stalker," not only left symbols of "devil worship" at the scenes of his crimes, but friends reported that he was obsessed

See William Martin, "Waiting for the End," *Atlantic Monthly*, June 1982, pp. 31-37. See also F.H. Knelman, *Reagan, God and the Bomb* (Buffalo, N.Y.: Prometheus Press, 1985), p. 182. Knelman quotes Jerry Falwell as informing his followers: "Well, nuclear war and the Second Coming of Christ, Armageddon, and the coming war with Russia, what does this have to do and say to me?...none of this should bring fear to your hearts, because we are all going up in the Rapture before any of it occurs."

with the satanic themes on a 1979 album by AC/DC called *Highway to Hell*.[59] And finally, from one extreme to another, from deliberately decadent rock 'n' roll to the parent company of that icon of American purity, Ivory Snow, satanophany has registered its effects. In 1985, Proctor & Gambel announced that it would change its "Man in the Moon" logo as a response to consistent rumors by certain religious groups who claimed that the logo was a sure indication of devil worship.[60]

Rumbles of impending doom, obsession with the devil, the consciousness of disaster, and even a perverse pleasure taken in the contemplation of destruction—all these, and the others already discussed, line up as those conditions which, as Ben-Yehuda suggested, might fertilize a "witch-hunting" ideology. However, not only does Ben-Yehuda fail to extrapolate to the present, but he also seriously misinterprets the actual efficacy of the witch ideology itself. For, ultimately, he falls back on righteously damning such scapegoating movements as hopelessly foolish and ineffectual, suggesting that all such ideological stratagems contain an internal self-destruct mechanism and are doomed to inevitable failure:

When a community so vehemently and desperately tries to restore its moral boundaries, sociologists can expect that the attempt is doomed to fail.... persecutions can be interpreted as a symbol of incapacity, of a system's failure, as "death throes" if you wish, and they might be viable proof that the previous equilibrium cannot be recaptured.[61]

His conclusion therefore is that the witch persecutions were not only dysfunctional, but also an outrageous failure, demonstrating only futility, useless sacrifice of life and moral degradation. He further notes that the craze "was a unique historical combination of accusations against people, especially women, of whom the overwhelming majority were probably completely innocent." We have now come full circle, landing once more on the spot of the "guilty" or "innocent" victim. And here also, we find the blind spot of this analysis.

Basically, we are being asked to accept that this massive movement, a movement which succeeded in killing anywhere from two hundred thousand to nine million people—most of whom were women—which succeeded in enlisting nearly all of Europe over three centuries in its beliefs, was really just some big mistake and "failure." If, as Ben-Yehuda argues, this was an ideology which scapegoated a convenient target— women—in some futile and mad attempt to halt history and freeze traditional structures against change, then the witch persecutions were indeed dysfunctional and qualify as a "craze" and not a reasoned movement. But there is an alternative interpretation, i.e. that the persecutions were perfectly synchronized with the values and needs of a patriarchal order and served a successful and triumphant function for that order and its future.

Patriarchy has been defined by Kate Millett as a system in which "every avenue of power within the society, including the coercive power of the police, is entirely in male hands."[62] This power must be continually maintained. Millett further cites Hannah Arendt's observation that power is kept either by consent (usually obtained through conditioning to an ideology) or is enforced through violence. Clearly, the witchcraft persecutions by men against women, and legitimized by an overtly misogynic ideology, could be interpreted as the successful exercise of violence, a war which was won in a campaign to consolidate patriarchal power in the midst of sweeping social changes. Perhaps, also, as radical feminist analysts argue, the persecutions were a direct response not only to "social change," but were also a systematic attack against women who were actively resisting the patriarchal church and state.[63]

Whether or not the majority of women executed as witches posed an individual threat or active resistance to patriarchy, or whether they were randomly selected targets aimed at solely on the basis of their sex, is too vast a question to be answered here. What I will argue is that within a patriarchal order the witch persecutions were ultimately logical, even *normal* considering that the witch ideology set the norms for over three centuries. Ben-Yehuda, among others, has stated that witchcraft was a "myth," i.e. a delusion or deception. But the deception is only continued when the phenomenon is everywhere called a *craze*, if that term is employed to suggest that it was a social aberration, some medieval delusion sponsored by looney old men or frustrated monks, or even, in a far more sophisticated analysis, a futile, spasmodic, ideological death gasp. Although Ben-Yehuda never uses the word *impotent*, he implies as much when he describes the persecutions as a "symbol of incapacity," a "system's failure," for these images are as glamorous as the impotencies that the *Malleus* so fondly reports on. The "Witchcraze" was a planned and powerful persecution, not an impotence but a completed violation.

As I have shown, we now live in an age which seems to closely parallel those crisis factors which surrounded the European Witchcraze. With this background in mind, I will turn to an examination of more of the correspondencies between that era and the current one of sex crime, pointing out not only structural similarities, but also a shared and continuing tradition, for the witch "craze" was by no means unique— nor has it ended.

Witch-Craze/Sex-Mania: The Mask of Insanity

We are not accustomed to associate patriarchy with force....Customarily, we view its brutalities in the past as exotic or "primitive" custom. Those of the present are regarded as the product of individual deviance, confined to pathological or exceptional behavior, and without general import.

Kate Millett[64]

Psychiatrists have concluded that Bundy is probably a psychopath, that his public persona—so clean cut, intelligent, attractive, charming, and normal—is, in fact, the most significant clue to the profound and disturbing abnormality beneath the surface....the psychopath characteristically wears a "mask of sanity"—in the words of Dr. Hervey M. Cleckley...who examined Bundy. And beneath this mask lies an emotional void.

James Horwitz, in *Cosmopolitan*[65]

Just as we customarily view the systematic brutalities of the gynocidal witch era as a "craze," we are now expected to understand the contemporary terrorization of women, not in political terms, but as the aberrant behavior of mysterious sexual maniacs, preternatural monsters, or in the most acceptable jargon, *psychopaths* or *sociopaths*. Currently, the mythic designation of "witchcraze" is echoed in the notion of "sexual psychopathy"—the most frequently voiced explanation for current trends in sexual murder. Both designations shrink behind a similar mask of *insanity* in order to defeat political analysis and understanding.

In *The Myth of Mental Illness*, Thomas Szasz proposed a thesis that remains anomalous to the modern psychiatric paradigm. He contended that mental illness is a "myth," i.e. an ideological invention of modern psychiatry, akin to the centuries earlier invention of devils and witches by the European religious establishment.[66] Once again, a clear parallel can be drawn between the European Witchcraze and the current Age of Sex Crime. In the Witchcraze, the ideologists manufactured the category of demonological witch in order to mystify and obscure the gynocidal intent. Currently, that same function is served by the widespread mythicization of the violator.

The notion of the psychopath originated with a nineteenth-century physician, J.C. Pritchard, who described patients who were "morally insane," but could still lead outwardly normal lives.[67] Throughout the twentieth century, the concept has been expanded, popularized, and widely integrated into common consciousness.* Particularly in characterizations of sexual murderers, the term is almost ubiquitously employed.** How it is used, however, can be extremely puzzling. For

*Perhaps the most significant popularizer and proponent of the diagnosis of psychopath is Dr. Hervey Cleckley. See his standard text, *The Mask of Sanity: An Attempt to Clarify Some Issues About the So-Called Psychopathic Personality*, 5th ed. (Saint Louis: C.V. Mosby, 1976).

**The case of the "Hillside Strangler" is revealing here. Psychologist John Watkins, the man who "discovered" Kenneth Bianchi's "multiple personality" and consistently argued for the validity of that diagnosis told *Time* that Bianchi was "a very pure psychopath (7 May 1979, p. 26). Yet Dr. Martin Orne, the man whose examination of Bianchi convinced him that the whole thing was a fabrication and whose testimony helped to topple Bianchi's scheme, nevertheless also defined Bianchi in just that same way. As he told PBS *Frontline* (27 March 1984): "Mr. Bianchi is a sexual psychopath."

example, readers of the earlier quoted description of Ted Bundy might be somewhat startled by the logic or lack thereof in the statement, i.e. that his highly normal public persona is actually the greatest clue to his abnormalcy, but this is precisely the standard approach. Writing in the *Journal of Police Science and Administration*, two FBI agents quote Robert E. Hardin—"an outstanding criminal psychologist...[on] the problem of the sociopath and sex offenses":

The individual [the sexual sociopath] is not psychotic, is not neurotic, is not mentally retarded, and frequently appears not only normal, but hypernormal.[68]

Here we are very close to an open admission of the normalcy of sexual violence to the phallocentric society. Indeed, one scholar (although using a definition of the psychopath as largely non-murderous) has examined the psychological literature and, after weighing the implications of his characteristic traits—*beguiling, guiltless, manipulating, cynical, primitive egocentricity, unempathic, professes conventional values, unperturbed, restless,* and *oriented in the present*[69]—has concluded that the psychopath cannot be considered "ill nor even seriously out of phase" with many typical American values. He proposes that the psychopath is not really an "antisocial personality" at all, but, on the contrary, is a "heavily socialized" one.[70]

The diagnosis of psychopath, although largely accepted within the American psychiatric community, has had its detractors.[71] A 1965 Kinsey report, for example, deemed it to be a "wastebasket classification which is used for persons whose actions are disapproved of or not understood by clinicians and the lay public."[72] It is also a classification which allows for the expedient disposal of truth and the elaborate manufacture of myth. Norman Mailer and others have hailed the psychopath as not only the paradigmatic personality, but also the "hero" of our age.[73] Along these lines, Alan Harrington, in his 1972 book, *Psychopaths*, further mystifies the type:

Detached and unconcerned—the mark of clinically diagnosed psychopaths everywhere, except during brief flareups of temper....destructive psychopathic force....at times almost magical, and in a terrible way almost religious....not merely dominating but....bewitching others.[74]*

Here the very close ties of modern psychiatric explanation to the favorite fictional portrayal of the sex killer as a supernatural devil or immortal monster are manifest. Moreover, the intent and effect of each myth is identical—to enshrine the sex killer as the man apart, as the extraordinary and inexplicable, though inevitable, presence.

*Again, we might recall journalists Michaud and Aynesworth's mumbo jumbo regarding Ted Bundy's "preternatural power to manipulate, a capacity whose effect was akin to magic."

Although the mystique surrounding the sexual psychopath is strikingly similar to that which traditionally has attended the christian devil (i.e. the magical, destructive, sexual, evil force), the psychopath, in his role of torturing and murdering women, is actually far more analagous to the godly witch hunter. Indeed, this fusion of both devil and pricker aspects in the contemporary psychopath points to that familiar false opposition of male types as it operated during the Witchcraze. Ironically, one of the most dire accusations that could be hurled against a woman was that she had made a pact with the devil. But then, as now, it was the patriarchs who made a pact with the devil— i.e., themselves, their ideological construct—to annihilate women whenever females threaten the supremacy of the Family of Man. (For a contemporary rendition of this script see the acclaimed 1985 film, *Prizzi's Honor*.)[75]

The witch killers were quite explicit about why they did what they did: they did it for God; they did it for Man; they did it to purify the "Body of Christ";[76] they did it because they felt threatened, they needed to "save the world," i.e. their world; they did it because it was the norm; they did it because they were ordered to do so by higher authorities; and they did it because they liked it. The reasons for contemporary gynocide are essentially similar, as the killers and their chroniclers reveal:

I love my work.

Jack the Ripper

Boy, it made me feel powerful...I was like
any other normal guy, trying to make out.

Albert De Salvo[77]

Everything I did was for survival.

Lawrence Singleton, convicted of raping a 15 year-old girl
and chopping off her arms with an ax[78]

To be honest, I pulled up her clothing to satisfy some
sort of sexual revenge upon her.

Peter Sutcliffe, explaining his mutilating attack[79]

Ever since I was a young boy I have wanted to torture
a beautiful young girl.

Donald Fearn, sex-murderer[80]

Bianchi: Yeah, I killed the first girl.
John Watkins (psychologist): You killed the first girl.
    Who was she? Did you know her?
Bianchi: Nah—that nigger.

Watkins: Oh?
Bianchi: Yeah—nice black witch.
Watkins: How did you happen to decide on her?
Bianchi: Well, I didn't see anything wrong with it.
   It was just there.[81]

Gradually, his sexual desire builds back up and joins,
as it were, those other unfulfilled desires, this
other need to totally possess her.

Ted Bundy[82]

I was death on women. I didn't feel they need [sic] to exist. I
hated them and wanted to destroy every one I could find. I
was doing a good job of it.

Henry Lee Lucas[83]

We had a profile of the women he did not like. They all
seemed to be women he could not date, women who were
unattainable. Most of them were small, petite young
women with long, dark hair and pretty faces...women
he could overpower and then *demonstrate his virility to.*

description of Leonard Paradiso, sex-murderer[84]
(emphasis mine)

We're looking for an intelligent person [sic], a person [sic] that might have animosity
against women in some way or perhaps has a biblical interpretation toward cleansing
women such as baptizing them in the river or whatever.

*Seattle police official describing
projected profile of the "Green River Killer"[85]*

I was just cleaning the place up a bit.

Peter Sutcliffe[86]

I was making life-and-death decisions...playing God
in their lives.

It was a command. I had a sign and I followed it...
Don't think that because you haven't heard from me that
I went to sleep. No, rather I am still here...
Thirsty, hungry, seldom stopping to rest; anxious to
please Sam. I love my work.

David Berkowitz[88]

The motivations behind gynocidal acts are mystified and obscured
when attributed to an aberrant, inexplicable psychopathy, or to normative
definitions of *sex* and *lust* as sensual desire. As these statements reveal,
other possible motivations include misogyny, sadism, obsession with
personal power, fear, fantasy fulfillment, revenge, dread of rejection, dread
of impotence, desire for purgation, and response to a "command." The
implications of none of these, however, will be grasped when the myth

of the mad, monstrous and always mysterious psychopath dominates perception.

British journalist Joan Smith has analyzed the operation of such characteristic mystification in the cultural saga of the "Yorkshire Ripper." As she sees it, the initial myth of the contemporary reincarnation of Jack the Ripper—the whore killer who adopts an adversarial relation to the police, sending them missives, taunting them, eluding capture with an uncanny ability—was the "artefact of a predominantly male police force transmitting its prejudices through a predominantly male press." After Sutcliffe was captured, his lawyers presented a defense claiming that he was schizophrenic, that he heard voices issuing from crosses on graveyards, commanding him to kill "scum" and "filth," i.e. prostitutes. The jury, however, did not buy it, found Sutcliffe sane, and convicted him. Smith writes:

It seemed possible that the myth would be destroyed...At long last it seemed to have been publicly acknowledged that we live in a society where sane men periodically embark upon the wholesale slaughter of women. But no, the outpouring of words after the trial— in newspaper features and three books—did as much as possible to mould Peter Sutcliffe into the Yorkshire Ripper...to prove he was some sort of monster. The Yorkshire Ripper was filed away as an aberration. The case is closed. The myth was won.*

While the predominantly male ideologues and media construct and disseminate a myth of the aberrant and the monstrous, women generally do worry about the *normal* state of affairs. Elizabeth Baron, Deputy Attorney General in California, recalls:

What was so frightening about the "Hillside Strangler" was that the picture I had in my mind was of the average, ordinary man, someone that could be my colleague in the office, someone that could be waiting on my table in a restaurant, somebody that could be taking my ticket in a theater. He was not going to be a monster. He was going to fade into anonymity among all the other people. He was going to be someone's loving son, loving husband, sweet brother, good neighbor. People were going to be surprised when we found out. And that was really frightening because you didn't have a way to guard yourself, to protect yourself. Because it could have been anybody.[89]

Similarly, Joan Smith noted that during the siege of the "Yorkshire

---

*Smith is also explicit on the function of that myth as well as the motivations behind it: "That myth is now being used to conceal the truth it momentarily threatened to reveal. It came into existence because men are unwilling to recognize a deep vein of straight-forward misogyny which sanctions a whole spectrum of violent behavior towards women, from knocking the wife about to rape to murder....If male violence is common and violators commonplace, then each man might have to take a worried look at himself. Better by far to endow the man who attacks women with characteristics that set him apart from other men." Joan Smith, "Getting Away With Murder," *New Socialist*, May/June 1982, pp. 10-12.

Ripper," one group of citizens did ignore the myth and sought the killer in the most familiar of men. She writes, "While the police were seeking a man apart, women were turning in their husbands and brothers." In nearly every case of highly publicized serial sexual murder, a similar phenomenon occurs. Paralleling the scores of men who "confess" to the crimes, are the many women who come to the police, expressing hesitant but grave doubts about the men with whom they are intimately involved. Actually, this is one of the ways that Ted Bundy was initially listed as a suspect in the "Ted murders." His girlfriend of six years had reported her misgivings about him to the Seattle police. She subsequently relates that experience in a book incredibly titled, *The Phantom Prince: My Life with Ted Bundy*.[90] The narrative is fairly predictable, but one factor stands out: this woman lived in constant fear and suspicion with a man she simultaneously "loved" for a number of years, always vacillating between romance and terror.[91] Her story is not unique; nor are the stories of the assorted men who call up the police, confessing themselves to be the current Strangler, Ripper, etc. What these parallel phenomena indicate is an abiding fear and violence at the core of a multitude of quintessentially "normal" relationships.

One researcher, Allan Griswold Johnson, has concluded that all girls now twelve years-old in this country stand a twenty to thirty percent chance of suffering a violent sexual attack in their lifetimes. He states:

It is difficult to believe that such widespread violence is the responsibility of a small lunatic fringe of psychopathic men. That sexual violence is so pervasive supports the view that the locus of violence against women rests squarely in the middle of what our culture defines as "normal" interactions between men and women.[92]

In a different vein, further testimony on the normalcy of sex crime is offered by two criminologists in a book on such crimes written specifically for police investigators:

In every neighborhood there are men who choke their wives or are choked by them, men who cut their wives slightly with a razor in order to see blood at the moment of ejaculation or are cut by them, men who stab a pillow alongside their partner's head with a butcher knife in order to stimulate to climax. It may be that during a major investigation police detectives will have to identify such people [sic] as part of the solution to the crime.*

Such, it seems, are the typical bedroom communities of the United States.

---

*A few pages later, these authors also advise the police, "The sadistic murderer is almost always male. Generally, do not waste time looking for a female." Robert H. Morneau and Robert R. Rockwell, *Sex, Motivation, and the Criminal Offender* (Springfield, Ill.: Charles Thomas Publishers, 1980), pp. 208,223.

The normalcy, indeed *hypernormalcy*, of the "psychopath," the ready identification so many men have with the sexual killer, the frequency of violence in the male-female relationship: all of these bespeak the network of phallic norms, mores, and institutions which ultimately legitimate and even command the gynocide of the Age of Sex Crime.

Finally, in considering this characteristic pursuit of the aberration, we might recognize, again, the operation of patriarchal glamour. For this mythic pursuit (like the fixation on the "terrible mother" or "blameworthy victims") not only distracts from the normalcy of sexual violence, but also casts an obscuring haze over what is actually the simplest and most obvious shared trait among all serial killers—that is, their sex, their maleness. And it is precisely this factor that has been most systematically ignored by criminologists and psychologists in their investigations into the causes of sexual murder. In a 1984 article, criminologist Steven Egger, after first noting that all known serial killers are male, goes on to observe:

This sexual differentiation may lead researchers to study maleness and its socialization as an etiological consideration. However, the lack of this obvious distinction has apparently precluded such study.[93]

This however, is somewhat obtuse. Perhaps researchers have not yet made that so obvious distinction because they do not wish to follow up on its necessary implications, because making such a distinction would inevitably introduce the issue of sexual politics into sexual murder.

Understanding the slaughters of both the Witchcraze and the Age of Sex Crime as political, we can continue to examine the underlying functions of both campaigns.

The Method to the "Madness"

Death by torture was the method of the church for the repression of woman's intellect, knowledge being held as evil and dangerous in her hands. Ignorance was regarded as an especial virtue in a woman, and fear held her in this condition. *Few women dared to be wise, after thousands of their sex had gone to death by drowning or burning because of their knowledge....* The witch was in reality the profoundest thinker, the most advanced scientist of those ages. (emphasis mine)

Matilda Joslyn Gage[94]

The Yorkshire Ripper did have a meaning for women—as a potent symbol of male violence toward them. The magnitude of his crimes forced into the open women's underlying fears about men. Even now, women in Leeds and elsewhere lead lives circumscribed by the threat he so starkly represented.

Joan Smith[95]

Feminist analysis looks at both the Witchcraze and contemporary sexual terrorism and sees these as no aberrations, but normative persecutions within the patriarchal order—persecutions fulfilling specific political functions. Historian H.C. Erik Midelfort has also explored the functions of the Witchcraze, but from his angle witch burnings were not only "functional" but "therapeutic" in that they were able to provide society with a means to control and eliminate a potentially disruptive and revolutionary element—i.e. non-patriarchally controlled women.

Midelfort first points out that the common stereotype of the witch as a single, eccentric, often old and isolated woman is largely an historically accurate one. For it was unmarried women, along with the widowed and divorced, who were the most likely targets of the hunters, particularly in the beginning phases of the era. He comments:

We can concede that the small trials may indeed have served a function, delineating the social thresholds of eccentricity tolerable to society, and registering fear of a socially indigestible group, unmarried women....Until single women found a more comfortable place in the concepts and communities of Western men, one could argue that they were a socially disruptive element, at least when they lived without family and without patriarchal control. In this restricted sense, *the small witch trial may have even been therapeutic, or functional.*[96] (emphasis mine)

Men may no longer profess a belief in witches, yet the founding phallic fears about "loose," i.e. uncontrolled, women are still issued, swallowed, and digested with ease. Moreover, it is clear that women who live "without family and without patriarchal control" are still threatening to the "concepts and communities of Western men." Thus, the phallocratic fear, discomfort, and need for control have found new expression in the Age of Sex Crime, an era in which random and virtually all-pervasive sexual terrorism functions in much the same way as did the witch burnings—to inhibit, circumscribe, reorder, and in some cases terminate the lives of women.

Comparing the two eras, these further correlations emerge:

Records: As previously noted, estimates of numbers killed in the Witch Hunts range from 200,000 to nine million. Such an extreme gap is similar to the one which exists today between reported incidence of sex crimes—ranging from physical abuse, through incest, rape, mutilation and murder—and their actual occurrence. We readily accept that no reliable records exist from past centuries, yet that same situation adheres today in regard to sex crime. Researchers continually point out that for abuses such as wife beating and rape there are simply no concrete statistics due to under-reportage, linked with (female) shame and society's (male police and court's) deliberate ignoring of their incidence.[97] Such systemic silences only serve the abusers/rapists, adding to the mystification of male violence, rendering it nebulous and unnamed, yet simultaneously omnipresent.

The situation is remarkably similar regarding sexual murder. In 1975 Susan Brownmiller pointed out that there were no available national figures on the yearly number of rape-murders because the act is treated as a homicide by the police and courts. She then speculated that there were perhaps four hundred rape-murders per year in this country.[98] (That figure would not register those lust-murders which do not include rape.) By the mid-1980s, police officials say that there are somewhere around five thousand serial murders annually in this country, most of them murders of women, although exact sex ratios are not given.[99] (That figure would not include the women who are "missing" or those who are victims of non-serial sex murder.) Yet if all of the sex murders (serial and non-serial) were accurately counted, if all of the instances of the women killed by their boyfriends[100] and the two to four thousand wives beaten to death annually by their husbands[101] were figured in, if sexual murders of boys and young men were reckoned,[102] if the massive incidence of nonlethal sexual assaults against women and girls were taken into account, if statistics from other countries were figured in, would we then recognize that we live in the midst of a period of intensified gynocide, equivalent in destruction to the European Witchcraze and recorded, if not in the inadequate or unavailable statistics, in the widespread embedding of sex crime and its ideology into legend, fiction, film, song, fashion, and, most of all, pornography.

Victims: As Joan Smith noted, it serves the myth of sex crime for it to be commonly believed that the murderer must have some "motive beyond simple hatred of women"[103]—e.g. he obsessively hates prostitutes, or women who remind him of his mother, or all girls with long, brown hair. However, analysts of sex crime would be best advised to go beyond these glamours and recognize the truly significant similarities among victims of sexual murder. First of all, they are women in a woman-hating world; their killers are men. Secondly, although some highly sensationalized serial killers (e.g. Bundy, Berkowitz, Wilder) do murder women on the basis of their correspondence to a pornographic/objectifying ideal, many more victims of serial murder are women who "share common characteristics of what are perceived to be prestigeless, powerless, and/or lower socioeconomic groups"[104]—i.e. women of color, prostitutes, runaways, vagrants, single and often elderly women. For example, the women killed by the "Boston Strangler" were single or widowed; they lived alone. The "Hillside Stranglers" at first picked on runaways, prostitutes, and streetwomen, not because they particularly hated these types, but because they made the easiest and least mourned prey. By virtue of age, race, occupation, living situation, nonmarital status and social class, such women are targeted as especially expendable, as "professional victims."*

Although some groups of women are branded as especially vulnerable, *all* women are meant to internalize the threat and message of sexual terrorism. Not all of the victims of the "Yorkshire Ripper" were prostitutes, but all of them, we are told, were women "the killer sighted outside at night."[105] Henry Lee Lucas, interviewed by Sylvia Chase on *ABC News 20/20*, told the vast nationwide audience** that he had tracked women across almost the entire United States, following them persistently, getting gas when they did, etc. Whether or not Lucas had actually done this, his message went out to millions. He concluded: "A woman alone ain't safe at all." At this juncture, Chase responds: "Mr. Lucas, what you say sends a chill through my bones; I do nothing but travel alone." He replies: "Yeah, but just think if I was out there. What if somebody like me be out there?"[106]

Just think indeed. The life or death injunctions could hardly be more explicit: stay off the streets at night; live behind locked doors; do not live alone; never travel alone; seek patriarchal "protection" (control); and maintain a nonthreatening position in the "concepts and communities of Western men" by keeping one's place in the institutions/confines of marriage and the family. Women who cannot or will not keep to these directives are told every day in a multitude of ways that their lives are expendable and could easily be destroyed.

Finally, the basic tenet of Susan Brownmiller's crucial study of rape, *Against Our Will*, bears repeating: "[Rape] is nothing more or less than a conscious process of intimidation by which *all men* keep *all women* in a state of fear."[107] And, indeed, patriarchy can be understood as the "State of Fear."[108] In that State, fear is the internalized cop, the secret policeman who arrests the movements of female minds and bodies. Fear is the fatherly judge, handing down injunctions not to be wise, not to be "eccentric" or independent, sentencing women to the confines of phallic institutions. Finally, in that State, fear is meant to be the ultimate governor/ruler of our entire lives, quashing any resistance with the spectre of the most violent and horrifying death.

---

*Of course, young, white middle-class women are also "expendable" although in smaller numbers. Certainly, their murders provide much of the material for the eroticization of gynocide—in both factual and fictional accounts. As Annie McCombs has written concerning the contemporary victims of sexual murder: "...while poverty set them up, being born a woman painted a target on them. And, while money or education can and does help, neither guarantees a woman's life." See "A Letter *Ms.*, Wouldn't Print," *Lesbian Ethics*, 1, No. 3 (1985), pp. 85-88, esp. 86.

**This particular installment of *20/20* got the top Nielson rating (the most watched show) of that week of July, 1984.

For if rape, along with physical abuse, street harassment,[109] incest, etc., are some of the more common means of maintaining fear in women, the threat of the mutilation/murder—epitomized in the culture-wide myth figure of Jack the Ripper—is meant to keep all women in a state of profound dread. This function of the mythic Ripper was inadvertently referred to by Derek Morgan in his review of Tom Cullen's history of the Ripper, *When London Walked in Terror*. Cullen had proposed failed barrister Montague Druitt as the identity of the killer. Morgan roundly rejects that proposition:

I don't believe a word of Mr. Cullen's theory anyhow. And don't, I must confess, particularly want to. I want my Ripper unknown, unimaginable, and incomparably terrifying...I shall go on scaring five-year-olds into eating their porridge by threatening them with "Saucy Jack."[110]

How unlovely is the sadistic Mr. Morgan's levity and how expedient that desire for "his" Ripper to be unknown, mysterious and incomparably terrifying for he, as an adult male, has virtually nothing to be terrified of in relation to sexual violence. How simple it is for men to boldly serve up incomparable terror not only to five-year-old children, but to women of all ages.

Typically, those bullies who have constructed the States of Fear and Confinement call them such things as the "Home of the Brave," or the "Land of the Free." Moreover, *courage* is proclaimed to be a masculine virtue, a standard measure of (male) heroism. Yet how much more real is the courage of women who brave the systematic misogyny of this State. June Jordan writes:

Nothing unusual: The writer leaves the house and heads into the evening, outside, for a walk to clear the mind. And what about that? Is there anything peculiar in that act? Well, yes: The writer is a woman, and Black, besides. Consequently the act of taking a walk means that she, this writer, will be perceived as a provocative/irresponsible/loose/insubordinate creature on the streets, by herself, moving along as though she had a natural right to wander around, after dark.

Acknowledging the danger, she points out that if the writer is raped, people will say, "Why was she there?" "Was she asking for it?" Jordan analogizes that individual rape to the rape of "Black and First World Peoples" about whom it is also said that the rapist was "invited," that the rapist was "saving" the raped ones, doing them a favor. She continues:

And the moon is full, everywhere, tonight: Southern Africa will become a haven, a situation of supreme safety for the multitudes now suffering rape. And here, in Manhattan, the streets will become a refuge, an agreeable alternative to the house for this particular Black woman, and for women generally, and do you know why I say that with so much calm?

Because all of us who are comparatively powerless, because we have decided that if you interfere, if you seek to intrude, if you undertake to terrorize and to subjugate and to stifle even one moment more of these, our only lives, we will take yours, or die, trying.

It's 12:30 A.M. and now I am going out, by myself, to put this in the mailbox, three blocks away. And, listen: I am not afraid.[111]

Religious/ Sexual Mania

On October 8, 1888, the *New York Times* gave its interpretation of the "Whitechapel Paranoiac," i.e. Jack the Ripper.[112] Although echoing the standard responses of incredulity and incomprehension, it also suggested two "manias" which might be motivating the killer—the "sexual" and the "religious"; these are, of course, precisely those "manias" which fueled the Witchcraze. By the "religious," the *Times* is referring, rather superficially, to a "moral" crusade against prostitution, but there are far deeper implications to the *sacred* or religious character of all gynocidal crusades.

If the European Witch Hunts were explicitly religious, the contemporary Age of Sex Crime is subliminally so. Certainly, much of traditional patriarchal religious propaganda—from the earliest "creation" myths through judeo-christian notions of female sexual filth, primordial blame, and evil—provide fundamental legitimation for the practices of modern sex crime. More deeply, we might realize along with Mary Daly that :

Patriarchy is itself the prevailing religion of the entire planet, and its essential message is necrophilia. All of the so-called religions legitimating patriarchy are mere sects subsumed under its vast umbrella/canopy....All are erected as parts of the male's shelter against anomie. And the symbolic message of all of the sects of the religion which is patriarchy is this: Women are the dreaded anomie. Consequently, women are the objects of male terror, the projected personifications of "The Enemy," the real objects under attack in all the wars of patriarchy.[113]

Contemporary sex crime is a continuation of that ongoing religious/ sexual warfare which is patriarchy. Sexual murder, essentially, is a sacred transgression.[114] It is a form of ritual murder—the ordained sacrifice of scapegoats, "professional victims." That ritual repeatedly decimates/ terrorizes the "Enemy," while propitiating the male godhead, i.e. the phallocentric world, invoking the continuance of that reign, the security of that reality.

Within modern western patriarchy, the sexual violation of women, although nominally despised and tabooed, is secretly desired, approved, institutionalized, and ultimately mandated. That *secrecy* is key. One of the most glaring distinctions between the European Witchcraze and the

Age of Sex Crime is that, while the Witchcraze was socially sacrosanct, blessed by both church and state, absolutely legal, overtly organized and propagated, the Age of Sex Crime is, instead, covertly organized and propagated. Knowledge of its scope, network, functions, even its ideological normalcy and actual support systems within the patriarchal culture is kept mysterious—hidden, fragmented, lied about, and ignored. Concomitantly, although the multiple interconnecting forms of sexual violence—including harassment, molestation, incest, battery, and rape, through torture, mutilation, and murder—are nominally "criminal" activities (and are tokenly punished), they are simultaneously depicted, embedded, romanticized, eroticized, and legitimated via much of the intellections, entertainments, and institutions of modern patriarchy. In the next two chapters, I will look at some of these subliminal modes for the presentation and enactment of sex crime ideology.

Chapter V

Companion Ideologies:
The Fetishes of Sex Crime

Witch/Doctor

The *Malleus Maleficarum* might, with a little editing serve as an excellent modern textbook of descriptive clinical psychiatry of the fifteenth century, if the word *witch* were substituted by the word patient, and the devil eliminated.

Gregory Zilboorg[1]

Sir Melville Macnaghten...was also convinced the Tabram murder was not the handiwork of Jack the Ripper....Tabram's throat had not been cut...nor did the wounds inflicted on her body show any anatomical skill. Seemingly, they were the work of a man in a blind frenzy, rather than that of the cool but misplaced *gynecologist that was Jack the Ripper.* (emphasis mine)

Tom Cullen[2]

They say I am a doctor now. Ha! Ha!

Jack the Ripper

The historical connection between witches and healing has been salvaged from neglect by various thinkers. Chief among these are Matilda Joslyn Gage, Thomas Szasz, Barbara Ehrenreich and Deirdre English. Their consensus is that to a large degree those burned as witches represented a group of folk lay healers, herbalists, midwives, counselors and abortionists.[3] Ehrenreich and English argue that the elimination of the witches through mass persecutions was a political movement, designed to clear the way for the establishment of a male professional elite:

Witches lived and were burned long before the development of modern medical technology. The great majority of them were lay healers serving the peasant population, and their suppression marks one of the opening struggles in the history of man's suppression of women as healers.[4]

Typically, however, the Freudian psychiatrist Gregory Zilboorg, in standard reverse gear, prefers to drive the persecuted into sick roles—hysterics and crazies. In a thoroughly outrageous move, he suggests that the *Malleus* (the book Ben-Yehuda described as the "textbook of the Inquisition") might "serve as an excellent modern textbook of descriptive clinical psychiatry for the fifteenth century." Such a proposal is immediately both absurd and horrifying; still there is perhaps more meaning here than he intends. If we extend Zilboorg's contention that the witches were the patients, we can infer that the role of doctor was played by the professional prickers, torturers and hunters. In the last chapter I suggested that the ideologies and practices of the Witch Hunts have never really ceased, but have instead assumed new forms. Guided by the knowledge that a political goal of the persecutions was to further the establishment of a male medical profession, it becomes easier to see how that new, and now entrenched, profession has remained true to its origins, continuing a damning and mutilating ideology of "sex"— meaning, again, the female sex.

Although Zilboorg wants to "eliminate the devil," we should, instead, be ready to reintroduce him in the mythic figure of Jack the Ripper, for that demon was also a "doctor." Challenging Zilboorg for the most outrageous assertion is Cullen in whose words the Ripper was a "cool but misplaced gynecologist." The connection of sex crime to gynecology is accurate enough, but could be observed in the form of an arrogant quip only by one who is saved by his gender from the ministrations of either Rippers or gynecologists. The notion of the Ripper as some kind of doctor is a pervasive one. In that favorite game of the Ripperophiles—guess his identity—the most popular and recurring answer of all is that of an M.D. That identity provided the first major theory and it remains the dominant fictional explanation; the most common image of the Ripper usually includes a little black doctor's bag as well as a knife. In *Time After Time*, the Ripper is *Dr.* John Stephenson; in Bloch's classic "Your's truly Jack the Ripper," he appears as a practicing psychiatrist.

The pricker, the ripper, the doctor—the witch, the whore, the patient: these threesomes form concentric triangles in the theory and practice of sex crime. Each pair—pricker and witch, ripper and whore, doctor and patient—restates a common and central structure of sexist mythology, perhaps the most fundamental structure as identified by Simone de Beauvoir in *The Second Sex*. This is the concept of the female as "Other." Citing recurring attitudes in male philosophies, such as this from Aristotle—"The female is a female by virtue of a certain lack of qualities; we should regard the female nature as afflicted with a natural defectiveness," or from Thomas Aquinas who pronounced woman to be an "imperfect man," an "incidental being," de Beauvoir concludes:

Thus humanity is male and man defines woman not in herself but as relative to him...she is simply what man decrees; thus she is called "the sex," by which is meant that she appears to man as a sexual being. For him she is sex—absolute sex, no less. She is defined and differentiated with reference to man and not he with reference to her; she is the incidental, the inessential as opposed to the essential. He is the Subject, he is the Absolute—she is the Other.[5]

That dualism has taken historical and destructive shape in pricker-witch, ripper-whore, doctor-patient: in all these manifestations the female represents "sex—absolute sex, no less." The witch was all "female," i.e. all female sexuality, insatiable carnal lust; correspondingly, all females were said to be witches. Lea reports that in Switzerland it was believed that "almost every woman is a witch."[6] The whore is not only the "professional victim," but as is implicit in this patriarchal dialectic, she is the professional *woman*, reduced to the most basic feminine role of sexual dispensary for men. Thus all women are said to be whores and, as pornographer/philosopher Georges Bataille writes, "prostitution is the logical consequence of the feminine attitude."[7] And finally, as will be expanded upon in this chapter, to the nineteenth century professional inventors of gynecology (and later psychology), "Women were 'the sex.' "[8]

The gynecological attitude is typical; the sum character of the female derives from her sex, precisely from her sex organs. Dr. Horatio Storer said in 1871 that woman "was what she is in health, in character, in her charms, alike of body, mind and soul because of her womb alone."[9] Moreover, the majority opinion held that their sex organs predisposed women to insanity (hysteria), disease, eroticism (considered pathological in the female) and even an inherent criminality. In 1866, Dr. Isaac Ray stated:

With women it is but a step from extreme nervous susceptibility to downright hysteria, and from that to overt insanity. In the sexual evolution, in pregnancy, in the parturient period, in lactation, strange thoughts extraordinary feelings, unseasonable appetites, *criminal impulses*, may haunt a mind at other times innocent and pure."[10] (emphasis mine)

Thus, just as the *witches*—and not their torturers and murderers—and the *prostitutes*—and not their johns—were/are regarded as the "sex criminals," so also were the female patients of the 19th-century gynecologists categorized as sexual criminals. Medical historian G.J. Barker-Benfield explains this perspective:

Membership of the body politic had always been limited by sex organs. The assumption of woman's special liability to mental sickness by way of her characteristic menstrual and reproductive functions pushed all women close to the criminal category: "an insane woman," in the words of Dr. William Goodell, Professor of Clinical Gynecology at the University of Pennsylvania, "is no more a member of the body politic than a criminal." If women were only sex organs, and female sex organs were by nature a menace to health unless run to earth by pregnancy, then women were by nature sick; and if woman's sickness was construed as intolerable social disorder, then to be a woman was a crime. For Gardner [gynecologist and author], menstruation was an "infirmity." He held that "it was a crime to be sick." Women, then, were criminals by nature.[11]

This nineteenth-century gynecological world view contains what for the patriarchy is the timeless meaning of *sex crime*, that is, the ordained criminality of the female sex. For what the phallocentrists perceive as "naturally defective,"i.e. in error, sinful, sick, perverse, and, in a word, unnatural, is to be a female in a world where the male is taken as the ultimate if not the only measure. Thus being female—the "Other"— is the root paradigm for the "unnatural act" which comprises the traditional definition of sex crime.

Heralding a new (though definitely derivative) type of sex crime, Jack the Ripper arrived on the scene in 1888. His innovations thus coincided with the respectable Victorian inventions of gynecology and Freudian psychology—both of which have been analyzed as counter-evolutionary responses to the feminist and sexual revolutions of that era. Indeed, it is in these two medical specialties that respectability and sex crime join hands for, like the witch persecutions, these medical phenomena can be recognized as institutionalized ideologies and behaviors which function to enforce patriarchal control.

Medical Sex Crime I: Gynecological Ideology

But first we must ask: what is a woman? "Tota mulier in utero," says one, "woman is a womb."

Simone de Beauvoir[12]

There were two things missing. Her rings had been wrenched from her fingers...and the uterus had been taken from the abdomen...the injuries had been made by someone who had considerable anatomical skill and knowledge....The amount missing would go into a breakfast cup....The difficulty in believing that the purport of the murderer was the possession of the missing abdominal organ was natural. It was abhorrent...that a life should be taken for so slight an object.

The Times (London) on the 1888
Ripper murder of Annie Chapman[13]

The specialized treatment for women known as gynecology arose in the nineteenth century as a direct response to the first wave of feminism....the purpose and *intent* of gynecology was/is not healing in a deep sense but violent enforcement of the sexual caste system....gynecological purification/castration of women is accomplished [by]...the fetishization of female parts....An example of this fetish destruction is the recent hysterectomy epidemic in the United States.

Mary Daly[14]

It might at first be difficult to conceive of something as legal, entrenched, and purportedly benign as gynecological medicine to be a category of sex crime, but it is important here to remember that the entire witch persecutions were all perfectly legal, fervently supported by the highest offices of the Church and State and the most learned men within the culture. Jack the Ripper is so frequently analogized to a gynecologist because his characteristic mutilations so precisely paralleled some of the most popular, legal, and purportedly benign operations of his era, many of which are still popular and performed today. As Mary Daly points out in her critique of patriarchal atrocities, *Gyn/Ecology:The Metaethics of Radical Feminism*, medical gynecology continues to function as an institutionalized arm of violence against women. As such it is generically linked to both the Witch Hunts and to contemporary criminal sexual terrorism.

Like the demonological theories of the fifteenth to eighteenth centuries, the founding precepts of gynecology had all the "characteristics of an effective ideology." The history of the rise of gynecology in America has been best tracked by G.J. Barker-Benfield in several articles and a book. In an analysis, which is, in this one respect, remarkably similar to Ben-Yehuda's of the Witchcraze, he considers gynecology to be an ideological response to social upheavals and tensions. Setting the historical "frame of reference" for its invention, he writes:

...."disenchanted" and "pessimistic" moods...seem to have run through American society generally in the late 1860s and 1870s....Among the identifiable symptoms of the breakdown were the failures and corruptions of Reconstruction, the longest depression in American history, insatiable business trusts, swarms of what were held to be sexually potent and racially inferior immigrants, and a government discredited at all levels....people responded to these changes with a reassertion of the "old bedrock values." These values were laced with the paranoia endemic to American history.[15]

But Barker-Benfield also incorporates an acute awareness of the misogynic motivations and primarily political functions of the new medical specialty:

Men's growing sense of vulnerability after the Civil War—their notion of social crisis and the concomitant gynecologic crescendo—cannot be disassociated from the increasing vociferousness of women at the same time, most noticeably on the suffrage front....Disorderly women were handed over to the gynecologists for castration and other kinds of radical treatment by husbands or fathers....The patient was returned to her menfolk's management, recycled, and taught to make the will of the male her own.[16]

Such treatments largely took the form of what Barker-Benfield calls "sexual surgery," or "the need to treat women's genital organs with knives and scissors."[17] Female castration (the removal of the ovaries) was the most common of all. Moreover, this operation/mutilation was clearly ideologically motivated:

Advocates and modifiers of wholesale female castration saw themselves *reimposing order,* of the kind conventionally expected of female behavior. Woman was supposed to be dependent, submissive, unquenchably supportive, smiling, imparting an irrelevant morality, regarding sex as something to be endured, and *her own organs as somehow a dirty if necessary disease.* (emphasis mine)[18]

Reducing woman to her sex and then identifying that sex as filthy and impure (criminal or diseased) is a joint ideology for both sex crime and gynecology; the outcome is to "destroy the sickness at its source."[19] Daly has identified such a process of female destruction as an interaction of fetishization and castration;[20] both of these processes are key concepts in the analysis of sex crime.

Gynecological Fetishes

3.5 million "Amateur Gynecologists" can't be wrong. Now you, too, can enter the exciting world of gynecology. And you don't have to put up with eight years of medical school and skyrocketing tuition rates.

For just $22 you can subscribe to HUSTLER and learn everything about female anatomy. HUSTLER exposes unexplored territories and shows you parts of a woman's body you thought were visible only during a hysterectomy operation.

> *Hustler* subscription ad, 1977[21]

Introducing the best handle of a spoon, I saw everything as no man had ever seen before.... The Speculum made it perfectly clear from the beginning.... I felt like an explorer in medicine who views a new and important territory.

> *J. Marion Sims,* 19th century
> "Father of American Gynecology"[22]

Each sexual assault was "peculiarly incomplete"... the actual wounds were nearly all similar lacerations which might have been caused by an instrument such as a speculum, used by gynecologists in examination of their patients, or by some other object.

> *Gerold Frank, The Boston Strangler*[*][23]

In August 1981, *Hustler* magazine featured an "intimate" report on the "Hillside Strangler." Here, Kenneth Bianchi, the confessed strangler, gave his side of the story:

When you fuck a broad, man, you take full charge.... You gotta treat em rough...there's no cunt good enough to hang on to man. Just variety....It wasn't fuckin' wrong. Why is it wrong to get rid of some fuckin' cunts?[24]

[*]An assumed victim of Ted Bundy was assaulted while sleeping. A heavy metal rod was used to thrash at her head while an actual speculum was "thrust brutally up inside her—a kind of frenzied bloody "examination" that caused extensive internal injuries." This woman did survive after several months in a coma. Stephen G. Michaud and Hugh Aynesworth, *The Only Living Witness* (New York: Simon and Schuster, 1983), pp. 30-31.

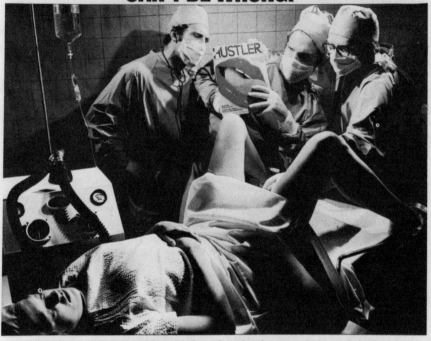

Bianchi is telling us that female equals cunt and how appropriate that he tells it to us in *Hustler*. That magazine's specialty is the so-called "beaver shot," the woman exposed with her legs widely spread, the shot which often causes *Hustler* to be facetiously described as "too gynecological," a comparison that the editors obviously play upon in their own ads and photo essays.[25]

Such attitudes are not restricted to intentionally obscene publications or the amateur philosophy of sex murderers, but are echoed among the most erudite and learned. Jean Paul Sartre, for example, in his essay succinctly titled, "The Hole," explains that, "The obscenity of the feminine sex is that of everything which 'gapes open.' It is an *appeal to being* as all holes are."[26] (emphasis in the original) Such dictums are the phallo-philosophical equivalents of the standard "obscenities" that *Hustler* regularly provides to its "amateur gynecologist" audience. Consider the recurring and characteristic pictorial composition of *Hustler*—the "beaver shot." This composition visually orders that the female is "a hole" and that therein lies the "obscenity" (read also *filth, carnality, lust, danger, disease,* and *criminality*) of the female sex. This message, like that of all gynocidal ideologies, reduces the woman to a fetishized sex organ; as in the witch annihilations, as in gynecology, as in sex crime, she is defined as "sex—absolute sex."

The commonality among pornography, gynecology, and sex crime is further underscored by the shared icon of the *spread-eagled*, i.e. the punished, debased, and defeated female body. This was the position in which the victims of both the Boston and Hillside stranglings were left. Journalist Harold Banks describes in detail the grotesque placement and decoration of the bodies of women who were killed by the "Boston Strangler," noting that they were left displayed in "what physicians call the gynecologic position" and that such a posture "could not have been more calculatedly degrading."[27] As this shared structure testifies, the sex criminal, the pornographer, and the gynecologist all share not only a common perspective on female degradation, but also a common fetish. Mary Daly has pointed out that expert use of the term *fetish* "restrict[s] the meaning...to non-genital parts of the body, deceptively ignoring/denying the fact that men fetishize genitals," a fetishization that she links to the active "purification/castration of women" by gynecologists.[28] This legal purification/mutilation of women by 19th and 20th century gynecologists first anticipated, and now participates, in the overtly criminal Age of Sex Crime.

Sexual Surgery

He [Jack the Ripper] does not seem to have had sexual intercourse with his victims, but very likely the murderous act and subsequent mutilation of the corpse were equivalents for the sexual act.

Richard von Krafft-Ebing[29]

There is, by the way, ample evidence that gynecologists saw their knives' cutting into women's generative tract as a form of sexual intercourse.

G.J. Barker-Benfield[30]

The new age of Ripper-style sex crime began precisely at the point of triumph for a new age of gynecological surgery, a movement that was characterized by the "flamboyant, drastic, risky, and instant use of the knife."[31] Between 1853 and 1883, four operations were invented: clitoridectomy, ovariotomy ("female castration"), hysterectomy, and radical mastectomy—the surgical removal of, respectively, clitoris, ovaries, womb and breast. These operations caught on with the force of a fashion and rapidly became standard procedure for the treatment, not only of physical complaints, but just as frequently for mental and moral disorders as well: "troublesomeness, eating like a ploughman, masturbation, attempted suicide, erotic tendencies, persecution mania, simple 'cussedness' and dysmenorrhea."[32] As these "symptoms" indicate, it was moral and mental disorders, i.e. *ideological* disorders, that so obsessed the gynecologists. One of the most disturbing of these was female lust: "Desire was regarded as a symptom indicating castration."[33] Other "mental disorders" and "sexual transgressions" that required surgical intervention included "masturbation, contraception, abortion, [and] orgasm."[34] To correct such disorders, women were "unsexed," the criminal taint of "femaleness" was literally rooted out. Such was the punishment for the sex crime of being female, for living in biological defiance to the Man's World.

These punishments/operations took place in overwhelming numbers. Ovariotomies were so frequently performed that in 1906 it was estimated that for each of the 150,000 doctors in the United States there was one castrated woman. Some doctors boasted that they had removed from fifteen hundred to two thousand ovaries. In the words of Barker-Benfield, they "handed them around at medical society meetings on plates like trophies."[35] Also by 1906, a major medical journal published an article, "The Fetich of the Ovary," bemoaning the ramifications of such operations on the nation's fertility and population growth.[36]

The fetish value and subsequent mutilation of women's sex organs remains operative in contemporary culture. The rage for ovariotomies has ceased, but has been largely replaced by unnecessary and mutilating procedures such as hysterectomies, routine caesarean sections, and radical mastectomies. Writing in the *New York Times*, Maggie Scarf relates this incident:

An acquaintance of mine, who was interning in an obstetrics-gynecology service, was assisting at a hysterectomy. The chief resident performed the operation with impeccable style and skill. But just afterward, as the patient lay unconscious upon the table, the physician held the newly detached uterus aloft. My friend glanced at his face and said quizzically, "You look...pleased?" "Ah yes, I am," he answered. "Another small victory in man's unending battle against the womb."[37]

That unending battle results in a count of more than 690,000 hysterectomies performed each year in the U.S. making it the second most frequently performed major operation. Almost half of all women over forty are advised to undergo it. The operation ends in death for 12,000 per year, a death rate higher than the death rate for uterine/cervical cancer. U.S. gynecologists perform proportionately twice as many hysterectomies as their British counterparts. This major operation is recommended as a "simple" solution for everything from backaches to contraception. Deborah Larned reports:

Several medical studies—one as early as 1946—have shown that at least one-third of all the hysterectomies in the U.S. have been performed on women with *normal* uteri. In many cases women who underwent hysterectomies had not presented any symptoms prior to surgery.[38]

The epidemic of hysterectomies began to be obvious to all in the profession around 1970. Still, in what is now remembered as the "Great Debate" at the 1971 annual meeting of the American College of Obstetrics and Gynecology, the popularity of the operation was widely affirmed. Following an exchange on the relative merits of the procedure, physicians were asked to register their approval or disapproval by their applause:

The acclaim for hysterilization lasted a full 25 seconds: the applause for the "no" position, only 10 seconds. What's more, according to *Audio Digest's* decibel meter, the intensity of the advocates' applause was double that of the opposition.[39]

Reasons for such inordinate enthusiasm are perhaps indicated in part by the attitude of Connecticut gynecologist Ralph C. Wright, an outspoken advocate of routine hysterectomy:

When the patient has completed her family, total hysterectomy should be performed as a prophylactic procedure. Under these circumstances, the *uterus* becomes a *useless, bleeding, symptom-producing, potentially cancer-bearing* organ and therefore should be removed.... To sterilize a woman and allow her to keep a useless and *potentially lethal organ* is incompatible with modern gynecological concepts.[40] (emphasis mine)

Obviously, some modern gynecological concepts are not all that different from the founding traditions of sexual surgery. There remains a strong fixation/fetishization of the sexual organs as well as a continuing hostility to female organs as "potentially lethal," dangerous, hence *criminal* zones which "should be removed."

Another "throwback" to Victorian gynecology is the Halstead Radical Mastectomy (invented in 1882), a mutilating but routine procedure that excises not only the breast and the lymph nodes, but also the pectoral muscles of the chest. Increasingly, in recent years, the routine performance of this operation has been called into question. Survival rate for patients who have received the radical procedure has been shown to be no greater than for those who had a simple mastectomy followed with radiation therapy.[41] An MIT biologist reported that although surgeons have by and large adopted radical mastectomy,* there is not sufficient data to justify its use. Rather, "there is abundant evidence supporting the proposal that more conservative procedures provide at least equal benefit with substantially less mutilation."[42]

It has been frequently noted that male surgeons might not be so quick to embrace such admittedly mutilating procedures if they were performed upon male sex organs.[43] Significant here is the statistic that ninety-seven per cent of all American gynecologists are men.[44] One gynecology textbook points out that, "Any operation can have symbolic meaning to the patient. This is especially true of surgery performed in the pelvic area."[45] Although this text conveniently skirts the question, it must also be asked what symbolic meanings these ritual operations on female pelvic regions have for the male surgeons who perform them. It is commonplace to suggest that American men have a "breast fetish," yet dare we connect this fetish to the popularity of the mutilating radical mastectomy, let alone the so-called prophylactic mastectomy (when a mastectomy is performed on a healthy woman in order to "prevent" cancer).[46] It is everywhere agreed that Jack the Ripper's desire to possess the "missing abdominal organ" (the uterus) was abnormal, abhorrent, criminal, incomprehensible, and incredible. Yet what of the actions of medical mutilators and the continuing crime of unnecessary hysterectomies performed on women patients? Barker-Benfield observed that the 19th-century gynecologists saw their knives cutting into women's

---

*Gena Corea reports: "When, after biopsy, American doctors detect a cancerous tumor, 90 percent of them perform a Halstead radical mastectomy. Most do not first inform their patients that breast-cancer treatment has been an unresolved controversy for decades. Neither do they mention that British surgeons perform half as many radical mastectomies (per 100,000 population) as American surgeons with comparable results. *The Hidden Malpractice: How American Medicine Mistreats women, Updated Edition* (New York: Harper and Row, 1977, 1985), p. 273. In this edition, Corea also documents other instances of current gynecological mutilation—unwarranted vulvectomies, clitoridectomies, and vaginal restructurings often performed without the patient's knowledge or consent. See pp. 311-28.

"generative tract" as a form of sexual intercourse. Here is the direct parallel between normative gynecology and the sex crime invented by Jack the Ripper in 1888—violence as sex, mutilation as the phallic "touch."

The knife or scalpel, after Freud, is commonly considered to be a "phallic symbol." Clearly the gynecological trespasses upon women in the nineteenth century contributed to that notion and, as Ehrenreich and English point out, it was the gynecological world view that anticipated and then was ultimately replaced by the psychoanalytic: "Under Freud's influence, the scalpel for the dissection of female nature eventually passed from the gynecologist to the psychiatrist."[47] Mary Daly has designated these psychiatrists as "mind-gynecologists" and, like their predecessors, these mind-gynecologists contributed generously to the ideology of sex crime.

Medical Sex Crime II: Psychology and Ideology

Some of Freud's opinions about women were not unlike those of Kramer and Sprenger [authors of the *Malleus*], as the following passage illustrates:

> It must be admitted that women have but little sense of justice, and this is no doubt connected with the preponderance of envy in their mental life; for the demands of justice are a modification of envy; they lay down the conditions under which one is willing to part with it. We also say of women that their social interests are weaker than those of men, and that their capacity for the sublimation of their instincts is less.

I cite this opinion of Freud's about women not so much to criticize it...but to emphasize the significance of scapegoating in the phenomena called witchcraft, hysteria, and mental illness.

Thomas Szasz[48]

I will simply claim for myself the rights of the gynecologist.

Sigmund Freud[49]

Slang dubs psychiatrists not only "head shrinkers," but also "witch doctors" and, as in the prior witch-pricker and gynecological ideologies, the basic view of women proffered by psychoanalysis is inherently oppressive. Jean Baker Miller has commented, "It is striking to realize that in the psychoanalytic writings on the *psychology* of women, the greatest amount of material is on the *sexuality* of women."[50] Once again, woman's character is equated with her sex; as in the other ideologies, woman is reduced to "absolute sex." In some ways, as Ehrenreich and English have observed, psychoanalysis represented at least an amelioration for women since it was not physically injurious as were the gynecological treatments. Nevertheless, it:

was in direct continuity with the gynecological view which it replaced. It held that the female personality was inherently defective, this time due to the absence of a penis, rather than to the presence of the domineering uterus. Women were still "sick," and their sickness was still totally predestined by their anatomy.[51]

Once again the concept of the female as the primordial "Other," the defect or deviation from the norm, provides the model for the explanation of female nature.

In this section, I will not be attempting a general critique of Freud. That has been done elsewhere, and often quite comprehensively, notably by Kate Millett who categorized Freudianism as the leading counter-revolutionary ideology in its reaction to nineteenth-century feminism.[52] Instead I will focus upon the key issues for sex crime—fetishism and castration—as they took shape in Freudian theory.

Psychological Fetishes

When Berkowitz assumed the position he did, he was not simply shooting the women. He was symbolically copulating with them, fucking them, if you will.

> *A psychotherapist on the "Son of Sam"*[53]

Most serial killers will kill with an ax or knife rather than a gun in order to achieve intimacy with the victim.

> *Richard Rappaport, Northwestern University Medical School*[54]

Young Cop (inspecting the body of a murdered and mutilated victim): Was this girl raped, Doc?
Doctor: There's no evidence of forcible entry.
Older, hero cop (played by Charles Bronson): I could have told you that, you know.
Doctor: On the basis of what?
Bronson: Well, if anybody does something like this, his knife has got to be his penis.

> *10 To Midnight* (J. Lee Thompson, 1980)

Like Jack the Ripper, many subsequent sex murderers never actually rape their victims, but use a characteristic violation as their "equivalent for the sexual act." What Jack the Ripper did was kill by slashing the throat and then severely mutilate the genitals, abdomen, breasts, and other organs; his method provided the prototype for the modern sex crime. Penetrating a woman with a bottle, broom or screwdriver, achieving "intimacy" with an ax or a knife, strangulation, shooting a woman with a .44 caliber gun or bashing her with an oak club: these provide the *sex* in sex crime. And when David Berkowitz states, "I only shoot pretty girls," everyone in this culture gets his meaning. A psychotherapist at a police conference on that killer told the gathering, "Gentlemen. Every time he shoots his gun, he's ejaculating."[55] We might groan at the pop Freudianism implicit in such a remark, but Freud's theories, particularly those on fetishism and castration are most relevant to the analysis of sex crime—particularly when we reverse the reversals inherent in those theories.

Intrinsic to Freud's theory of fetishism is the notion that because women do not have penises, they are perceived by both men and women as castrated males, a perception supposedly formed in each sex by the first sight of the other's genitals. For women, according to Freud, this experience leads immediately to "penis envy"—she has seen it and knows that she is without it and wants to have it. The male reaction comes a bit later; two approaches are possible—"horror of the mutilated creature or triumphant contempt for her."[56] The fetishist is one of the horrified. He refuses to acknowledge that women do not have penises because if he did admit that, he would have to entertain the possibility that he could also be castrated. Therefore, "He takes hold of something else instead—a part of the body, or some other object—and assigns it the role of the penis which he cannot do without."[57]

The fetishist uses the body part or object, for example a shoe, as a substitute for the "missing" female penis. As long as that shoe is there he can feel safe from a castration threat. A shoe fetish may seem like a relatively harmless offense, but the consequences of such a mythology do not end at the feet. Angela Carter has written:

Female castration is an imaginary fact that pervades the whole of men's attitudes toward women and our attitude to ourselves, that transforms women from human beings into wounded creatures who were born to bleed.[58]

Although Freud asserts that the belief in female castration is a neurotic notion, his own language betrays him and he consistently refers to the "unwelcome fact of women's castration." And within his framework, that imaginary fact has indubitably superseded the reality. Freudian psychology constructs a paradigm which poses the female genital to be innately in a state of mutilation; if the female genital is a wound, a product of an imagined or fantasized mutilation, sex crime is the concrete manifestation of that imaginary fact, the acting out of that fantasy, in the real world. The characteristic act of the Ripper and those in his mold is the actual mutilation of the vulva. The psychology fits the crime.

Numerous post-Freudians, including the women among them, have continued to promote this ideology. Phyllis Greenacre, for example, has analogized the traumatic sight of the female genital to the "witnessing of some particularly mutilating event: a mutilating death or accident, operation, abortion or birth in the home."[59] And Greenacre is far from the worst of the offenders. Consider what another follower, Leonard Sillman, does with his application of psychoanalytic precepts.

In an article entitled, "Femininity and Paranoidism," Sillman attempts to explain why so many women show a rejection of femininity and a "profound aversion to their husband who...becomes to her a tormentor, a 'jailer,' a feared and detested object....each attempt on his part to make love constitutes rape."[60] Rather than acknowledge the widespread reality (and *legality*) of marital rape as well as the actual imprisoning of women by abusive husbands,[61] Sillman concludes that such women are paranoid and that their rejection of men stems from the fact that the male superiority of the husband deals many blows to his wife's narcissism. She becomes profoundly envious of his superior strength and power "as well as his posture in the sexual act which becomes the symbol of his superior aggressivity." Not reality but the male fantasy of female penis envy is the ruling structure here. Indeed, according to Sillman, the phallus is worshipped by the unconscious of both sexes as representing " 'the power and the glory,' the intellect and all superior capacities." Because women sadly lack this very thing, a repudiation of femininity arises in both men and women for:

Not only is a woman a "castrated" animal to the unconscious, but—far worse—instead of being equipped for attack, she is designed to "be attacked," and as part of her female instincts invites it. This is the origin of the profound connotation of derogation which arises from a man's being called "womanly" or a fairy, and the same unconscious attitude makes the term "fuck" such an opprobrious one. The woman's genital organ is designed to be a receptacle subordinate to the male's, and from his and her exaltation of aggression and its symbol—the phallus, she becomes turned by the unconscious into a thing to be "used," "enslaved" and subjected to the "superior" male · (emphasis mine)

This idea that the female is "designed to be attacked" is one of the most choice poisons of Freudian and neo-Freudian ideology. It is qualitatively identical to the idea that "all witchcraft comes from carnal lust which is in women insatiable." If what men defined and then persecuted as witchcraft came from within the "evil" female herself, men were themselves blameless. Equally, men can easily absolve themselves of any blame for their subjugation, enslavement and mutilation of women when they propagate the belief that "her instincts invite it."

Freud himself best expressed this legitimation of violence and mutilation in his discussion of "sexual symbols." He wrote:

The more striking and for both sexes the more interesting component of the genitals, the male organ, finds symbolic substitutes in the first instance in things that resemble it in shape...further, in objects which share with the thing they represent the characteristic of penetrating into the body and injuring—thus sharp *weapons* of every kind, *knives*, *daggers*, *spears*, *sabres*, but also *fire-arms*, *rifles*, *pistols*, and *revolvers* (particularly suitable owing to their shape). In the anxiety dreams of girls, being followed by a man with a knife or a fire-arm plays a large part.[62]

Of course, the girl's "anxiety dream" seems to be the boys' pleasurable fantasy since this scenario is a conventional scene in any number of mass media productions. Furthermore, Freud's conception of the penis proceeds from what Kate Millett has called "a fancy of sexuality as a lethal assault,"— *a fancy* that has nonetheless preoccupied and replaced reality in the hetero-relational world.[63]

Along with *fuck* and *screw*, other slang terms indicate the recurrence of this male dream. For example, common nicknames for the penis include *rod, tool, weapon, gun, screwdriver, pile driver, club,* and *gear;* corresponding slang terms for the vulva include *slash, wound, gash.*[64] Consider also this stunning cultural coincidence. During that summer of 1977 when David Berkowitz was shooting "pretty girls" in the streets of New York, the so-called "Sex Pistols," the exemplars of British punk rock, simultaneously hit the New York scene. The *New York Times* applauded their arrival, "The Sex Pistols deliver a non-stop assault of loud, tight, fast song."[65] At this point we must stop and wonder how dissimilar the performance "assault" of the "Sex Pistols" is from the sexual shootings of the "Son of Sam." Both phenomena are fired by an identical and glamorous mystique of sex-and-violence, aggressive male sexuality and an *assaulted** victim or audience. Entertainment here neatly bonds with psychological ideology in the social construction of sex crime.

The identification of the penis with weaponry is continually broadcast through every avenue of popular culture: *happiness,* as the Beatles sang it, is a warm gun. We might also again consider the traditional American hero, the fellow whom D.H. Lawrence described as "the essential American [read *male* American] soul...hard, isolate, stoic, and a killer," the characteristically celibate "saint with a gun."[66] And from Deerslayer through Mickey Spillane's Mike Hammer, John Wayne's Ethan Edwards (*The Searchers*, John Ford, 1956) and Clint Eastwood's *Dirty Harry* (Don Siegal, 1971) that character recurs in American masculine romance. Moreover, his *gun*, particularly with Mike Hammer and Dirty Harry, has become ever more obviously and ridiculously phallic.

Mickey Spillane's *I, The Jury* (1947), long a record-holder for largest novel sales in America, features the hero's gun used in the expressly sexual murder of his lover. In this story, Mike Hammer's one-armed war buddy has been murdered in a particularly vicious manner—shot in the stomach and then psychologically tormented. Mike vows vengeance and sets out to find the killer. In the midst of his investigation he meets and falls in love with a psychiatrist, Charlotte, a stereotypic "blonde bombshell" and "femme fatale." About eight murders later, the quick-

---

*assault (n): 1. a violent attack....2. rape: a euphemism, *Webster's New World Dictionary*, 1982.

witted Mike figures out that she is the killer. Arriving at her vacant apartment, he awaits her return with his gun out, cocked and ready. She comes back, finds him there, and immediately realizes that he knows she is guilty. The ensuing scene is pivotal in the tradition of pornographic murder. Hoping to forestall Mike, Charlotte begins to strip. Up until this point the two, although expressly in love, have not yet had sex; the crude yet knight-like Mike has preferred to wait until they have been married. Now, however, Charlotte is offering him her highly prized sex. As he chants the details of her violences, she correspondingly reveals her body, giving no answer, only stripping. Finally, she is almost nude and Mike is winding down his litany:

No. Charlotte. I'm the jury now, and the judge, and I have a promise to keep. Beautiful as you are, and as much as I almost loved you, I sentence you to death.

(Her thumbs hooked in the fragile silk of the panties and pulled them down. She stepped out of them as delicately as one coming from a bathtub. She was completely naked now. A sun-tanned goddess giving herself to her lover. With arms outstretched she walked over toward me. Lightly, her tongue ran over her lips, making them glisten with passion. The smell of her was like an exhilarating perfume. Slowly, a sigh escaped her, making the hemispheres of her breasts quiver. She leaned forward to kiss me, her arms going out to encircle my neck.)

The roar of the .45 shook the room. Charlotte staggered back a step. Her eyes were a symphony of incredulity, an unbelieving witness to truth. Slowly she looked down at the ugly swelling on her naked belly where the bullet went in. A thin trickle of blood welled out.

At this point, Mike looks behind his head and notices that there is a gun on the table. Her arms weren't really going out to embrace him, but to grab the gun and shoot him; once again gynocide is presented as merely a form of male self-defense:

A face that was waiting to be kissed was really waiting to be splattered with blood when she blew my head off.
My blood. When I heard her fall I turned around. Her eyes had pain in them now, the pain preceding death.
Pain and unbelief.
   "How c-could you," she gasped.
   I only had a moment before talking to a corpse, but I got it in.
   "It was easy," I said.[67]

Hammer's bullet to Charlotte's lower belly with his cocked and ready .45 is a thin symbolism for his actual target—her vulva. The eroticized violence of this scene is the only sexual consummation between the two lovers that is desired by the male character, author, and presumably readers.* Moreover, the annihilation of women is not only heroic, necessary, and gratifying—it's easy.

Another all-American hero in the mold of Hammer, Clint Eastwood's "Dirty Harry" never tires of telling us that he totes a Magnum .357, "the largest and most powerful handgun in the world." Of course his shadow/double, the maniac killer, understands perfectly and even compliments him when he takes it out. "My, that's a big one," he croons.**

At the beginning of the technological era, Sigmund Freud was comparing the penis to knives, sabres, swords, and revolvers. Consider the consequences to female life now that phallic equivalents have taken symbolic shape in the likes of the MX missile. Consider, as well, the parallel consequences to the life of the planet.

Missile Envy

I recently watched a filmed launching of an MX missile. It rose slowly out of the ground, surrounded by smoke and flames and elongated into the air—it was indeed a very sexual sight, and when armed with the ten warheads it will explode with the most almighty orgasm. The names that the military uses are laden with psychosexual overtones: missile erector, thrust-to-weight ratio, soft lay down, deep penetration, hard line and soft line.

Helen Caldicott, *Missile Envy*[68]

A political cartoon by Lou Myers shows two military men dueling with extended penises, actually missiles, one marked *U.S.*, the other, *U.S.S.R.*[69] *Public Illumination* magazine, a small artists' publication, serves up its version of nuclear safety: a drawing of an exploding mushroom cloud with a diaphragm attempting to contain it. "Better Safe Than Sorry," they advise.[70] What these mock, however, a 1984 ad for a Northrop Tigershark fighter plane reverently genuflects to. This ad (appearing in the *Atlantic,* Jan. 1984), features a black and white picture, not of the plane but of its "control stick." That stick, in huge close-up, dominates the page. The copy reads:

Pilot and aircraft are one. He thinks; the plane responds.... Systems and human engineering by Northrop Corporation's Aircraft Division have coupled the pilot with the world's most advanced avionics through an anatomically designed control stick. All vital controls are strategically positioned on the stick and throttle.... The competitive edge is his.

*Again, I am reminded of *Prizzi's Honor* (John Huston, 1985). The male hero once more kills his lover in a symbolic interaction suggesting intercourse; we can assume it is more exciting for the patriarchal audience when the man kills a woman he genuinely "loves."

**Joan Mellon also understands. In *Big Bad Wolves: Masculinity in the American Film* (New York: Pantheon, 1977), p. 296, she comments: "The .357 Magnum Harry carries is a surrogate penis, gigantic and under his complete control, a fantasy of the terrified and the impotent."

Copyright © Lou Myers. Reprinted with permission.

Copyright © 1982 by *Public Illumination* Magazine. Reprinted by permission of the artist, Mimi Smith.

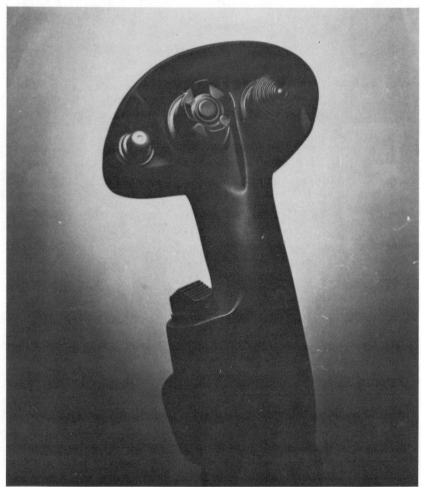

Pilot and aircraft are one. He thinks; the plane responds.
The plane is Northrop's F-20 Tigershark, America's newest fighter. Systems and
human engineering by Northrop Corporation's Aircraft Division have coupled the
pilot with the world's most advanced avionics through an anatomically designed control
stick. All vital controls are strategically positioned on the stick and throttle.
The Tigershark flies at his fingertips. He concentrates on the mission,
not the functioning of his aircraft. The competitive edge is his.

Northrop Corporation, 1800 Century Park East, Los Angeles, California 90067 USA

NORTHROP
Making advanced technology work

Here Northrop tells us that pure "joy" (as epitomized by the flaunted phallic "joystick") can be found in the phallotechnic fusion of man to killing machine. And this is manifestly a fantasy of sexual violation/pleasure. The key image is the "anatomically designed" stick—one lovingly fashioned in the image and likeness of man and thereby eliciting, or intending to elicit, a biological identification, a species bonding, loyalty, and support.

Ronald Reagan encouraged a similar fantasy during his post-game remarks at Superbowl 1984. Speaking on split screen television to Coach Flores of the Los Angeles Raiders, Mr. Reagan said, "I've already gotten a call from Moscow. They think Marcus Allen is a new secret weapon. They insist we dismantle it." Warming to his metaphors, the Great Communicator continued, stating that the game had "given me an idea about that team of yours. If you would turn them over to us, we'd put them in silos and we wouldn't have to build the MX missile."[71] Idealized virility is thus gleefully fused to weaponry and to an unprecedented and Earth-destroying lethality. The logical conclusion of this pervasive metaphor can only suggest world nuclear holocaust as the ultimate form of sexual murder. Indeed, listening closely, we might realize that whenever Ronald Reagan or anyone else sexualizes/fetishizes his weaponry, he is actually pronouncing himself the political equivalent of Jack the Ripper.

Similarly, Mr. Reagan has also promoted his Strategic Defense Initiative (the projected space-based nuclear defense system, strategically nicknamed "Star Wars") as a means of rendering nuclear weapons "impotent and obsolete."[72] Yet however much Reagan and company want to emasculate their rivals, they desire only to bone up the home team.* Indeed, laser expert John D.G. Rather, a strong advocate of the military extravaganza "Star Wars," wrote in a 1982 article that any country that was the sole possessor of space lasers would thus possess the "longest 'big stick' in history."[73] This marked male obsession with lengths, "big ones," measurements, and competitive comparisons of "sticks," points to one further supreme reversal. It is not *women* who have penis envy.

Joysticks, MX missiles, space lasers or sex pistols—Freud's concept of the sexual "symbol" demands further explication. Again like Jack the Ripper, many sex murderers never actually rape their victims; instead of using their penis as a weapon, they use a weapon as their penis—a knife (Jack the Ripper), brooms and bottles (the "Boston Strangler"),

---

*About ten percent of the multi-billion dollar "Star Wars" budget is *explicitly* for nuclear weapons (and the rest of the research might at any time be applied to offensive weapons and strategies). Such research includes items such as advanced "penetration aids" to help the still virile American missiles reach their intended targets as well as the futuristic laser and particle beam weapons.

oak clubs (Ted Bundy), machine tools (the "Yorkshire Ripper"), or the gun (the "Son of Sam"). These weapons are not functioning simply or even solely as symbols, but would much more accurately be described as *fetishes*—not in the only sense that Freud would have admitted, i.e. as substitutes for the imaginary female penis, but, rather, as replacements for the *male penis*. Thus the weapon—the *rod, tool, instrument*—becomes the operative male organ in a staggering replacement of the real by the symbolic. This conquest by the symbolic haunts the entire sex crime phenomenon. Consider also the mass pervasion in the white man's culture of castration anxiety, symbolized everywhere in language, literature, myth, psychology, philosophy, humor, and art.

Castration Fantasies

We have already shown that they can take away the male organ, not indeed by actually despoiling the human body of it, but by concealing it with some glamour.

Kramer and Sprenger, Malleus Maleficarum

Beyond any doubt her sex is a mouth and a voracious mouth which devours the penis—a fact which can easily lead to the idea of castration.

Jean-Paul Sartre[74]

The psychiatric castrators...drawing upon their inexhaustible reversal reflex mechanisms, manipulate their female patients into believing that they, their mothers, and women in general are castrators of *men*. This reversal rivals the story of Eve's birth from Adam for top rank among the Great Hoaxes of history.

Mary Daly[75]

Everywhere in patriarchy, we are told the lie of the female as the dangerous and deadly sex.* This deceptive archeype is concentrated in the peculiar notion of the female as castrator of the male—a phallocentric archetype which animates all the figures of the overbearing mothers, the insatiable lovers, the scheming vamps, Mrs. Macombers, ballbusters, glamorous witches and castrating bitches. Of course, this fantastic ideological reversal greatly fuels the reality of sex crime, for when women are proclaimed the mutilating and lethal aggressor against men, the men are given absolute justification for their actual annihilation of women. Indeed, mass propagation of faith in the notion of woman as castrator has accompanied nearly all gynocidal campaigns. As Peter Gay has observed:

*Danger derives from the Ofr. *danger*, absolute power of an overlord and L. *dominum*, lordship, *dominus*, master. As the etymology indicates it is the domineering, hierarchical, patriarchal male who is the "dangerous sex." For a treatment of the myth, see H.R. Hays, *The Dangerous Sex: The Myth of Feminine Evil* (New York: G.P. Putnam's Sons, 1964). One thing is certain: no century depicted woman as vampire, as castrator, as killer so consistently, so programatically, and so nakedly as the nineteenth.[76]

One thing is certain: no century depicted woman as vampire, as castrator, as killer so consistently, so programatically, and so nakedly as the nineteenth.[76]

Such was the context from which Jack the Ripper emerged; moreover, such naked portrayals have continued unabated into the twentieth century.[77]

Such imagery for example is rife in popular song and is particularly noticeable when acted out in the video tunes of Music Television (MTV).* In one survey of the female stereotypes in the "love songs" on MTV, Annie Goldson found four predominant motifs. In order of frequency, these are: "cold bitches, love objects, maneaters, and victims."[78] All of these manifestly propagate the attitudes of sex crime, the first and third expressly through their evocation of castration doubledream.[79]

A song called simply "Maneater" was one of the very top hits of the early 1980s. It was recorded by Hall and Oates, consistently rated as the most popular duo in the country. Here, male loyalty comes to the fore in their warning to all the other boys:

Whoah, here she comes; watch out boys she'll chew you up.
Whoah, here she comes; she's a maneater.

They continue with appropriate phallocentric euphemism:

She's deadly man, she could really rip your world apart.[80]

Another rock group, Van Stephenson, beat out the ritual refrain with some additional detail. They sing of a "Modern Day Delilah" who "keeps her scissors laser sharp," loving men like "lions," but leaving them like "lambs." This song is found on an album entitled "Righteous Anger."[81] The cover depicts a barely clad woman staring coldly off, her back to the viewers. Etched into that unyielding back is the tormented face of a man; his hands chained and handcuffed, reach out in agony. The message is unmistakeable. She is the captor, the deadly one; he is the captive, the victim. Nevertheless, as the title promises, this man, filled with his "righteous anger" will soon exact his revenge. Such reversals, although ludicrous, are nonetheless extremely chilling for it is precisely such sentiments that fuel the actual enactments of sex crime.

During Peter Sutcliffe's trial, he revealed that he first murdered after a prostitute accused him of being "fucking useless" when he was unable to get an erection. After this humiliation, he said he experienced a

---

*MTV is an independent cable network devoted to "24-hour rock video," an extremely popular and much imitated media phenomenon. See also the video by The Tubes, "She's a Beauty," (Kenny Ortega, 1983) for a graphic depiction of woman as castrator of the male and vampire on male vigor and life.

"seething rage" and attacked, killed, and mutilated her. As Wendy Holloway reported, other men easily identified with his emotions and responded sympathetically. Sir Michael Havers, the prosecuting attorney, said of the prostitute's behavior, "Was this not a classic example of provocation?" The *Observer* commented:

It is not hard to see how this cocktail of frustration, guilt and humiliation could lead to fury, and the fury to an urge not just for revenge but for the satisfaction in spirit if not in body of his sexual urge.[82]

As Sutcliffe himself said, "To be honest I pulled up her clothing to satisfy some sort of sexual revenge on her." Mutilation was his form of "spiritual" satisfaction, gynocide the means of venting his "righteous anger."

The notion that women are responsible for men's impotence is a direct descendent from the ideology of the Witch Hunts, a connection which becomes immediately apparent when reading Christopher Lasch's *Culture of Narcissism* (1979). In his chapter, "The Flight From Feeling: Sociopsychology of the Sex War," Lasch tells us that while women are now more accessible as sexual partners to men, they are also far more threatening. If women once seemed to lack sexual response (under 19th century gynecological ideology), after Masters and Johnson they seem to be "sexually insatiable, inexhaustible in their capacity to experience orgasm after orgasm." Reverberations from the *Malleus* begin here, only to deepen as Lasch continues. He identifies what he calls a "spector of impotence" haunting the "contemporary [male] imagination," activated by the "apparently aggressive overtures of sexually liberated woman." Lasch, however, ultimately rejects feminism as the root cause of this "spector," feeling that feminism alone is too weak to generate such profound fears. Rather, as he see it, impotence is based in primitive male emotions and fears, fathomless unconscious archetypes. Getting right into that "castrating woman of male fantasy," Lasch writes with feeling of the "possessive, suffocating, devouring, and castrating" mother who swims in the swampy recesses of the masculine mind. It seems that all men live in barely restrained terror of:

...the vagina which threatens to eat them alive; of the legs with which popular imagination endows the American heroine, legs which can presumably strangle or scissor victims to death...[83]

That reference to the "vagina which threatens to eat them alive" brings us face to face with the most concentrated icon of men's self-serving fears—the *vagina dentata*, the toothed, i.e. castrating, vagina of archetypal myth. This motif can be traced in legend and fantasy from the oldest patriarchal narratives and images right up into the mandatory spike heels on the otherwise naked and vulnerable women in pornography, from medieval iconography of the gates of hell through the gaping mouth of the great white shark in the enormously popular film, *Jaws* (Steven Spielberg, 1975).*

Elsewhere I have analyzed the underlying structure of *Jaws* to be the ritual and heroic annihilation of a symbolic female, the monstrous female of male dreams, epitomized by the great white shark.[84] The key image is the shark's mouth "bristling with teeth," for that is the characteristic icon of the patriarchal archetype of the "Terrible Mother" and her *vagina dentata*.[85] The identification of the shark with the *bad* mother is evident throughout the film, particularly in its choice of victims. Except for the very first victim, all others—indeed anyone who is subsequently threatened by the shark—are boys and men. The action takes place in the ocean, the primal source of life, but this symbolic womb is full of blood, gore, danger, and death. There are graphic scenes of dismembered male limbs, legs falling off into the deep, etc. The trinity of male heroes in *Jaws* become archetypically heroic** via their pursuit and annihilation of that most terrible enemy—the castrating female, the terrible, murderous mother of patriarchal nightmare and myth.

Jaws serves up to men, however subliminally, a huge dose of dread and hatred for the female. Yet what of women who watch the film— what symbolic messages are transmitted, what cords struck? I suggest that women watching the film also recoil in deep horror, but not from the fear of the *vagina dentata* which we know to be a figment. Rather, a different message of terror is communicated to women. For the shark functions as a fundamentally ambivalent symbol, suggesting not only the archetypal castration threat to the male viewer, but simultaneously signalling the gynocidal masculine to the female. We can recall that the *Reader's Digest* likened Ted Bundy to a "shark patrolling a beach." And the theme of sexual murder is indeed intrinsic to *Jaws*; actually, the film opens with just such a scene.

---

*The recurring belief in the *vagina dentata* surfaced again in Vietnam in legends that Vietnamese prostitutes had placed razor blades or grenades in their vaginas in order to castrate customers. Again, this is a most hideous reversal, for it was the military men who were using, abusing, raping and mutilating Vietnamese women, even placing weapons such as grenades in their vaginas and blowing them up. For information on the legend see, Monte Gulzow and Carol Mitchell, " 'Vagina Dentata' and 'Incurable Venereal Disease': Legends from the Viet Nam War," *Western Folklore*, 24, No. 4 (Oct. 1980), 306-16.

**Well, two of them do anyway, achieving manhood via that classic trial of monster-slaying. The other (played by Robert Shaw) actually loses his manhood when he is bitten off at the waist by the shark. As Christopher Sharp writing in *Women's Wear Daily* (16 June 1975) observed, " 'Jaws' is the perfect movie for anyone with a larger-than-life castration complex."

A group of teenagers sit around a campfire smoking and drinking. One boy keeps giving a girl the eye. She gets up and begins to run toward the beach, tossing off her clothes as she goes. He gives chase, continually calling to her to "Slow down. I'm coming." Reaching the water naked, the girl enters for a swim. By this point, the boy has reached the beach and lies down on the sand. The camera lingers on the girl's long legs and semi-visible naked body. She calls out, asking him to join her in the water, but the boy refuses. Suddenly the shark attacks, whirling the girl on a long, drawn-out circle of death through the water. She screams and some of her words, through scrambled, can be made out. She is yelling, "It hurts, it hurts." At precisely this moment, the camera cuts to the boy, stretched out on the beach and intoning, "I'm coming, I'm coming." No doubt he was.

Because of the suspense and horror of this scene, the implications of the dialogue and succession of events are difficult to consciously grasp. But logically there is no reason for the boy to still be repeating "I'm coming" when they have already spoken and ascertained that he was, in fact, on the beach. Are we supposed to think that he had, within seconds, slumped into a drunken stupor, oblivious to her piercing cries, and that his loaded words were really quite meaningless? Frankly, this scene reeks with meaning and the scent is unmistakably one of sexual murder. (An actual suggestion of sex crime is inserted into the dialogue later when men viewing her remains joke about Jack the Ripper.) And however covert the presentation of that message, some women indubitably did receive it. In 1979, twelve Black women were murdered within six months in a very small area of Boston. One woman from that area commented:

I think of it like "Jaws." I saw "Jaws," and I didn't go swimming in the ocean. It's like something you're conscious about. When I'm with a man, I don't know what will trigger him off.[86]

Jaws, then, functions as examplary propaganda for sex crime ideology in that it so neatly intermeshes those two companion themes: men's symbolic and frankly delusory fear of castration at the hands of the "terrible female," and women's genuine fear of sexual attack, castration, and murder at the hands of the ordinary man. Moreover, to reiterate, these two motifs are mutually reinforcing in that the mass *fiction* of female castration of the male works to legitimate, encourage, and even command the actual castration of women by men.

We can observe the tandem operation of these two themes in another key pictorial—the cover of George Stade's sex crime novel, *Confessions of a Lady-Killer*. The "Avenger" is portrayed as a knight. In one arm he grips his hard and mighty sword; in the other he brandishes the severed head of the Medusa (the archaic Gorgon Goddess whose gaze was said to turn men to stone* and whom Freud, tellingly, reduced to a symbol of the maternal genital). And within the confines of phallic symbolism, the ideological message of this illustration is clear—her "genital," i.e. life, power, and being, must be severed and destroyed so that his might be saved.

Although this schema might seem too melodramatic and far-fetched, it was enacted with a precise and vicious reality in California in 1979. There, Lawrence Singleton picked up fifteen-year old hitchhiker, Mary Bell Vincent, ultimately raping her and then chopping off both of her arms with an axe. As Amanda Spake reports, in Singleton's view (as revealed by his writings and testimony in court) it was *he* who was under attack by the girl. Singleton felt that Mary Vincent had somehow "threatened to emasculate me." He described the episode, "My night of terror had begun. Everything I did was for survival....She forcibly kidnapped me, also threatening me with rape charges." Singleton, of course, emerged from his "ordeal" unscathed while the girl was raped and mutilated. Spake further reports:

Singleton's last letter to me about the case was chilling. In it, he rewrote the exact, legal language of the kidnapping count as he was convicted of it. Above each place that his name, Lawrence Singleton, appeared, he had written the name of the new perpetrator of the crime: "Mary Bell Vincent."[87]

Women do not often kidnap, strangle or castrate men in reality. Indeed men are usually castrated only in their dreams. When such mutilation does happen to men, it is inflicted upon oppressed, or younger, men *by other men*. The "Trashbag Murderers," for example raped and castrated young boys they picked up hitchhiking on California highways

---

*In a stirring article, Emily Erwin Culpepper analyses the significance of the Gorgon face as a symbol of contemporary women's *rage* against sexual violation and terrorism. Culpepper relates an incident which occurred one night as she sat alone, working on her dissertation. Someone knocked at the door and she, after looking out and thinking that it was a friend of her neighbor's, opened the door. The man came in and attacked her. Culpepper, at first unprepared, gathered herself and fought back, throwing out the would-be attacker. She includes a selection from her journal recalling this incident:

NO! DANGER! Right here! NOW! PUSH his body BACK! KNOCK his hand AWAY! Shove and—loud—yell, 'GET OUT! GET OUT! GET OUT!'

I am staring him out, pushing with my eyes too. My face is bursting, contorting with terrible teeth, flaming breath, erupting into ridges and contours of rage, hair hissing. It is over in a flash. I still see his eyes, stunned, wide and staring, almost as if *I* am acting strange, as if *I* were acting wrong!

Culpepper speaks of her will to fight, her "Gorgon spirit," which petrified her attacker, her *Rage* which saved her. See Emily Erwin Culpepper, "Ancient Gorgons: A Face for Contemporary Women's Rage," *Woman of Power: A Magazine of Feminism, Spirituality, and Politics*, 3 (Spring 1986), 22-24, 40.

throughout the 1970s. The tortures inflicted by these murderers as well as those by Dean Corll (Texas, mid-1970s) and John Wayne Gacy were gruesome to the extreme. Furthermore, the history of lynchings and castrations of Black men and equivalent atrocities against other scapegoated groups, reveals yet another tradition of sex crime. Beth Day writes:

An examination of the way the lynchings were conducted suggests an overriding sexual theme. Castration, sexual mutilation, and sexual torture were common components, no matter what the alleged crime....It was the body of the black that obsessed the lynch mob. The symbolic desexing of the victim suggests, as black sociologist Calvin Hernton has pointed out, "a lover gone mad."[88]

The female and male victims of Ripper-style crimes are similarly castrated, tortured and murdered. Gynecological surgery simultaneously approaches women's sex organs with "scissors and knives"; nowhere, medically, is the male organ comparatively threatened. All the talk of female castration of men is clearly pure deception, masculine glamour, total reversal. What is demonstrable is the recurring incidence of both female and male castration *by males.*

What we might then realize is that all the incessant babble about male "fear of women" serves in many ways as a cover up for their deep and abiding fear of each other. That fear is further obscured by the solid taboo that silences discussion of the male-on-male sex murders in cultural myth narratives—the fictions and formulas of the mass media. Consider. Why are there no thinly veiled fictionalizations of the lives and times of Dean Corll or John Wayne Gacy to match that glut of stories featuring Bundy and Berkowitz-like killers? Why no television specials on the "Trashbag Murderers"?* Why no "boy in danger" movies among the current glut of slasher films, stirring the imaginations and feeding the fantasies of any potential "Bluebeards"[89] in the audience?

Actually Freud was right about the fact that sons fear fathers—for might really castrate and rape them. And, likewise, fathers do fear sons—for who ultimately will replace them. Certainly, there is mythic legitimation for such antagonisms—who is it but the supreme christian father god who demands the sacrificial torture and death of his own son. Andrea Dworkin has written:

The fathers, wombless perpetuators of their own image, know themselves; that is, they know that they are dangerous, purveyors of raw violence and constant death. They know that male desire is the stuff of murder, not love. They know that male eroticism, atrophied

---

*There has been a television special about the "Atlanta Child Killer," but this is because it is more acceptable to the status quo to show Black males as victims.

in the mummified penis, is sadistic; that the penis itself is as they have named it, a knife, a sword, a weapon. They know too that the sexual aggression of men against each other, especially sons against fathers, once let loose would destroy them.

...The fathers truly fear the potency of the sons. Knowing fully the torture chambers of male imagination, they see themselves, legs splayed, rectum split, torn, shredded by the saber they have enshrined.

Do it to her, they whisper; do it to her, they command.[90]

All fantasies aside, it is the male who qualifies as the "dangerous sex," harmful not only to women, animals, and the planet, but also to other males. Thus the command, "Do it to her," becomes the perpetual refrain in the Age of Sex Crime.

In order to ensure that proper targeting, the female sex is archetypally objectified, stripped of reality, and reduced to an essentially symbolic function. This recurrent assault on the real by the phallosymbolic— reminiscent of the masculine glamour—is ubiquitous throughout sex crime ideology. It operates, for example, in: the killer's use of the fetish/ weapon as his penis; the belief in the imaginary fact of female castration; the further belief in the female castrator and not the documentable male mutilator; the extraordinary reversal which makes woman the "dangerous sex;" and, finally the process which ensures the generation of genuine evil as the consequence of patriarchy's characteristic heroic crusades against its own constructed/fetishized "evil."

The Symbolic Sex

I never quite understood it—this sex symbol—I always thought symbols were those things you clash together! That's the trouble, a sex symbol becomes a thing. I just hate to be a thing, but if I'm going to be a symbol of something I'd rather have it sex than some other things they've got symbols of.

Marilyn Monroe[91]

In New York City in 1922...a statue called "Civic Virtue" was erected in City Hall Park. It represented a man standing victorious over a heap of conquered temptations in the form of women. For at least two decades this work drew the ire of feminists who resented the suggestion that "man symbolizes virtue and woman vice."

Margaret Cheney[92]

He went over there, ripped her clothes off, and took a knife and cut from her vagina almost all the way up....Then he stooped and knelt over and commenced to peel every bit of skin off her body and left her there as a *sign* of something or other.

account of a U.S. war crime in Vietnam[93]

Man would have nothing to lose, quite the contrary, if he gave up disguising woman as a symbol.

Simone de Beauvoir[94]

In that dialectic which names man as Subject and woman as Other, man becomes not only the self, the essential, but also the real. Correspondingly, woman becomes the inessential, the object, the unreal or the symbolic. In New York City in the summer of 1981, a nun was raped and a number of crosses were carved into her body. In the war crime described above, the woman's body was used as purely symbolic matter. Such symbolizations are violent and extreme but are nevertheless wholly consistent with the all-out use of the image of woman as the primary stuff of symbolism in this culture. As James Laver, authority on fashion, has commented, "Woman is the mould into which the spirit of the age pours itself."[95] Considering the reigning spirit of this age, Laver's proposition is grim enough, but it becomes even more so as it becomes clear that it is just this assumption and appropriation of the female sex *as symbol* that underlies and sustains patriarchy and the Age of Sex Crime.

Consider an issue of *Esquire* from February 1967, a monthly which in those days still billed itself as a "magazine for men" (now they call themselves "Man at His Best"). The cover photo is a nude woman stuffed into a garbage can, her face and legs sticking out, her expression mournful. The caption reads: "The New American Woman: Through at 21." Inside, an unsigned article inveighs against this supposedly new and representative female type, although the entire concept is a concoction of the author's mind. We are told that this new breed is epitomized by the "L.A. Woman," a rootless being without standards who is hedonistic and morally vacant—in short, a danger to Man, a disease which must be eliminated and destroyed:

The town and the woman are intertwined; one could never have been born without the other....the L.A. woman henceforth to be known as the American Woman. She is sick, and she is also a sickness. Their germs are already spreading out of Los Angeles across the country in the usual forms and with the usual potency.*[96]

Thus, the symbol selected to convey the corruption and decay of the modern, man-made city is a young, and as the article demands, short-lived woman. Furthermore, the composition of the cover shot implies a means by which this sickening woman might ultimately be disposed of. That means is none other than sex crime, for the image of a nude woman dumped into a garbage can is a recurring icon of sexual murder,[97] second only to that of the nude woman in the "gynecological" position.

Another telling illustration of the use of woman as the symbolic

---

*See also the song by the Canadian rock group, The Guess Who, entitled "American Woman," in which American women are blamed for "their" country's "war machine," "ghetto scene," etc. The Guess Who, "American Woman," written by Bachman/Cummings, *American Woman*, Victor Records, AYLI-3673, 1969.

sex can be found in the history of the 1946 film *Gilda*, starring Rita Hayworth in what was to become her definitive role as film star and sex symbol. Throughout most of the movie we are unsure if we can trust her character, suspecting that she will turn out to be another of the conventionally lying and castrating *femme fatales* so massively propagated in the detective fiction and *film noir* of the post-war period.[98] Indeed, the song she sings, "Put the Blame on Mame," suggests as much for in its lyrics a woman is blamed for the Chicago fire, the San Francisco earthquake, and the freezing over of Manhattan. It is clearly implied that Gilda is yet another visitation of the archetypal Eve, the eternal evil feminine.

But in this one film, the heroine surprisingly does not turn out to be a liar, killer, or bringer of doom who must be righteously eliminated by the hero. Nevertheless, as film critic Michael Wood has pointed out, the myth of woman as disaster triumphed and the phallocracy memorialized Gilda by giving her name to an atomic bomb. Wood comments:

The symbolism is enough to frighten off any but the most intrepid Freudians: the bomb dropped on Bikini was called Gilda and had a picture of Rita Hayworth painted on it. The phallic agent of destruction underwent a sex change, and the delight and terror of our new power were channeled into an old and familiar story: our fear and love of women. We got rid of guilt, too. If women are always to blame, starting with Eve perhaps, or Mother Nature, then men can't be to blame.[99]

In *reality*, of course, it was men who conceived of the bomb project, largely planned and accomplished its construction, and later chose to use it. But *symbolically*, the destructiveness of the bomb was linked to the female sex. Rita Hayworth was henceforth known in France as the "Atomic Star"; women have been called "blonde bombshells" ever since; and, in memory of the island that was split in half during that test, the name *bikini* was given to the overtly sexual two-piece bathing suit worn by women.

If women "are" the bomb, why not make women war itself. Another *Esquire* cover, this time from November 1984, does precisely that. Drawing attention to its inside story, "Why Men Love War," the cover photo shows a dazed woman, garbed in army fatigues and helmet. She is carefully made up and wears diamond earrings, but her expression is frozen, discomfiting. Her eyes open into a glassy state of shock; perhaps she sees some approaching troops getting ready to fire upon her. This projected personification of woman as war indicates once more that women are the true enemy, the true objects of attack in all phallic warfares. Once again, phallocracy is setting up a victim, a target, subliminally suggesting/commanding: *"Do it to her."*

Reprinted with permission by Esquire Associates. Copyright © 1967 by *Esquire*.

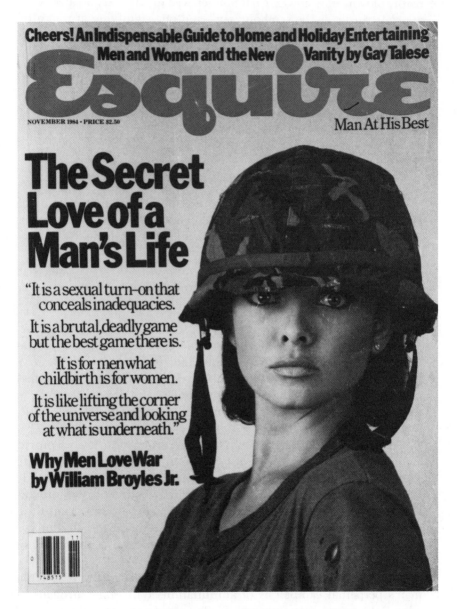

Reprinted with permission by Esquire Associates. Copyright © 1984 by *Esquire*.

Ceaseless violence can be directed against female flesh because the reality of women is nowhere felt nor believed in, precisely because women are constructed as the symbolic sex—and one signifying at root all the ultimate dangers: castration; disease; war; death—in short, evil.

The Final Fetish

Down from the waist they are Centaurs,
Though woman all above:
But to the girdle do the Gods inherit,
Beneath is all the fiend's: there's hell, there's darkness,
There is the sulphurous pit—burning, scalding,
Stench, consumption; fie, fie, fie! pah, pah!

Shakespeare, *King Lear*

The authors of the *Malleus* paused briefly in their fulminations against women as witches to comment upon the relation of the male sex to that most heinous sin. They immediately find themselves absolved and praise god:

And blessed be the Highest Who has so far preserved the male sex from so great a crime; for since He was willing to be born and to suffer for us, therefore He has granted to men this privilege.

The Freudians take up a similar theme centuries later and proclaim that all of the creative, the "power and the glory," essentially the *divine* have been corralled by the phallus. Correspondingly, it remains the lot of women to represent the dangerous and essentially the demonic and this symbolic double standard provides a cornerstone for the ideology and practice of sex crime.

A mid-seventies poster for the New York Erotic Film Festival provided a choice image for the Age of Sex Crime. In this illustration a few lines suggest a female body from mid-torso to mid-thigh; no head or legs below the knee are included and that partial body is drawn only as a mere outline. The genital area, however, is scrupulously detailed; it is the face of the devil. Once more woman is reduced to "absolute sex" and the vulva, here and elsewhere, is fetishized as a concentrated sign of evil.

In his last book, *Escape From Evil*, Ernest Becker attempted to explain man's perpetual campaigns of annihilation. With some arrogance, he adopts the perspective that man is above/different from the rest of the world in that he alone has made death conscious. Men fear death and therefore see evil in everything that wounds, causes ill health, brings displeasure, or threatens life. They become preoccupied with the idea of evil and feel compelled to "fetishize evil," that is to locate the threat to life in some place where it can be placated or controlled, i.e. scapegoated and destroyed. According to Becker, a logic of the heroic develops out of this fetishization for man then assumes his highest role to be a heroic struggle against that isolated threat (which he conveniently forgets that he originally fabricated). The Earth is made into a theater for his heroism; he throws his life into acts which will transcend that evil and, at least symbolically, conquer death. As Becker sees it, this is man's great tragedy. Because he alone is conscious of death, he struggles to be immune to it. By being able to fetishize evil and thus "lash out in all directions against imagined danger," he actually produces real evil in that process.[100]

Women, of course, are chief among the male-imagined "dangers" and Becker's script, in some ways, provides a philosophical underwriting for sex crime. As Margaret Cheney remarked regarding matricide Edmund Kemper, "To kill a scapegoat is to become a hero."[101] And the fictional murderer, Victor Grant, in George Stade's *Confessions of a Lady-Killer*, loudly and precisely articulates just this brand of self-absolution. His first victim, the feminist Jude Karnofsky, is presented throughout the novel as an archetypal monster:

The monster who held Samantha in thrall was the Dragon of the Apocalypse herself. Karnofsky had at her disposal all the demonic forces released by the collapse of a civilization, our civilization.

Reverberations from both the Witch Hunts as well as the contemporary movement of christian fundamentalism can be heard here.[102] In this novel, as in the Witchcraze, male terrorization and execution of women are given sacred legitimation, promulgated as necessary for male survival, indeed, as requisite for the survival of "our" civilization.* Thus the slaughter of "monstrous" women—be they feminists, prostitutes, patients or witches—becomes a culturally prescribed action, a manly and heroic deed, a bulwark against chaos, a maintenance of things as they are, an act of brotherly love. As Stade's protagonist (after revealing that he has taken the Mike Hammer "Avenger" character in *I, The Jury* as his role model) confesses with unswerving assurance:

And I, Victor Grant, avenger, defiantly assert that I have been your hero, whether you know it or not, whether you accept it or not. What I did, I did for you.[103]

De Beauvoir is right; men must give up disguising women as symbols. But, concomitantly, they will have to relinquish their favorite disguise— the mask of the hero.

---

*As Virginia Woolf advised, women must never cease to think and question "What is this civilization in which we find ourselves," for it is assuredly not *our* civilization. See Virginia Woolf, *Three Guineas* (New York: Harcourt, Brace & World, 1938; Harbinger Books, 1966), p. 109.

Chapter VI
The Age of Sex Crime

I cannot repeat this too often any one is of one's period....And each of us in our own way are bound to express what the world in which we are living is doing.

Gertrude Stein

I ask you to consider the development of weaponry in the last eighty years, nuclear bombs, poisonous gases, laser beams, noise bombs, and the like, and to question the development of technology in relation to women.

Andrea Dworkin[1]

Sex crime indubitably has its archetypal and historical referents, its grounding in the social verities of male-made gods and heroes, scapegoating, and religious sacrifice. Yet sex crime in the form of the serial mutilation murder is a modern practice. By claiming the current period to be an "age" of sex crime, I claim sex crime to be a key sign of the times, a root paradigm, a practice that expresses precisely what the patriarchal world in which we are living and dying is doing.

Still, sex crime is not the only such paradigm. To assemble others, we can begin by invoking that shared designator, "The Age of..." In so doing, we immediately gather Mechanical Reproduction, the Media, the Camera, Pornography, Fashion, Television, the Computer, Plastic, Technology, Space, and, most insistently, the Nuclear. All of these typically modern products and phenomena comprise a cultural composition, a cluster of interrelated and mutually reinforcing parts. As such, each could be examined for its particular relation to sex crime. Such an examination—a contextualization of the phenomenon of serial sex murder—will be the focus here. Moreover, I will be guided by Dworkin's suggestion that we consider the development of technology in relation to women, concentrating on technologies not only of mass destruction, but also on those of mass communication and replication.

The Messages of the Media

A man has an argument with his girl-friend. The man leaves. The woman gets ready for bed. Later that night, the man returns, breaks into the apartment, stabs the woman to death and stuffs her body into a plastic garbage bag. The man carries the bag downstairs to the alley where he dumps it into a large metal trash receptacle. The man walks off into the night.

—plot synopsis, proposed 3-minute student film, 1979[2]

Michelle Citron and Ellen Seiter describe the above as a "fairly typical synopsis of a student film treatment in a university film production class." As precisely that typicality demonstrates, sexual violence has become inseparably blurred into the assumptions and projections of the image media. In film, fashion, pornography, advertising, television, and photographic "art,"[3] gynocide has become standard subject material, entertainment convention, and three-minute melodramatic cliché.

Television critic Michael Arlen has designated the modern era as the "Camera Age," and in her study of photography Susan Sontag has concluded that the culture-wide obsession with that form indicates that this is a society of "image-junkies."[4] While such mass addiction/ intoxication is frequently either trivialized or abhorred, it should also be considered in its *sacred* dimension. A variety of analysts have argued that the mass media comprise a modern religion.[5] Harold Lasswell, for example, has written that the image media function for the modern populace much as the medieval cathedrals with their stained glass windows, statuary, icons, and carvings did for an illiterate peasantry.[6] George Gerbner claims television in particular as the new religion:

...in the sense of preindustrial pre-Reformation religion in the sense of one's having no choice—a cosmic force or symbolic environment that one was born into, and whose assumptions one accepted without much questioning.[7]

Like traditional religions, the mass media provide those repetitious pictures and stories which ritually demonstrate the basic order of the culture. In so doing (again like traditional religions), they socially construct reality,[8] ingraining appropriate values and beliefs while simultaneously cultivating resistance to social change, a surrender to "things as they are."

In patriarchal religions, both condemnation (the identification of women with evil) as well as exclusion (the institution of an all-male godhead) characterize the treatment of women. Not too surprisingly, those same modes dominate the patriarchal media as well. Gerbner and Gaye Tuchman use the term "symbolic annihilation" to describe the systematic treatment of female images in the mass media.[9] Such annihilation is commonly expressed through stereotyping: women are projected in images which are condemnatory ("bad" women are deadlier and more vicious than even the "bad" men), belittling (women are shown as incompetent, silly, or merely decorative), or victimizing (women are made the helpless, fated victims of male violence).[10]

Another method of symbolic annihilation, what Gerbner and Tuchman term *absence*, takes shape in the systematic obliteration of female presence in significant areas of the mass-mediated world. For example, content analysis of television reveals that male characters consistently outnumber female characters three to one on prime time, two to one overall.* Most viewers are not consciously aware of this distortion, but through habitual viewing simply assimilate and internalize its assumptions. Gerbner holds that representation in the sacred/symbolic world of televised imagery signifies "social existence"—power, importance, significance, in short, *reality*. Absence, on the other hand, connotes powerlessness, invalidation, *unreality*.**

Thus, in the Camera/TV/Film Age, women are not only systematically immured in annihilating stereotypes, but are, as well, simultaneously symbolically disappeared. The common non-sense generally holds that such projections and deletions in the symbolic world simply "reflect" or editorialize on a pre-existing reality. But instead, such imagery, like that of traditional religions, continually, if subliminally, functions to ritually shape both "reality" and "unreality."

Marilyn Monroe, remarking upon people's frequently bizarre behavior toward her, once lamented. "I realize some people want to see if you're real."[11] Andrea Dworkin has written:

Neither men nor women believe in the existence of women as significant beings. It is impossible to remember as real the suffering of...someone who is in fact viewed as some thing, an object or an absence.[12]

In 1964, thirty-eight people ignored Kitty Genovese's repeated cries for help and instead watched (some even pulled up chairs to their windows) as Robert Mosley (whom the *Times* described as a "family man") stalked, stabbed, raped, and murdered her.[13] Public and professional opinion have widely blamed fear, urban alienation, and passive viewing habits induced by watching television, for such callous behavior. Yet there is far more to this story, for these people were also watching the annihilation of an "insignificant" being in a sequence that mirrored one of the most ritually repeated performances of the patriarchal symbolic world.

Sex crime propagandist Brian De Palma blithely notes that "using women in situations where they are killed or sexually attacked" is simply a "genre convention...like using violins when people look at each other."[14] In 1983 alone, one in eight commercially released films in this country depicted violent acts by men against women.[15] Such conventional portrayals similarly pervade advertising, rock 'n' roll song lyrics and

---

*Such erasure of women is endemic to all areas of patriarchal "reality," e.g. history, art, literature, etc. In the world of the media, consider as well such films as *Jaws* or *Star Wars*. Each are typical in that there is at best one woman in what is otherwise a completely male filmscape.

**These same methods are used against all who are "other" to the dominant reality, i.e. the non-white, non-affluent, non-American, the poor, the aged, etc.

album covers, billboards, display windows, etc.[16] The fashion pages also regularly flash back the gynocidal scene; in *Vogue, Harper's Bazaar, Glamour,* etc., women are shown dead, laid out, suffocated, shot, run over by cars—all in the course of advertising products such as stockings, perfume and shoes.[17] These symbolic annihilations of female images perform much the same functions and have many of the same general effects as actual male violence. They too demonstrate the rules of patriarchal power, help to generate the State of Fear, eroticize violence, give ideas to violent-prone men, and ceaselessly suggest obliteration to women. Such imagery is the necessary symbolic counterpoint to the lethal actualization—its mirror reflection, "inspirational dream," and motivating myth.

We might recognize such media manifestations of misogyny as a "pornography of everyday life," for it is, of course, express pornography which sets the trends, pushes the limits, and provides the ultimate source for all other victimizing and degrading images of women in the media.[18] Radical feminist critiques of pornography have been offered in great depth elsewhere,[19] and my purpose here is not to duplicate those analyses, but to suggest some of the ways in which the institution of modern pornography is central to the practice of sexual murder.

Documenting Sex Crime

In the United States, it [pornography] is an $8-billion trade in sexual exploitation.

It is women turned into subhumans, beaver, pussy, body parts, genitals exposed, buttocks, breasts, mouths opened and throats penetrated, covered in semen, pissed on, shitted on, hung from light fixtures, tortured, maimed, bleeding, disemboweled, killed....

It is every torture in every prison cell in the world, done to women and sold as sexual entertainment....

---

*I would not, of course, argue that pornography is a sole cause of violence against women. Rather, each form of gynocide is accompanied by a specific type of propaganda. Because the Witchcraze was religiously mandated and socially sanctioned, its propaganda consisted of sacred texts such as papal bulls and inquisitorial manuals, as well as elite art which, ironically much like contemporary pornography, fixated upon gross caricatures of female sexuality. In keeping with the subliminal and categorically criminal character of the Age of Sex Crime, its principal form of propaganda—pornography—assumes a largely underground, "taboo," and mysterious aspect. Clearly, a gynocidal intent could also be set forth in a patriarchally based anti-pornography crusade—one which based that stance upon an ideology of female sexual filth, religious purity, the sanctity of marriage and the family, and the containment of women in male-controlled institutions. Indubitably, the anti-pornography stances of traditional religions as well as the "New Right" are based in just such an ideology. Once again we are confronted by seeming opposites (e.g. *Hustler* vs. the "Moral Majority") which actually serve to demarcate the boundaries of patriarchy, functioning cyclically, in one way or another, to keep women securely within those bounds.

PHOTOGRAPHS: GUY BOURDIN

CHARLES JOURDAN

Fabrice   85 $
Fabrice
Fabrice
Fabrice

30

1977

MAUD FRIZON

Two Ten East 60th St. New York, New York 10022

It is physical injury and physical humiliation and physical pain: to the women against whom it is used after it is made; to the women used to make it.

Andrea Dworkin[20]

The core assumption of the Age of Sex Crime is the equation of "sex" with the male mutilation and murder of a woman. So too, the essence of pornography consists in the conditioning of male arousal to female subordination, humiliation, objectification, pain, rape, mutilation, and even murder.[21] It is largely because of pornography that members of contemporary culture can see the torture of women and think *sex*. It is in pornography that the basic meanings of sex crime are distilled—the female body fetishized, displayed, sacralized, only so that she can be hated, possessed, profaned, sacrificed. Moreover, although the entire range of sexual violations are nominally defined as despised and taboo acts, these very same acts, portrayed in pornography, are the very stuff of this massive "entertainment" industry.

Not surprisingly, the case histories and personal testimonies of sex killers almost universally reveal not only a regular use of pornography,[22] but also the enactment of a fantasy of making and participating in pornography itself. The following represent a sampling of these cases:

In 1957, Harvey Glatman impersonated a professional photographer and hired female models to pose in typical detective magazine "distress" scenes, i.e. the woman bound and gagged. After binding a woman, Glatman would repeatedly rape and photograph her before finally murdering her. He later decorated the walls of his apartment with the photographs. Glatman was caught when one woman, Lorraine Vigil, fought with him, getting his gun away from him and flagging down the police. He had killed three women— Judy Dull, Shirley Anne Bridgeford, and Ruth Rita Mercado. Glatman was executed in 1959.[23]

When David Berkowitz, the "Son of Sam," was arrested, police searched his apartment and found that it was filled with pornography.

Pornographic films and literature were also found among the possessions of both Kenneth Bianchi and Angelo Buono, the "Hillside Strangler." (One reporter even tells us that Buono had papered the walls of his bathroom with *Penthouse* centerfolds.) Buono and Bianchi had started out working together as pimps, using methods of deception, coercion, and ceaseless physical/sexual abuse to keep young women in servitude to them.* They also took nude photographs of these women which served a multitude of purposes: blackmail; advertisement to potential clients; and for the pimps' own pleasure. When Buono and Bianchi began to torture and murder women, they continued to take photographs of their victims. And finally, the pornographic imperative comes full circle when, in much of the popular reporting of these murders, the narrative takes the tone of a pornographic recitation, clearly intended to arouse the male reader.[24]

---

*For an analysis of these common practices see Kathleen Barry, *Female Sexual Slavery* (Englewood Cliffs, N.J.: Prentice-Hall, 1979), especially pp. 73-102.

In December 1984, *Penthouse* published a "photo essay" on Asian female bondage in which several nude Asian women—several of whom seemed to be dead—were shown tied up, hung from trees, and hurled onto rocks. In North Carolina in January, 1985, an eight-year-old Chinese girl was found hanging upside-down from a tree. She had been raped and murdered.[25]

Newsweek, in a special report on serial murder, found that: "Many serial killers found an outlet for their vivid sexual fantasies in pornography. Kemper [Edmund, the "Coed Killer"] scoured detective magazines for pictures of corpses and frequented 'snuff' movies in which intercourse is a prelude to murder. 'That didn't make me mean,' he says. 'It just fueled the fire.' "[26]

In 1982, two teenagers, Beth Jones and Margaret Krueger, who thought they were getting five hundred dollars to appear in a pornographic film, were apparently murdered during the making of a snuff film. Pornographers Fred Berre Douglas and Richard Hernandez were arrested.[27]

The wealthy playboy, Christopher Wilder, would tell women that he was a professional photographer and that, if they would pose for him, he would get them modeling assignments. Wilder would then drug, sexually abuse, and photograph women and girls in his Florida home. Before his murder spree in 1984, Wilder had already committed at least three sex offenses and was on probation for crimes that included rape, kidnapping, and forcing women and girls to pose for nude photographs. In 1979, Wilder kidnapped a 17-year-old, fed her drug-laced food, and then put her in various outfits so that he could photograph her. A Florida sheriff reports that Wilder told the girl, "My eyes are the camera."[28]

When Lawrence Bittaker and Roy Norris were arrested for the murders of five teenage girls in California, police found over 500 photographs of teenage girls among their possessions. These men not only took photographs of the tortures and mutilations of their five, murdered victims, but also recorded the pleas and screams of Shirley Lynette Ledford on cassette tape for their later enjoyment.[29]

Two other killers, Leonard Lake and Charles Ng used a cabin in rural California as a site for torture and murder of their kidnapped victims. Evidence removed from the site included pornographic photos, handcuffs, and homemade videotapes of sexual torture involving Lake, Ng, and several of their female victims causing one police official to remark that it was all like "a horror film."[30]

Finally, Ted Bundy, describing to an interviewer the "entity" who would commit multiple sexual murder, told of that third person's gradual formative progression through the pornographic continuum. The interviewer reports:

He told me that long before there was a need to kill there were juvenile fantasies fed by photos of women in skin magazines, suntan oil advertisements, or jiggly starlets on talk shows. He was transfixed by the sight of women's bodies on provocative display....Crime stories fascinated him. He read pulp detective magazines and gradually developed a store of knowledge about criminal techniques—what worked and what didn't. That learning remained incidental to the central thrill of reading about the abuse of female images, but nevertheless he was schooling himself.*

Next, Bundy speaks for himself:

Maybe he [the "entity"] focused on pornography as a vicarious way of experiencing what his peers were experiencing in reality. . . . Then he got sucked into the more sinister doctrines that are implicit in pornography—the use, the abuse, the possession of women as objects. . . . A certain percentage of it [pornography] is devoted toward literature that explores situations where a man, in the context of a sexual encounter, in one way or another engages in some sort of violence toward a woman, or the victim. There are, of course, a whole host of substitutions that could come under that particular heading. Your girlfriend, your wife, a stranger, children—whatever—a whole host of victims are found in this literature. And in this kind of literature, they are treated as victims.[31]

Bundy is perhaps the most explicit witness, but as all such testimony reveals, pornography functions as advertisement, school and fuel for sex crime. Moreover, as many of these cases further demonstrate, pornography is not only the fantasy prelude to an actual violation, but pornography also *is* the veritable enactment and recording of sex crime.

That factor was also much in evidence during the public hearings conducted in Minneapolis (1983) on the effects of pornography.** Here, testimony from women who had themselves been victims of sexual abuse, counselors from rape-crisis centers and battered womens' shelters, and clinicians who work with sex offenders, all pointed to pornography as central to a vast amount of all types of sexual violation. Pornography is used by men prior to sexual abuse, during the abuse, and then, afterward,

---

*A 1986 NBC mini-series, *Bundy: The Deliberate Stranger*, ironically, was filled with images of "women's bodies on provocative display"—particularly as the killer stalked them in preparation for sexual murder. Once again the patriarchal media aligns itself precisely with the point of view of the sex killer.

**These hearings were organized by, among others, Andrea Dworkin and Catharine MacKinnon to show cause and provide support for their anti-pornography civil-rights ordinance. This law defines *pornography* as "the graphic sexually explicit subordination of women through pictures and/or words" that includes one or more of a set of eight qualifiers such as "women are presented as sexual objects who experience sexual pleasure in being raped." The Minneapolis City Council has twice passed this law, but it was vetoed each time by the mayor. The uniqueness of this law is that it is not a censorship bill or a traditional obscenity statute (which the right-wing has traditionally favored) but a civil-rights ordinance allowing victims of pornography to sue for harm. To see the complete law as well as a description of the hearings see *Women Against Pornography Newsreport*, 6, No. 1 (Spring/Summer 1984), or Andrea Dworkin, "Censorship, Pornography, and Equality," *Harvard Women's Law Journal* 8 (1985), reprinted in *Trivia: A Journal of Ideas*, 7 (Summer 1985), pp. 11-32.

the abuse itself having been recorded or during a recounting can itself be used and/or sold as pornography. All such testimonies, as well as those of the sex killers themselves, expose a fact which patriarchal glamour consistently obscures: the pictures of pornography are not all simulation and play acting. Rather, they frequently depict real acts. It is real women and often children who actually are being coerced, actually are being bound, gagged, pissed on, whipped, raped, mutilated, and even murdered.[32]

Yet even when such acts are "merely" dramatizations/simulations, we cannot ignore the function of such imagery in the social construction of sex crime. Kathleen Barry writes:

Pornography is a *practice* of cultural sadism as well as a means of diffusing it into the mainstream of accepted behavior and therefore into the private lives of individuals. It is the principal medium through which cultural sadism becomes part of the sexual *practices* of individuals.[33] (emphasis mine)

Of course, many eminently reasonable people persist in denying pornography as practice, preferring to bracket it as *only* "fantasy," as if the symbolic and material worlds, ideology and behavior, could ever be so neatly, even surgically, disconnected.

In human cultures, there is often a traditional belief in the power of the image over material reality. Summing up that belief, Montague Summers writes in his 1928 introduction to the *Malleus Maleficarum*:

To effect the death of a man [sic] or to injure him by making an image in his likeness, and mutilating or destroying his image, is a *practice* found throughout the whole wide world from its earliest days.[34] (emphasis mine)

Although (like the tales of malefic glamour) this may be dismissed as hopelessly quaint or irrelevant to the modern world, that *practice*, based in a causal relation between image and reality, is still very much a part, albeit a masked one, of this contemporary society of image-junkies. The persuasive power of an image, its propensity to call forth emulation,* the need of an observer to translate image into act, to become the image: these principles clearly underlie and propel the modern institutions of fashion, advertising, the star system, and, of course, politics. Few would question the efficacy of persuasive imagery in any of those areas. Yet when the institution of pornography enters the picture, the casual relation between image and behavior becomes the subject of seemingly endless

---

*Frankly, the image of the *actual* sex killer historically has functioned to call forth direct emulation, as demonstrated by the ubiquitous phenomenon of "copycat killings."

controversy.*

Finally, it is in that quintessential pornographic product—the "snuff film"—that the wavering dividing line between patriarchal fantasy and patriarchal reality purely dissolves. In these films, an actress is told that she will appear in a scene of simulated murder, but then, with the camera running, the woman is actually tortured, murdered, dismembered. Here, clearly, the image not only potentially elicits the act, but is absolutely inseparable from the act.

At the core of pornography is dissimulation—the lie that women are symbols, objects, possessions, dolls, i.e. that women are not real, and, correspondingly, the pervasive assumption that pornography isn't real either, that it is "fantasy." Typically then, much of the debate aroused in patriarchal circles regarding snuff films is whether or not they are genuine or indeed whether any genuine snuff films can be proven to exist.[35] Consider the following taken from a book on sex crime written largely for police investigators:

One large law enforcement agency now has in its possession a new film reportedly made in a foreign country that looks extremely realistic. The death scene shows a nude woman lifted several feet off the ground by ropes tied to her wrists. While suspended, her intestines are ripped out through her vagina and she then hangs there bleeding to death while another woman dances underneath her, drinking some of the blood that flows out. Whether or not this is a real snuff film, it is important to keep in mind the kind of sadistic personality that will be buying copies of this film.[36]

Amidst the incomprehensibility of the horror itself, is yet another incomprehensible factor. There seems to be no sure way to discern on film what is a faked murder and what is a real one, which is a "symbolic annihilation" and which is an actual one. Here the characteristic messages of the unreality of sexual violence and the insignificance/unreality of women fuse purely with the properties of the medium as the camera

---

*Whether or not there is a causal connection between sexual violence and sexually violent imagery remains an issue of intense controversy and dispute. A 1970 National Commission on Obscenity and Pornography concluded that there was no such connection. As this book goes to press, a 1986 Attorney General's Commission has reversed that finding and suggests a causal relation between certain kinds of pornography and acts of sexual violence. See Robert Pear, "Panel Calls on Citizens to Wage National Assault on Pornography," *New York Times*, 10 July 1986, Sec. A., p. 1, col. 2. See also *Pornography and Sexual Aggression*, ed. Edward Donnerstein and Neil Malamuth (Orlando, Fl.: Academic Press, 1984) as well as works by Barry, Russell, and Lederer in note 19 of this chapter for detailed summaries and analyses on the results of such research throughout the past twenty-five years.

itself works to confound the eye. This truly is phallic glamour.*

In his classic 1935 essay, "The Work of Art in the Age of Mechanical Reproduction," Walter Benjamin noted that, "During long periods of history, the mode of human sense perception changes with humanity's entire mode of existence."[37] He continued with an analysis of how the medium of the camera—particularly in its use in the film—has altered sense perceptions. Currently, the Ages of the Camera, Mechanical Reproduction, and Sex Crime shake hands in tacit collusion on the destruction of female reality. For clearly, it is not only the content of the patriarchal media (the stereotypings, erasures, subordinations, and victimizations) which further the world view of sex crime, but also something about the forms and properties of the media themselves. Marshall McLuhan insisted that the medium *is* the message, then, in nearly the same breath, defined those media as the "extensions of man."[38] And, in the Age of Sex Crime, these extensions frequently take on the familiar phallic form and function of the fetish/weapon.

The Camera Age: The Medium as Message

Just as the camera is a sublimation of the gun, to photograph someone is a sublimated murder....the act of taking pictures is a semblance of appropriation, a semblance of rape.

Susan Sontag[39]

I've got your picture. I've got your picture,
I've got a million of them all by myself.
I'd like a doctor to take your picture,
So I could look at you from inside as well.

"Turning Japanese," The Vapors, 1980[40]

There are two specific properties of the camera as it is wielded and understood within patriarchy that are particularly relevant to sex crime. The first is the sublimation of rapist/murderous actions into the taking and using of photographs. The second is the camera's role in the objectification of women.

In patriarchal discussion of the camera, that media extension is often seen as an operative double for the penis. For example, David Thompson, writing in *Film Comment*, deplores a tendency among young American male directors to reduce the women in their films to "still photographs," i.e. one-dimensional objects for voyeurism and little else. Still, he cautions:

---

*The authors of the *Malleus* call upon the authority of a saint Isidore to define *glamour*: "For a glamour is nothing but a certain delusion of the senses, and especially of the eyes." See James Sprenger and Heinrich Kramer, *The Malleus Maleficarum*, trans, and with an Introd. and notes by Montague Summers (c. 1928; New York: Dover, 1971), p. 59.

I would not want this article to be read as a feminist tract.... I am not sure that women can use the camera with the force and energy it has in the hands of, say, Martin Scorcese. That may be because photography itself is an invention, an art, and a trauma that comes from and speaks to man.[41]

Once again, any medium of creativity—be it a pen, paintbrush,* musical instrument, or camera—is seen as the direct emanation of man and the manly. The camera then seems, in the hands of a woman, to constitute an unnatural act, if not a castration. Yet Thompson surely is double-thinking here for, after so firmly identifying the camera with the masculine, i.e. the phallus, how can he then be surprised to find it used as a medium of sublimated sex crime, ranging from that objectifying voyeurism into rape and murder.

Such voyeurism (what we might call *eye-balling*)[42] is forthrightly spoken for by photographyer Bert Stern. He avers:

Making love and making photographs were closely connected in my mind when it came to women. Not that I made love to the women I photographed—but if I wanted a woman, a photograph was a very special way of having her.

Just a few months before Marilyn Monroe killed herself, Stern managed to arrange a photographic session with her. In his account of that session, Stern torridly confesses his enormous expectations of Monroe, his long-standing sexual fantasies concerning her, his dream of "shooting" her nude. According to him, he not only broke down her resistance and got her to take off her clothes, but that she then wanted to make love to him. This modern prince, however, took that opportunity to reject his no longer symbolic, fantastic, and sleeping beauty. He explains:

My desire for her was too pure, it bordered on awe. To make love to her would have been too much...and not enough.

But, of course, "making love" to her—despite the requisite lip service to Monroe's ultimate desirability—was not at all what he wanted. Like the sex killers, Stern preferred his fetish to his penis, a symbol to female reality. Indeed, Stern wanted precisely a symbolic possession and, again according to him, he got just that:

I saw what I wanted. I pressed the button, and she was mine....My love affair with Marilyn had been photographic. It had all the energies a love affair should have and none of the problems.[43]

*Auguste Renoir reportedly declared that he painted with his penis. See Sandra M. Gilbert and Susan Gubar, *The Madwoman in the Attic: The Woman Writer and the Nineteenth Century Literary Imagination* (New Haven: Yale University Press, 1979), p. 6.

What Stern reports as an ecstatic and fulfilling experience, if true, probably left Monroe only with a familiar and deepening alienation as once again she was reduced to the photograph, the sex object, the sex symbol, the thing.[44]

The implicit rapism and necrophilia of Stern's camera work are further elaborated by two other camera-men, and in another photographic medium, the film. In Michael Powell's *Peeping Tom* and Alfred Hitchcock's *Psycho* (both from 1960), the fundamental correspondencies between the Ages of the Camera and Sex Crime are made explicit.

Powell's *Peeping Tom* was at first roundly condemned as a degenerate production, but critical opinion has gradually shifted and it is now widely hailed as an avant-garde classic, a cinematic gem. In a publicity blurb, its distributor, Corinth films, cites Andrew Sarris to the effect that *Peeping Tom* has been "an inspiration to a whole new generation of American filmmakers....a cult film to end all cult films."[45] Insofar as American filmmakers, both mainstream and pornographic, depend upon gynocidal imagery and themes, this is absolutely correct.

Peeping Tom's plot concerns a man (made murderous due to his early traumatization by his father) who works in a film studio by day, but at night shoots pornographic movies. These are actually snuff films, for he murders the women as he films them; indeed, he literally kills them *with* his camera for there is a spear attached to it. Moreover, a mirror is positioned on the camera so that the victim must watch her own murder. After thus stealing her life, turning her being into his possessed image and her death into a scene, the killer then entertains himself by viewing his product. Director Michael Powell blithely assures us: "*Peeping Tom* is a very tender film, a very nice one. Almost a romantic film. I felt very close to the hero."[46]

That same year, Alfred Hitchcock released his "fun" picture, *Psycho*. This immediately popular and critically acclaimed movie actually addressed those very same issues of voyeurism, sexual murder, and the annihilating role of the camera as did *Peeping Tom*. *Psycho*, however, did it for the mainstream.

As has been frequently observed, a motif of voyeurism is integral to *Psycho*. In the very first scene of the film, we are confronted with the structural voyeurism of the camera itself as it scans the city of Phoenix, searching until it finally peers in a hotel window to gaze at half-dressed lovers. Next, there is the explicit voyeurism of the killer, Norman Bates (Anthony Perkins) who, as a prelude to sexual murder, stares through a peephole at Marion Crane (Janet Leigh) as she undresses for a shower. And finally, there is the implicit voyeurism of the film viewer. As Hitchcock himself described the intentional style of this film, "It allows the viewer to become a Peeping Tom."[47]

It is when the violence always lurking in voyeurism actually breaks out, that the key scene of the film occurs—the slashing murder of Marion Crane as she showers. This is the depiction that Raymond Durgnat classified as "pornographic murder," declaring that, in spite of himself, "the murder was too erotic not to enjoy."[48] This sexualization of female murder is one of the most elementary fixtures in sex crime propaganda.* In countless depictions of this type, the gynocidal scene is invariably accompanied by the standard conventions of pornographic depiction, the generic cues for sexual arousal. The female victim is shown undressing, bathing, even caressing herself and masturbating, unaware that (along with the film viewers) the sex killer is watching her. With the audience properly primed for a "sex scene," the killer then makes his entrance and embarks upon the conventional terrorization, mutilation, and murder.[49] Here sex and violence are ritually fused; gynocide becomes sexual climax for the film audience as well as the screen killer.

The "shower scene" in *Psycho* is the classic film depiction of such sex/murder. Still, this scene stands apart in that Hitchcock did not rely either upon graphic nudity or a detailed, bloody portrayal (as is more or less standard in the slasher films). Rather, he filmed in black and white and transmitted the message of sexual violence not only via the narrative, but also through cinematic technique. The murder scene runs for only forty-five seconds, but it consists of over seventy separate shots, all rapidly intercut. These show fragments of the woman's naked body, the knife, the killer, parts of the shower, etc. Only once do we see the knife against bare abdomen, and even then we do not see it actually cut the flesh. No explicit nudity or violence is shown at all. Regardless, the pornographic impact of this death scene can everywhere be measured in the responses of both critics and audiences.[50]

Hitchcock has widely congratulated himself for making such a "cinematic" film, a wonder of directorial virtuosity, a film *for* filmmakers. In an interview with Francois Truffaut he commented:

I feel it's tremendously satisfying for us to be able to use the cinematic art to achieve something of a mass emotion. And with *Psycho* we most definitely achieved this. It wasn't a message that stirred the audience, nor was it a great performance or their enjoyment of the novel. *They were aroused by pure film.* (emphasis mine)

To this, Truffaut responds, "Yes, that's true."[51]

Yet the two filmmakers are telling only half-truths. It is a flagrant lie that the content of the scene—the sexual murder of a woman, the paradigmatic gynocidal spectacle—is irrelevant to "audience" arousal.

*This structure is also, of course, evident in the murder scene in Mickey Spillane's *I, The Jury* (see Chapter V).

Rather, the power of the scene derives from Hitchcock's careful and pure fusion of medium and message. For in *Psycho*, Hitchcock is using the film itself as a "body double"—a double for the female body. Just as the director matches his camera "eye" to the voyeuristic killer's eye, he also wields his camera as a phallus/fetish/weapon in a direct parallel to the killer's wielding of the knife, thereby treating the film exactly as the killer treats the woman's body. The "message" of this scene tells of the cutting and slicing of a female body and Hitchcock, in a twin editorial frenzy, cuts, slashes, slices, and fragments the film itself. If in *Peeping Tom*, the woman is overtly killed *by* the camera, so too is she in *Psycho* although somewhat more abstractly. Moreover, by completely identifying the female body with his text, Hitchcock keeps perfect time with the traditions of sex crime, reducing woman to pure symbolic matter—his form, his production, his representation, his medium and his message.

"Representation of the world," writes de Beauvoir, "like the world itself, is the work of men; they describe it from their own point of view, which they confuse with absolute truth." Commenting on this, Catharine MacKinnon bluntly defines that viewpoint, "Woman through male eyes is sex object."[52] And that objectification has only hardened as men have further extended their views with electronic eyes.

Sex Objects

To photograph people is to violate them, by seeing them as they never see themselves, by having knowledge of them they can never have; it turns people into objects that can be symbolically possessed.

Susan Sontag[53]

He should have recognized that what really fascinated him was... to a degree, possessing them physically as one would possess a potted plant, a painting, or a Porsche. Owning, as it were, this individual.

Ted Bundy[54]

I saw what I wanted. I pressed the button, and she [Monroe] was mine.

Bert Stern

When they were being killed, there wasn't anything going on in my mind except that they were going to be mine.... That was the only way they could be mine.

Edmund Kemper[55]

The entrapment/possession of the female via her image is, of course, not a modern phenomenon. In *Ways of Seeing*, John Berger analyses the traditional depictions of women in European oil painting and the continuation of these conventions into contemporary imagery, especially advertising. He concludes that such depictions are structured by a world view and social reality in which:

> To be born a woman has been to be born within an allotted and confined space, into the keeping of men....A woman must continually watch herself. She is almost continually accompanied by her own image of herself.

Thus, in the eyes of both women and men, she is turned into an "object of vision: a sight."[56]

Similarly, Laura Mulvey in her critique of phallocentric film argues that under patriarchy men hold the gaze and make women into spectacles, objects of that gaze through a variety of forms and rituals: the nude in art, strip shows, chorus lines, beauty contests, "cheesecake," "girl-watching," fashion, personal mirror gazing, pornography, etc.[57] Of course, women are turned not only into the object, i.e. *aim*, of that gaze, but also into objects, i.e. *artifacts* for and by that gaze. Writing in *Critical Inquiry*, Susan Gubar stresses that men have made women into "art objects," "icons," and "dolls." As she sees it, this consists of being 'killed' into art," frozen into immanence as object or product, not creator or artist.[58]

In 1935, Walter Benjamin pointed to a radical change in the art object and the nature of art itself as a consequence of the new technologies of mechanical reproduction, particularly photography and the cinema. As he saw it, these technologies made obsolete the value once ascribed to the "originality," authenticity and uniqueness of the work of art. What, after all, can be said to be the original photograph, the original film? As a result of such technologies, a plurality of identical copies could be substituted for the unique existence of the art object. As such, uniqueness itself becomes devalued, meaningless, and correspondingly, "that which withers in the age of mechanical reproduction is the aura of the work of art."[59]

What then, we might wonder, have been the ramifications of this age on the perceived auras/reality of actual women, already reduced in the patriarchal world view to art objects, icons, symbols? Over thirty years ago, Marshall McLuhan noticed that something like the processes of mechanical reproduction were being applied to images of women. He spoke of a "love-goddess assembly line," a media mechanism whereby female images were churned out in a string of endless identical copies, clone-like, doll-like replacement parts.[60] Thus, accompanying the symbolic annihilation of genuine female presence, even distracting us from noticing it, is the concomitant manufacture of a ubiquity of interchangeable, unmemorable, literally fashioned, veritably glamorous "girls"—the cover girls,* poster girls, calendar girls, centerfolds, pinups,** boy toys, and animated Barbies fabricated and propagated throughout all avenues of mass imagery.

Ted Bundy speaks directly to the connections between these machinations/annihilations and those of his own. In his interviews with Michaud and Aynesworth, he was asked to explain the attitude of his "entity" toward the women he had murdered. The interviewer begins:

"Victims," I said. "You indicated that they would be symbols and images. But I'm not really sure. Images of what?"

"Of women!" he exclaimed. "I mean of the idealized woman.
What else can I say?"

"A stereotype?"

"No. They wouldn't be stereotypes necessarily. But they would be reasonable facsimiles to women as a class. A class not of women, per se, but a class that has almost been created through the mythology of women and how they are used as objects.[61]

After months of such discussion, Aynesworth and Michaud remark, "The girls that Ted Bundy talked about had no more flesh-and-blood reality to their killer than a Coppertone billboard."*** Yet is this really so safely aberrant, so "psychopathic," so rare? Many normal men and popular cultural conduits frequently and proudly convey those same malperceptions—expressing desires for dead women (be they Marilyn Monroe or Snow-white),[62] falling in love with pictures ("the girl I love is on a magazine cover"),[63] and seemingly unwilling or unable to

---

*For example, the cover girl makeup line passed from Cybil Shepard as the premier "cover girl" right into Cheryl Tiegs and then Christie Brinkley with scarcely a perceptible blink of its blonde, blue-eyed, and obviously racist, image.

**The slaughter of Dorothy Stratten by her ex-husband and promoter, Paul Snider, exemplifies the intermeshing of pornography, photography, and gynocide. Snider promoted Stratten (then eighteen) into *Playboy* fame, first as the found object of its "bunny hunt" and later as "Pinup of the Year." Stratten married Snider, but left him after a year. But Snider was obsessed with the continued possession of the woman he had, with the help of Hugh Hefner, fashioned into a pornographic object. He ultimately murdered Stratten, strapping her into a homemade bondage device and raping her both before and after fatally shooting her. He then killed himself, In the filmic retelling, *Star 80* (1983), director Bob Fosse insists that we make a connection between the incessant photographing of Stratten and the sexual shooting/murder of her. Snider is shown as obsessed with her photographic image, constantly taking pictures of her and using these to paper the walls of his apartment. Still, the film itself becomes pornographic, not only presenting Stratten herself (played by Mariel Hemingway) as the consummate dumb blonde, but getting all the necrophilic titillation it can out of the last gynocidal scene.

***Actually, a commercial played regularly on MTV throughout the last half of 1984 featuring a bikini-clad blonde in a sun-tan ad billboard "coming to life" and joining two cruising boys in a convertible.

distinguish between phalloglamour and female reality (as Van Halen sings it, "Are you for real, it's so hard to tell, from just a magazine").[64]

Bundy referred to his victims not only as "symbols," "images," and "the object," but also as "puppets" and "dolls." And matching the symbolic capture/annihilation of women through photographic imagery, is the three-dimensional construction of more solid advertisements for female unreality—the quintessentially "plastic woman"—the pornographic doll or mannequin.

"Living" Dolls

...if I killed them, you know, they couldn't reject me as a man. It was more or less making a doll out of a human being...and carrying out my fantasies with a doll, a living human doll.

Edmund Kemper[65]

I'd rather have a paper doll to call my own than have a fickle-minded real live girl.

The Mills Brothers, 1943[66]

As Simone de Beauvoir observed, "One is not born, but rather becomes, a woman."[67] The most basic symbol of this procedure is the doll or mannequin, an icon that stretches from the patriarchal myth of Pandora through the miniature sex object Barbie.[68] Moreover, this icon is, as Susan Griffin writes, "the pornographic object's most quintessential form":

Pornography is replete with images and evocations of the "doll," an actual plastic copy of a woman, made to replace a woman, and to give a man pleasure without the discomfort of female presence. In fantasy, this object appears everywhere in poetry, in stories, in novels. And in fact, we find that the "doll" is actually sold through pornographic shops.[69]

The doll is so classic an icon to patriarchal/pornographic culture because it not only profanes the once sacred female body and image, but also because it so purely betokens the man-made woman, the truly *fashionable* woman,* the veritable object of possession.

Moreover, the doll is a central icon to the Age of Sex Crime, an age in which men turn women into objects/toys for their so-called "recreational murders." Significantly, that age has been marked by a proliferation of pornographic doll fantasies. One, *The Future Eve* (1887) concerns a rejected young lover going to the inventor Thomas Edison, imploring him to scientifically remedy his plight. The inventor complies with his wishes and constructs a perfect mechanical replica of the lost love.[70] Eighty years later, Ira Levin parodied this recurrent theme in

---

Fashion is derived from the Latin *facere*—to make, shape. Hence the "fashionable woman" is the one who can best be made, shaped, contrived.

his novel, *The Stepford Wives*.[71] In the affluent haven of Stepford Connecticut, all is not well. The family men have bonded into a "Men's Association" which manufactures a nearly indistinguishable, though ineffably more glamorous, robot replica of the members' wives, allowing the husband to personally kill his wife and simultaneously acquire a mechanical replacement. The artificial substitute is preferred not only for its better looks and longer shelf life, but also for its more compatible personality, superb sexual performance, and superior housekeeping abilities.

Another doll fantasy dating from the nineteenth century, *La Femme Endormie* (The Benumbed Woman, 1899) is excerpted by the Kronhausens in their history of erotic fantasies. The story concerns a shy, middle-aged man who commissions an artist to build him a doll sex partner. Delighted with the object, he christens it "Mea," i.e. *mine*. The Kronhausens noncritically relate this "idea of manufacturing and using an artificial woman" to the concomitant manufacture of "inflatable or foam-rubber vaginas." They cite as illustration this ad from a French magazine in the late 1890s:

FEMALE BELLY
With Artificial Vagina

Designed to give the man the perfect illusion of a real woman by providing him with just as sweet and voluptuous sensations as she herself.

Outwardly, the apparatus represents a woman's abdomen, minus the legs....

This female tummy with lubrication is the only apparatus that duplicates exactly the copulatory organs of the woman [and is therefore the only one] capable of giving the perfect illusion of reality.

Being readily inflatable and deflatable, the apparatus can be as easily hidden in the pocket as a handkerchief or any other toilet article.[72]

Here the doll motif, the imagined manufacture of a "total woman," blends seamlessly with the marked pornographic penchant for "parts"— detachable female parts. Jack the Ripper explicitly enacted the sexual violence implicit in all such imaginings and apparatuses. He actually did carry away the "copulatory organs" of his victims; moreover, he mutilated their bodies so badly that they were then inevitably described as "broken dolls."[73]

If the doll—the perfect, plastic illusion of a woman—is clearly central to the masculine realm of pornography, so too is the doll—as mannequin—an elementary fixture of feminine fashion. Moreover, women are exhorted to make that mannequin their model in more ways than one. An article on master designer Christian Dior revealed that,

"The greatest of M. Dior's virtues, of course, is his burning desire to make all women beautiful. 'My desire,' he says, 'is to save them from nature.' "[74] Who, however, will save us from M. Dior, for conformity to that pornographic ideal of "beauty," often requires both the artificialization and the veritable mutilation of the natural female body.[75]

The always implicit commingling of fashion and pornography has become increasingly conspicuous in the past decade as the more rakish fashion photographers regularly spike their shots with nudity, scenes of sado-masochism, and suggestions of sexual violation.[76] Perhaps the most flagrant of these is Helmut Newton, a regular contributor to French and American *Vogue*, as well as to *Playboy* and *Oui*. One of Newton's trademarks, along with the use of prosthetic devices on his models and scenes of sexual slavery and ritual murder, is the photography of wax mannequins as if they were living women. Edward Behr, an editor of European *Newsweek*, introduces one of Newton's books, *Sleepless Nights*:

But above all, here is a man who loves women so passionately, so completely, that he has to carry this love to its ultimate conclusion. Look, he says, in a brace, a plaster cast, even in an artificial limb, she remains beautiful and desirable. And since models and mannequins are objects, to be manipulated at will, why not attempt the final manipulation, the mingling of real life and wax models? Do we really know the difference—not only here, but also in real life?[77]

Such "love" is reminiscent of the "love" of Jack the Ripper for his "work." Moreover, as Mr. Behr so self-satisfiedly proclaims, the boundaries between the real and the artificial, the being and the object, are being intentionally and successfully confused. Such themes of overt objectification have become increasingly common in all types of fashion imagery—from the everyday to the avant-garde.[78] Moreover, in the three-dimensional world, actual women are hired to work as so-called "living dolls," "robot models" who stand around in stores pretending to be mannequins.[79] Meanwhile, store designers scorn the use of male mannequins because, as one put it, "they never look real."[80] Female fakes, it seems, easily look "real," just as actual women can easily be made to look fake, because women have so long and so systematically been propagandized as artificial, because one of the top ten commandments of the gynocidal state is a disbelief in the reality of women.

Donald Lunde, Stanford University expert on mass murder, tells us, "To the sex murderer the victims may be viewed as 'life-size' dolls rather than fellow human beings."[81] Concomitantly, Irving Berlin pens (and multitudes sing along), "A doll I can carry, the girl that I marry must be."[82] Obviously, the projection of women as dolls is not only a penchant of the sex killer, nor exclusively a pornographic icon. Rather, the "female doll" is so pervasive a projection that it serves to identify the fundamentally pornographic character of this culture itself. And finally, it is the icon of the doll, the artificial replacement/simulation of a woman, that reveals the most elementary bonds among the Ages of Mechanical Reproduction, Technology, Plastic, Nuclearism, and Sex Crime. To begin to unravel these connections, we can turn once again to Marshall McLuhan who designated a female dummy, what he termed the "mechanical bride," as the most telling symbol of the modern, technological era.

Just Like A Woman

I'm gonna make me a girl machine/and build me a doll that looks like a dream....
"Girl Machine," *Warner Weidler*, 1961[83]

Why Is A Beautiful Woman Like A Nuclear Power Plant?
In order to remain beautiful she must take good care of herself... she schedules her rest regularly...when she is not feeling well she sees her doctor...she never lets herself get out of shape...she is as trim now as she was ten years ago...in other words, *she is a perfect example of preventative maintenance.*
—ad for the Crouse group of companies, 1976[84]

He said: Isn't *it*. Isn't *it* just. Isn't *it* just like a woman?
"It Tango," *Laurie Anderson*, 1981[85]

In 1951, in *The Mechanical Bride: Folklore of Industrial Man,* McLuhan pointed to what he found to be "one of the most peculiar features of our world—the interfusion of sex and technology....a widely occurring cluster image of sex, technology, and death which constitutes the mystery of the mechanical bride."[86] At the heart of this mystery, according to McLuhan, rests: 1) the pervasive sexualization* of technology—engines, cars "bodies by Fisher," even a nuclear bomb nicknamed "Gilda" after reigning sex symbol Rita Hayworth; and 2) the corresponding mechanization of the female body into a set of fragmented, fetishized, and replaceable parts—legs, breasts, buttocks, forming what is basically a plastic mechanism, a hot number, a sex object, sex bomb, living doll, love machine. McLuhan relates this interfusion of technology, sex, and death to a hunger to "explore and enlarge the domain of sex by mechanical technique, on the one hand, and, on the other to possess machines in a sexually gratifying way." He draws our attention to the increasing movement, in both fact and fiction, toward the use of sadistic violence as both sexual thrill and metaphysical invasion and suggests that technology plays a critical role

---

*By *sexualization*, McLuhan actually means *feminization* and hence ignores for the large part the masculinization of technology, particularly weaponry, as discussed in Chapter Five.

in creating this hunger for ever more intense thrills, resulting in a ghoulish public mentality that:

> ...reaches out for the *inside* story smoking hot from the entrails of vice or innocence. That may well be what draws people to the death shows of the speedways and fills the press and magazines with close-ups of executions, suicides, and smashed bodies. A metaphysical hunger to experience everything sexually, to pluck out the heart of the mystery for a super-thrill.[87]

Cognizant of the paradigmatic character of sex crime, we can recognize this not only as a technological, but also as a Ripper way of knowledge.

Since 1951, the patterns that McLuhan pinpointed have only intensified and proliferated; in ads, fashion and pornography, on television, in popular novels, films and songs—the mechanical bride is everywhere. To cite only a few of the more telling examples for his first category, the technological container for feminine symbolism, I would refer to an ongoing motif of feminization in any number of car ads. A 1964 Pontiac ad, for example, told its expectant buyers, "Any car that is this responsive, obedient, and satisfying to drive simply has no right to be this good looking." More recently, ads for Volvo urge, "Fall in love in 6.8 seconds flat," (1983) while one for Nissan informs us, "The headlights wink; the engine growls; the styling flirts."* (1983) Recall as well National Airlines' sensational 1971 "Fly Me" campaign in which a woman and an airplane are posited as identical. A 1980s ad for Technics portable stereo shows its product surrounded by curling smoke and attended by a black cat; the copy reads, "Technology Made Seductive."

The second of McLuhan's categories—the mechanization/fragmentation of images of women, the dissection of woman into "parts," continues full force. One of McLuhan's original illustrations is an ad for nylon stockings depicting the frankly disembodied "legs on a pedestal." Of course, this symbolic dismemberment of women has always been normative in pornography. Still, it is illuminating to realize how common the pornographic composition is in mainstream imagery; indeed such imagery is nearly invisible due to its ubiquity. For example, a smiling ad for "Tame" hair conditioner (1979) routinely chops up a female body image in order to ask, "Is there a part of you that's overconditioned?" One, for Almay eye shadow, (1981), simply presents a V-shaped design

---

*Most stunning is a 1984 television ad for Mercury Cougar. With Frank Sinatra crooning romantically in the background, a man is shown strolling through various outdoor locations accompanied by a woman. But they are not alone. He is being stalked persistently and amorously by a Mercury Cougar that 'winks,' purrs and relentlessly pursues him. The attention of the man is continually diverted from the woman and drawn irresistibly to his dream lover—the car.

of disembodied, though colorful, female eyes. Another for Yves Saint Laurent stockings (1980) shows a pair of high-heeled legs, cut off at the waist and waving in the air. If these are subliminally disturbing, fashion photographer Guy Bourdin is explicitly so. In a fashion shot for shoes, he presents a pair of detached mannequin legs striding into a room to join another pair of dummy legs seated at a table.[88]

The intent and effect of all such fashionable and pornographic symbolic dismemberments can best be understood by listening to an actual murderer/dismemberer describe the meaning of his actions:

Then I cut her throat so she would not scream...at this time I wanted to cut her body so she would not look like a person and destroy her so she would not exist. I began to cut on her body. I remember cutting her breasts off. After this, all I remember is that I kept cutting on her body.... I did not rape the girl. I only wanted to destroy her.[89]

Clearly, the "fantastic," partial, plastic, objectified, unreal, dead and dismembered women of fashion and pornography reflect and propagate the ripper-eye-view of the world, the reality of sex crime. Indeed, the "lust-murder" is characteristically defined as one in which there is an extreme fetishization of sexualized parts, frequently accompanied by the actual dismemberment of the body.[90] Still, MuLuhan insists that the mechanical bride is a symbol of *technology*. Following this icon further, we might then puzzle out the ways in which technology and sex crime interconnect.

Legitimate popular imagery is as rife with full-blown presentations of artificial women/mechanical brides as pornography is with evocations of the doll. For example, a 1985 advertisement from the Canned Food Information Council (in both print and video versions*) displays a shiny, curvaceous, aluminum-like fembot,[91] eyeless but wearing lipstick and high heels, to transmit their message that, "In the year 3000, food will come in...cans."

Of course, that is by far not the only message communicated by this consummate icon. A 1982 ad for Fuji audiocassettes is more direct. Against a grid of lines superimposed upon black space, a shiny faceless mechanical woman is curled up in fetal position. The copy reads: "Imagination Has Just Become Reality." Here the admen tell us frankly whereas many social scientists can only equivocate. Fantasy does effect/become reality; imaginations are, and are meant to be, enacted. Indeed, it is partially through the pervasion of such images that a new phallotechnic reality is being summoned into existence.

The character of that reality, as well as the connections between the Ages of Technology and Sex Crime, become ever more apparent as we read on:

Audiocassettes of such remarkable accuracy and clarity that *differences between original and recording virtually vanish.* (emphasis mine)

Similarly, Memorex audio and video tapes swear that their products will leave us forever wondering, "Is it live, or is it Memorex?", while an ad for Gould Electronics, a company which proclaims that it is "leading the way in nuclear power plant simulations," avers in a 1983 ad, "At Gould Simulation Is Reality." Of course, all such promises are uncannily similar to: 1) the 1890s pornographic apparatus which proffered a "perfect illusion of a real woman"; 2) the phalloglamorous images and "final manipulations" of photographer Helmut Newton; and 3) the mindset

---

*The video version was showcased during Superbowl, 1985.

of a sex murderer such as Ted Bundy who apparently couldn't or wouldn't distinguish between an image and a living female being.

If the world of mechanical reproduction clearly claims the mechanical bride as its own, so too does the world of nuclear arms. In early 1984, the *New York Times* reported on a group of dedicated young scientists hard at work on "Star Wars" research at the Lawrence Livermore Laboratory. We learn that these young men work six or seven days a week on top-secret projects "aimed at creating the next generation of nuclear weapons." At the same time, "Their dream, they say, is to end the nuclear arms race." Moreover:

Here the average scientist is in his 20s and few, if any, wear wedding rings. *No women are present* except for secretaries. The kitchen has a microwave oven, a hot plate, a refrigerator, and a mountain of empty Coke bottles.[92] (emphasis mine)

Here, surrounded by culinary evocations of the mechanical bride (but no real women to disturb their security), these young priests swallow Coke, dream of their weapons, and tinker with world destruction. Their desires are for potency; they want to father that third generation of nuclear weapons. They happily follow the fathers before them: Robert Oppenheimer (named "Father of the Year" by the American Baby Association in 1945 for his "Little Boy"—the nickname for the Hiroshima bomb); the five fathers of plutonium;[93] Edward Teller (father of the Hydrogen bomb) and, of course, Dr. Victor Frankenstein. It can still give one pause to realize how prophetic, how hauntingly accurate Mary Shelley was when she conceived the exemplary monster of technological myth to be a purely fathered (from dead flesh) creation.

Here also, we can receive intense intuitions on McLuhan's "mystery" of the mechanical bride. For this symbol is one which links technology to creation/fertility via an artificial woman. It thus betokens the utter enmity which phallotechnic man declares for living flesh and blood creation—motherhood, the womb, nature, the Earth itself. The mechanical bride, then, is mechanical *reproduction.** As such, it is not only the indistinguishable copy, but also the nuclear breeder, the artificial womb. As an icon, it signals the longed-for replacement of the elemental and organic world by an artificial, indistinguishable substitute, a perfect

---

*Gena Corea notes that various critics have made the point that contemporary culture has adopted the factory term *reproduction* to refer to procreation. She also provides a feminist analysis of the male technologies which attempt to both control and replace the female womb in *The Mother Machine: Reproductive Technologies from Artificial Insemination to Artificial Wombs* (New York: Harper and Row, 1985).

delivered from the "Future Eve,"*   the controlled womb/tomb of the mechanical bride. And this is a curious form of all-male mating for the mechanical bride is absolutely empty of any genuine femaleness, as false as Norman Bates' "mother" in *Psycho*, as plastic as a pornographic doll. Actually, the mechanical bride is a technological "Tootsie"; it is veritably a transsexed image of themselves and their technology for whom these young priests lust. It is "she" to whom they are truly wed, "she" with whom they mate to produce their inventions/generations/sons/ monsters. And finally, a core meaning of the mechanical bride is that— like the Lawrence Livermore Lab, like the sacred media world, and like the Stepford world the fathers are wishing us into—no women are *present*.

Obviously a parallel animus marks the Age of Sex Crime. For, as the patriarchs cast women into the role of the symbolic sex, all that they enact upon nature and the world is ritually enacted upon women. Not only are many of the contemporary sex killers actual matricides, but one of the most telling acts of the mythic forefather, Jack the Ripper, was both the mutilation of the womb as well as the actual theft of that organ from one of his victims. The violation and possession of the womb— be it in the form of knife attacks on the victim of a sexual murder or phallotechnic assaults on the metaphorical Mother Earth—form parallel processions to that proposed final/funereal marriage of mankind to the mechanical bride. The only possible consummation of such a union would be the total contamination and/or destruction of the elemental Earth and a final ensconsement in an artificial and dead environment— again, something like the parable of the Stepford husbands who preferred to murder their living wives and bury themselves into man-made mechanical brides, and, again, something like the ritual action of the sex killer who attacks and destroys the womb, the place of original generation.

The pornographic imagination of such utter destructiveness brings us, inevitably, to the Nuclear Age.

Mass Murders

As for being a mass killer, does not the world encourage it?
Is it not building weapons of destruction for the sole purpose of mass killing? Has it not blown unsuspecting women and little children to pieces and done it very scientifically? As a mass killer, I am an amateur by comparison.

Monsieur Verdoux (Charles Chaplin, 1947)

---

*As the well-known logo from Apple Computer—the artificial apple with the bite taken out—wordlessly testifies, the coming "paradise" is an artificial one.

The world has caught up with me and surpassed me. Ninety years ago I was a freak...now I'm an amateur.

Jack the Ripper, in *Time After Time* (N. Meyer, 1979)

Although the interconnections between sexual and phallotechnic violences are rarely explicitly addressed in contemporary critical thinking, they do surface from time to time in the popular culture.

Monsieur Verdoux (1947) was Charles Chaplin's last film made in the United States. Before *Verdoux*, Chaplin, through his much beloved character of the Little Tramp, had come to be the quintessential symbol of the "common man," innocence, survival, and the soul or spirit.[94] After 1936, however, Chaplin abandoned the Tramp character and by the time of *Verdoux* had opted to present himself as a far more serious man—a bank clerk who, having lost his job due to economic depression, matter-of-factly begins a new career of marrying wealthy widows and murdering them. This was the least popular of Chaplin's feature films. His public, apparently, did not wish to hear his message that the common man no longer had much of a soul, was no longer an innocent but had become a mass murderer. Critics too, in general, expressed distaste for *Monsieur Verdoux*, especially for the last scene where Verdoux, having allowed himself to be caught, makes a courtroom speech explicitly analogizing his mass murders of women to those mass killings so recently accomplished by the atomic bomb.

Some years later, Stanley Kubrick released his morbid comedy, *Dr. Strangelove: Or How I Learned to Stop Worrying and Love the Bomb* (1963).* In this film, the madman militarist who triggers world nuclear holocaust is the appropriately named General Jack D. Ripper. The General, obsessed with what he sees as a worldwide Communist plot to pollute his "purity of essence" through fluoridation of water, decides to wipe out the Soviet Union on his own initiative. He triggers "Plan R" (R for Romeo), instructing airborne bombers to launch a nuclear attack. This move ultimately results in the detonation of the Soviet's deterrence device, the "Doomsday Machine." The film thus ends with the end of the world, but before doomsday, Ripper elaborates his ideas to his captive, Colonel Mandrake:

Mandrake: Tell, me, Jack, when did you first become, well, develop this theory.

Ripper: Well, I first became aware of it, Mandrake, during the physical act of love— yes—a profound sense of fatigue, a feeling of emptiness followed. Luckily, I was able to interpret those feelings correctly—loss of essence. I can assure you it has not recurred.

---

*The title is somewhat reminiscent of traditional advice to rape victims, "If you're going to be raped, why don't you just lie back and enjoy it."

Women, women sense my power and they seek the life essence. I do not avoid women, Mandrake, but I do deny them my essence.

Like his prototype and namesake, General Ripper does not believe in "sexual intercourse with his victims, but very likely the murderous act and subsequent mutilation of the corpse were equivalents for the sexual act" (Krafft-Ebing). In the General's case, however, the mutilation murder is an all-out nuclear attack and the female corpse in the planet Earth.

The Dead Zone, Stephen King's best-selling novel, not only showcases the fashionable myth of the sex killer's monstrous mother, but poses yet another correlation between nuclear annihilation and serial sexual murder.[95] The story concerns a psychic, Johnny Smith, who is able to envision the future of anyone he touches. In the course of the novel, Smith is called upon first to solve and then to prevent two modern forms of mass murder. The first is the serial sex killings of young girls in a small Maine Town; the second is world nuclear war.

To solve the first, Smith identifies Maine's "Castle Rock Killer" as Frank Dodd, a trusted member of the local police force. Afterwards, he finds himself somewhat unaccountably attending political rallies, seeking out opportunities to shake the hands of politicians. Smith soon realizes that he has unconsciously connected the "patterned destructive madness of Frank Dodd" to some parallel madness he senses in the political arena. He confirms this intuition when grasping the hand of rising demagogue, Greg Stillson, and receiving a nightmare vision of that man as future president "pushing the button," initiating nuclear war, and going down as the "greatest mass murderer in world history." Now understanding Stillson to be what he calls "the political equivalent of Frank Dodd," Smith sets out to stop him and, somewhat waywardly, he does.

As all of these dreamlike themes and images from popular culture suggest, the Nuclear Age is intricately bound to the Age of Sex Crime.

Dangers of the Same Kind

Love is a danger of a different kind,
Takes you away and leaves you far behind....
It's savage and it's cruel and it shines like destruction.

"Love is a Stranger," *The Eurythmics*, 1983[96]

Nuclear Energy—Safer than Sex!

slogan of Safe (Society for the Advancement of Fission Energy)[97]

The bonds between the Nuclear Age and the Age of Sex Crime—the correlations between patriarchal conceptualizations of weaponry, worship, safety and danger, the sacred and the profane, women, taboo, the Earth and nature—are far too complex to be explored in their entirety here and will be reserved for a later work. For now, I will indicate only the most basic associations between nuclearism and "sex," perhaps the two extremities of danger in the modern world.

Five decades ago, Walter Benjamin understood that sense perceptions have been ineluctably altered by technology, resulting in a situation whereby:

Mankind, which in Homer's time was an object of contemplation for the Olympian gods, now is one for itself. Its self-alienation has reached such a degree that it can experience its own destruction as an aesthetic pleasure of the first order.[98]

It has been, perhaps, a lesser degree of that same "self-alienation" which accounts for mankind's historical tendency to experience the destruction of Others as an aesthetic, even erotic, pleasure of the first order. Now even mankind itself is faced with destruction, and the technologies of mass annihilation have exposed not only the gynocidal/biocidal/genocidal obsessions of patriarchy, but also the suicidal.

Robert Jay Lifton, one of the most insightful commentators on the Nuclear Age, has identified what he calls a "nuclear high" mindset—a culture-wide impression "of the nuclear explosion as the ultimate 'high state,' as the "only form of transcendence worthy of the age."[99] Such an enjoyment, aestheticization, even worship, of destruction glares out from William L. Laurence's Pulitzer prize-winning eyewitness report of the bombing of Nagasaki, an essentially celebratory account of the "thing of beauty" that snuffed out the lives of so many beings in that city. Laurence was aboard the flight of the bomber, the *Great Artiste*, and gave this sky-view of the blast (expediently ignoring any realization of the agony below):

...there came shooting out of the top a giant mushroom that increased the height of the pillar to a total of forty-five thousand feet. The mushroom top was even more alive than the pillar, seething and boiling in a white fury of creamy foam....As the first mushroom floated off into the blue it changed its shape into a flower-like form, its giant petals curving downward, dreamy white outside, rose-colored inside."[100]

If the Age of Sex Crime is fundamentally marked by an eroticization/enjoyment of agony and destruction, so too is the Nuclear Age.

And just as men are conditioned through pornography to equate arousal to subordination and violence, a pornography of nuclearism widely propagates the rapturous degradation, diminishment, replacement and destruction of the Earth. From science fiction *(Childhood's End)* through that good old-time religion *(The Late Great Planet Earth)*[101] and into advertising imagery, the demise of the Earth is everywhere and often enthusiastically imagined.

In the summer of 1984, for example, two very telling ads appeared in the business pages of the *New York Times*. The first (25 June 1984) was for Saudia Airlines. A split screen composition was used. On the left hung an image of the Earth, the globe as if seen from space. It was captioned, "The Problem." On the right are pictured four long jet planes, made to seem as if they are larger than the planet itself and aiming directly at the Earth. They were captioned, "And how we got round it." On the very next day (26 June 1984), *Science* magazine took out an ad to promote its upcoming 5th anniversary issue, one to be devoted to "20 Discoveries That Shaped The 20th Century." To impress that upon their viewers, they visualized two gigantic male hands, grasping, shaping, crushing and dwarfing a puny, malleable, pathetic and vulnerable Earth. Other recent ads resound the message. To cite only a few, one for Perrier water (1984) shows a giant bottle triumphantly bursting out of the top of a now dwarfed and violated planet. Another for Cobra phone answering machines (1984) pictures that machine floating over the surface of a planet which is no longer even composed of land and water, but, instead, of Cobra phone answering machines. Another, for a *Newsweek* publication (1984) chops the globe in half, announcing that it is "On Top Down Under." Finally, an ad for Rockwell International* (1985) headlines itself with the deformed word "man-ij" in boldface, assuring us that Rockwell is "not out to change the world. Just to supply the technology it takes to make it better." To illustrate this well man-ijed planet (and to counterpoint the mangled word) the Earth is depicted as if it were a projection on a computer screen. The top half of the sphere is sectioned into four pieces; the bottom disappears into the omnipresent abstract grid. Bolts penetrate the planet at both axes as well as through the middle.

These are all advertising images, but it is two non-advertising illustrations that bring us round to the core meaning of all such depictions and at the same time manifest the deep connections between the Age of Sex Crime and the Nuclear Age. The first takes form in a political cartoon in the *Nation*, 25 February 1984. It shows a grinning Henry Kissinger, naked but draped with the American flag, raping a woman whose head is the planet Earth. This is *motherfucking* precisely and the image graphically illustrates why *motherfucker* is the most charged word in the English language. Although nominally obscene, taboo, this is consummate patriarchal reversal for this curse is actually a command— and one heard and obeyed by the most sensationalized sex criminals as well as the most powerful politicians. Moreover, as companion to the Age of Sex Crime, the Nuclear Age presages the escalation of the

*Rockwell is a major contractor for both the MX missile and the B-1 bomber.

Reprinted with the permission of
Rockwell International.

paradigmatic rape of the mother into a rape-murder, i.e. total annihilation.

The second image is from the cover of the *Atlantic*, November 1984, and refers to an inside article on nuclear winter.* The illustration depicts a man (we see only his military arms labeled *U.S.*) holding an irradiated, glowing Earth in his hands. Moreover, the shrunken planet is now serving as the dot under a hovering question mark of black smoke. Once again, *he* has the whole world in his hands; once again, the planet is diminutive to the man. And just as the woman on her back with legs spread-eagled is the characteristic icon of female defeat in the Age of Sex Crime, these images of the diminished and violated Earth are the characteristic icons in a pornography of the Nuclear Age.

While the pornography of the Age of Sex Crime pictures women as plastic, displayed, dead, dismembered victims/objects, its Nuclear Age counterpart depicts the Earth as a threatened, abused, halved, shrunken, malleable, replaceable, and ultimately artificial object. Such visualizations form part of a ubiquitous phallotechnic propaganda, images meant not only to sell a particular product or illustrate a certain concept, but also to sell and embed a mindset in which those products and conceptions can attain a reality. These pictures are the working images of the phallotechnic state, acts of faith in its own existence and prayers for its continuing and future control of reality. Each set of synergetic visualizations legitimates the joint possession and destruction of both women and nature, heralds and promotes the plasticization, re-formation and replacement of the natural environment.**

This close association between gynocide and scientific practices and propaganda is not unique to the current era but was, as well, an essential feature of the European Witchcraze. As Carolyn Merchant has argued, those atrocities were synchronous with a scientific revolution and

---

*The flow sequence in this issue is quite stunning. Following the cover article, titled "Nuclear Winter and Nuclear Strategy," are a number of pages titled the "Atlantic Winter [Vacation] Travel Planner."

**Currently some scientists, locating themselves in what they term the "infancy of the Space Age," speak of the necessity of redesigning the Earth and other planets to better suit man's needs. They call this process "terraforming" or "planetary engineering." It is something like cosmic cosmetic surgery by archetypal rippers. Methods proposed including setting off nuclear bombs on Mars to melt the polar ice caps, etc. A recent book on this subject offered some Orwellian advice to such potential engineers: "Terra-formers may think of themselves as restoring the planet rather than raping it." See James Edward Oberg, *New Earths: Restructuring Earth and Other Planets* (New York: New American Library, 1981), p. 157.

NOVEMBER 1984
$2.00
The Atlantic
MTM AS THE FIRST YUPPIE / THE SEARCH FOR EXTRATERRESTRIAL LIFE
IS NUCLEAR WAR "IMPOSSIBLE"?
BY THOMAS POWERS
If the "nuclear winter" theory is correct, superpower war plans are obsolete
U.S.

resultant revisioning of world view whereby the dominant metaphors of the Earth as a living organism and Nature as a benevolent female principle were overthrown and replaced by a projection of the Earth and Nature as chaotic and unruly, wild and dangerous forces that men had to rule and control. The ideologically constructed witch was made into the central symbol of such wild and dangerous "evil," functioning as the most "suasive" scapegoat of the reconstructed world view. Indeed, the basic movement of the scientific revolution was ritually played out in the very structures and practices of the Witchcraze. The courtroom inquisitions, the ceaseless interrogations, the torture of women with mechanical devices: all of these precisely paralleled the emerging scientific model of men's supreme power over Nature, the mandate to probe and interrogate her "mysteries," to use science and mechanism as the method by which men could extract her deeply guarded secrets.[102]

Just as the gynocidal myths and methods of the Witchcraze paralleled those of the scientific revolution, so do similar correspondencies now exist between the Ages of Sex Crime and Techno-Nuclearism. Now too, there are vast shifts in the phallocentric world view, major alterations in the definitions of creation and reproduction, the said boundaries of the natural and the artificial, the original and the copy, in the meanings of sex and violence, in feelings about the Earth and space. Again, parallel annihilating stereotypes are being pasted onto both women and Nature, with the mechanical bride emerging as a central symbol in both the phallotechnic and sex crime ideologies. That most "suasive" projection is then re-visioned in the imagineered visualizations of the Earth as the "man-ijed," plasticized, and reconstructed planet. Equally, the pornographic culture's image of woman as object/victim is precisely analogous to the phallotechnic attitude of use, contamination, and destruction of the natural environment. The fetish-weapons wielded by sex killers all too gruesomely recall the jealously appropriated tools of national "defense." And finally, the actual torture, ravagements, mutilations, and annihilations of individual women by sex murderers function as parallel rituals to the larger phallotechnic "crimes against nature," the sex crimes, i.e. sexually political crimes, committed daily against "Mother Earth." Thus, the core identifying link between the Age of Sex Crime and the Nuclear Age is the cosmic stretching of the patriarchal imagination of destruction and a concomitant lust to mutilate the very origin and source of Life—a lust which can be enacted upon a concrete female body or directed against the Earth itself by the strategists, technicians, and politicians of nuclearism.

And for those of us who find ourselves, to our inexpressible grief, both living and dying in the joint Ages of Sex Crime and Nuclearism, we must recognize that "Jack the Ripper" sits not only at the head of the chamber of commerce, but behind the camera, in the halls of government, in the Pentagon, and in the laboratories. Moreover, what the newscaster called his "ghost"* hovers not only over Washington, D.C., but over all the man-made world and its institutions. In all of these interconnecting manifestations, he must be exposed, denounced, and exorcised. He must be stopped.

*See Chapter 1.

Epilogue

Those sisters are the "disappeared" of the women's movement. I *will* call out their names until the day comes when sex means something *else* besides women's dead bodies. I live for that day. On that day, I will be silent. I will remember those sisters who have been permanently silenced. Then, I will thank those who changed the world.

Annie McCombs[1]

...in addition all women who died or who demonstrated remarkable courage & integrity during rape attacks are given congressional medals of honor/ or the purple heart/ we shall have streets and monuments named after/ these women & children they died for their country.

Ntozake Shange[2]

My purpose here has been to demonstrate that modern, Western, serial sex murder is gynocide, sexually political murder, an extreme form of terrorism in the service of the patriarchal state. That state maintains control not only through such guided terrorism, but also by means of a tandem phalloglamour—the imposition of illusion, the severance of sense knowledge and perception from experience, something akin to what Robert Lifton was talking about when he wrote of the "psychic numbing" which characterizes consciousness in the Nuclear Age.[3] Thus, we live in the midst of a twentieth-century witchcraze and nowhere in the official consciousness is that recognized. Rarely even in the common consciousness is that knowledge fully comprehended, that outrage completely realized, the connections freely and fully drawn among this manifestation of patriarchal annihilation and its brother expressions, past and present.

In *Gyn/Ecology: The Metaethics of Radical Feminism*, Mary Daly exposed and analyzed five "sado-rituals." These are actions which recreate and reinforce the primordial patriarchal mythic event—the murder and dismemberment of the Goddess. As Daly writes, these are rituals which attempt to annihilate the "Self-affirming be-ing"—creative divine life and integrity—in *all* women by their targeted destruction of a number of concrete, existing women.[4] She examines such sado-rituals as Indian suttee, Chinese footbinding, the European witchburnings, African genital mutilations, and American gynecological practices. Sifting out the interconnections among these, Daly arrives at a "Sado-Ritual Syndrome," a set of intermeshed components of such rites which can be used as

198

a framework to manifest the deep interconnections among all such patriarchal atrocities. Thus the generic identity of sex crime to other gynocidal rites can be demonstrated by applying the seven points of that Syndrome to this contemporary criminal phenomenon.

"In the Sado-Ritual we find, first, an obsession with purity." The theme of the sexual killer obsessed with cleansing or rooting out impure women, paradigmatically prostitutes, dates from the origin myth and method of Jack the Ripper. Just as that killer is the archetype of the sex murderer, his chosen prey, the prostitute, remains phallocracy's archetypal victim/scapegoat—the man-made bad girl, the consecrated token of the sexual impurity which patriarchal culture tacitly imputes to all women. As such, not only the killer himself frequently is obsessed with destroying those whom he views as "scum" and "filth," but those tastemakers of phallic morality in the professions and media display many of the same obsessions as the killers, carefully classifying the victims as "good" or "bad," "pure" or "impure."

"Second, there is total erasure of responsibility for the atrocities performed through such rituals." The widely accepted diagnosis of *psychopath* to define those who perform these rites functions not only to absolve the individual killers themselves (who are then implicitly innocent "by reason of insanity"), but that mythic diagnosis similarly protects society itself. If the men who perform such actions are inexplicable aberrations, no one need look to social norms, institutions, and ideologies to find the bases of sexual murder. In aberration/insanity no one is responsible, no one left to blame...except, of course, the victims themselves.

"Third, gynocidal ritual practices have an inherent tendency to 'catch on' and spread since they appeal to imaginations conditioned by the omnipresent ideology of male domination." Thus although the paradigmatic victim of stranger sex-killings is the prostitute, the practice has spread to affect all classes of women. Next, it has "caught on" still further and a subculture of male-on-younger male attackers has developed, particularly throughout the 1970s. Moreover, recent serial killer Richard Ramirez, the "Night Stalker," confounded traditional patterns when he showed little regard for the stereotypic niceties and attacked anyone he could find asleep in a house at night, male or female, old or young.

"Fourth, women are used as scapegoats and token torturers." This facet is most obvious in the ubiquitous phenomenon of mother-blaming, indulged in not only by the killers, but by psychiatrists and the media mythographers. Secondly, we see this aspect in the tendency to blame the female victims for their own deaths.

"Fifth, we find compulsive orderliness, obsessive repetitiveness and fixation upon minute details which divert attention from the horror."

Sexual murder, like other rituals, is marked by a studied attention to repetition and detail, e.g. the specific fetishes of the killer, his (often elaborate) signature style of mutilation and murder, the victim type, etc. The media and/or police then can become similarly lost in detail—moral outrage expediently disappearing amidst the fascination with melodrama and minutiae. Similarly, there frequently is a movement to fixate upon (or concoct) details which seem to link a modern killer with the mythic forefather, Jack the Ripper. The contemporary killer is then proclaimed a "new" Jack the Ripper. Fact and fiction are blithely blurred; the reality of gynocide is overshadowed by mass fascination with the personality of the killer. Another common means of diluting realization of the gynocidal horror is to present the case as a "war" between the master killer and some celebrated "old man" or hero of a particular police force.[5] The female victims again become mere symbolic backdrop and the "hunt" between the two dichotomized males becomes the focal point. Finally, although there actually can be some similarities among the victims of a particular killer, the media and/or police frequently exaggerate or manufacture these. For example, we are told that all of the victims were "girls with long brown hair," all "beauty queens," "redheads," etc. Such fetishizations not only obscure the horror of the murders, but turn them into pornographic fantasies even as the killer is still "on the loose."

"*Sixth, behavior which at other times and places is unacceptable become acceptable and even normative as a consequence of conditioning through the ritual atrocity.*" Hence by the late 20th century, the situation in the United States alone is such that women are supposed to accept it as a "normal," unavoidable consequence of modern life that we must conduct our lives in constant vigilance and fear, restricting our movements, staying inside at night, etc. An article in *Science News*, reporting on the connection between pornography and violence against women, opened with a succinct articulation of a mindset produced and conditioned via the repetition of the ritual atrocity of sex crime:

Sexual attacks against women—our newspapers, magazines, novels, movies and television shows are full of such incidents. Considering the long history and continued prevalence of this kind of violence, it might seem that little can be done to curb it.[6]

Of course, common sense might be able to spot the reversal in this logic and suggest that the very fact that "our" newspapers, movies, etc. are filled with such depictions is itself a causal factor for sex crime. Indeed, throughout the Age of Sex Crime, not only have the actual incidences and types of sexual violence become environmentalized, normalized, but so have their depictions throughout all channels of public communication. Gynocidal themes and imagery have become commonplace not only in overt pornography, but have moved comfortably and ubiquitously into mainstream products as well.

"*Seventh, there is a legitimation of the ritual by the rituals of 'objective scholarship'—despite appearances of disapproval.*" It has been the psychiatric profession which has propagated the legitimating myths of the psychopathic killer as well as the causal mother. In other areas (e.g. history, sociology, etc.), there remains a dearth of scholarly analysis of serial sex crime. This is due not only to the currency of the phenomenon, but also to its continuing role as an effective form of phallic terrorism. As such, sexual murder remains mystified, a topic shielded by a largely unacknowledged taboo.

What research exists, moreover, also functions to mask the gynocidal character of sexual murder by ignoring the implications of the sexual differentiation between the violators and the victims.[7] Indeed, even when this factor is recognized, its meanings can still be expediently erased. For example, two professors at Northeastern University recently published a book on mass murder (the tone of this tome is epitomized by a back cover photo of the two standing in a graveyard). This book is largely a narrative survey of various forms and cases of mass murder, including serial sex murder. On that topic we are told:

It is obvious that certain types of mass killing—for example, serial raping and murdering— are the sole province of men. The fact that sex offenders, including rapists, child molesters and serial killers, are almost without exception male derives primarily from their greater need to dominate. While society allows a woman to maintain a submissive role, a male who feels weak, passive, or inadequate may feel strong pressure to live up to the powerful role that he believes he is expected to fulfill.[8]

According to this analysis, it is those males who *cannot* meet patriarchal expectations of manliness who become sex criminals. Yet, on the contrary, these criminals are the examplars of phallic manliness; they are everything that the patriarchal culture, at root, says a man to be. Moreover, society is presented as thoroughly generous in "allowing" women to "maintain a submissive role." No thought, it seems, has been given to exploring how that very role is meant to forever fix women into victim status.

Each of these seven points could be further amplified, yet still it remains clear that serial sex crime follows in the patterns of other gynocidal rituals no matter how distant in time and place. And like those other atrocities, sex crime functions not only to obliterate individual female lives, but, in keeping with the primordial patriarchal imperative, simultaneously aims to continually murder female divinity, i.e. the creativity, integrity, and spirit of living women. Finally, such rites continually provide a model for and reflection of phallocracy's planned appropriation/annihilation of the Earth itself.

. . . .

Jack the Ripper, along with many of his followers, has achieved legendary status. Such men have become world famous, awesomely regarded cultural figures. They are more than remembered; they are immortalized. Typically though, their victims, the uncounted women who have been terrorized, mutilated, and murdered are rendered profoundly nameless. Most are soon forgotten, catalogued as only just another photograph in the standard picturing of the victims, just another notch in the belt of the master killer. These women, particularly those who are non-white, poor, elderly, prostitutes, or streetwomen—are noted only as brief news items against the daily parade of "important" worldly events. Still others are never even named, left only as unidentified bodies in morgues across the country. And some are simply never found and remain listed as "missing," permanently *missing* (e.g. many of the suspected victims of Ted Bundy and Christopher Wilder). As Annie McCombs has accurately called it, all of these women, all of these victims of male sexual violence, are indeed our *missing*; precisely, they are our *disappeared*—the targets of an unnamed, ongoing, and mystified political terrorism, an undeclared, though perpetual, patriarchal warfare.

I write, then, to remember these women who, as Ntozake Shange so pointedly observed, "died for their country"—women and girls including Elizabeth Ann Landcraft, Shirley Lynette Ledford, Beverly Samans, Patricia Bisette, Yolanda Washington, Andrea Hall, Jane Sullivan, Anna Slesers, Helen Black, Dolores Cepeda, Sonja Johnson, Cindy Lee Hudspeth, Annie Chapman, Mary Ann Nichols, Elizabeth Stride, Mary Jane Kelly, Susan Perry, Patricia Walsh, Stacey Moscowitz, Donna Lauria, Christine Freund, Dawn Svocak, Virginia Voskerichian, Aiko Koo, Anita Luchessa, Mary Ann Pesce, Rosalind Thorpe, Alice Liu, Judy Dull, Shirley Ann Bridgeford, Ruth Rita Mercado, Wendy Coffield, Josephine Whitaker, Elena Rytka, Jayne MacDonald, Barbara Leach, Wilma McCann, Joan Mary Harrison, Emily Jackson, Jean Royle, Vera Millard, Yvonne Pearson, Teresa Ferguson, Suzanne Logan, Terry Diane Walden, Rosario Gonzalez, Donna Manson, Susan Rancourt, Janice Ott, Georgeann Hawkins, Roberta Kathleen Parks, Lynda Ann Healy, Brenda Ball, Margaret Bowman, Lisa Levy, Kimberly Leach, Denise Naslund, Caryn Campbell, Kristina Weckler, Jane King, Judith Miller, Sheila Burris, Gail Ficklin, Frankie Bell, Patricia Dennis, Lilian Stoval, Patsy Webb, Cathy Gystaveson, Linda Daniels, and all other women who have been sacrificed in gynocidal rituals. I call out their names in fury, in grief, and in the spirit of Nemesis that we *can* change the world, that all such atrocities will cease to be, will cease to deny female be-ing.[9]

Notes

Introduction

[1]Carolyn Moulton, "Editorial," *Fireweed: A Feminist Quarterly*, 14, (Fall 1982), 5-7.

[2]Catharine A. MacKinnon, "Toward Feminist Jurisprudence," *Stanford Law Review*, 34 (1982), 703.

[3]Jimmy McDonough, "I Can Teach You How to Read the Book of Life," *Bill Landis' Sleazoid Express*, 3, No. 7 (1984), 3-5.

[4]See Robert Lindsey, "Officials cite rise in killers who roam U.S. for victims," *New York Times*, 21 Jan. 1984, Sec. A, p. 1, col. 5. See also Peter Johnson, "Computers to help track repeat slayers," *USA Today*, 17 April 1984, p. 3A.

[5]Quoted in Lindsey, p. 7.

[6]There are no known serial killers who are female. Also, there seems to be no readily available statistics which break down the sex ratio of victims of serial killers, although the general consensus is that the great majority are females. Criminologist Steven Egger writes: "There are no known instances in which a serial killer is a female. . . . In a preponderance of known cases, the victims are young females chosen to satisfy the lust of the serial murderer. In some cases the victims are young males." See Steven A. Egger, "A Working Definition of Serial Murder and the Reduction of Linkage Blindness," *Journal of Police Science and Administration*, 12, No. 3 (Sept. 1984), 348-357, esp. 351. See also Donald T. Lunde, *Murder and Madness* (Stanford, Ca.: Stanford Alumni Association, 1975), p. 47; Joseph Berger, "Traits Shared by Mass Killers Remain Unknown to Experts," *New York Times*, 27 Aug. 1984, Sec. A, p.1, col. 1; Brad Darrach and Joel Norris, "An American Tragedy," *Life*, Aug. 1984, pp. 58.

[7]See Kate Millett, *Sexual Politics* (Garden City, N.Y.: Doubleday, 1970), p. 25. Millett writes: "The principles of patriarchy appear to be two-fold: male shall dominate female, elder male shall dominate younger."

[8]*Albuquerque Tribune*, 14 April 1984, p. A-2.

[9]As *People Weekly* reported: "The FBI has drawn the veil on the most graphic details of his assaults. 'Unfortunately,' says Assistant Director O.B. 'Buck' Revell, 'the more bizarre the acts the more likely you are to find copy cats. And inevitably there are going to be more Wilders out there.' " See "Journey of Terror," *People Weekly*, 30 April 1984, pp. 38-43.

[10]For an analysis of "male mystery" see Mary Daly in cahoots with Jane Caputi, *Websters' First New Intergalactic Wickedary of the English Language* (forthcoming, Beacon Press, 1987).

[11]Millett, pp. 44-5.

[12]See Susan Griffin, "Rape: The All-American Crime," *Ramparts, 10 Sept. 1971,*

pp. 26-35; reprinted in Susan Griffin, Made From this Earth: An Anthology of Writings (New York: Harper and Row, 1983), pp. 39-58. See Millett, *Sexual Politics.* See Andrea Dworkin, *Our Blood: Prophecies and Discourses on Sexual Politics* (New York: Harper and Row, 1976). See Diana E.H. Russell, *The Politics of Rape: The Victim's Perspective* (New York: Stein and Day, 1975). See Susan Brownmiller, *Against Our Will: Men, Women and Rape* (New York: Simon and Schuster, 1975).

[13]Mary Daly, *Beyond God the Father: Toward a Philosophy of Women's Liberation* (Boston: Beacon Press, 1973), p. 194. For a more extensive definition see Daly and Caputi, *Websters' Intergalactic Wickedary.*

[14]Dworkin, *Our Blood*, pp. 16, 19.

[15]See references in note #12. See also Diana E.H. Russell, *Sexual Exploitation: Rape, Child Sexual Abuse, and Workplace Harassment*, Sage Library of Social Research, Vol. 155 (Beverly Hills, Calif.: Sage Publication, 1984). Russell includes an extensive bibliography.

[16]See "Study Details Family Violence," *New York Times*, 24 April 1984, Sec. A, p. 17, col. 1.

[17]Tom A. Cullen, *When London Walked in Terror* (Boston: Houghton Mifflin, 1965), p. 285.

[18]Mircea Eliade, *Myths, Rites, Symbols: A Mircea Eliade Reader*, ed. Wendell C. Beane and William G. Doty (New York: Harper and Row, 1976), I, 3.

[19]Colin Wilson, Introd., *The Complete Jack the Ripper*, by Donald Rumbelow (Boston: New York Graphic Society, 1975), p. vii.

[20]See *Crimes and Punishment: A Pictorial Encyclopedia of Aberrant Behavior* (England: Phoebus Publishing, 1973), I, 85. This encyclopedia claims the phenomenon of what it terms "lady-killing" to be an explicitly modern crime:

> Of the hundreds of criminal cases contained in such compilations as *Lives of the Most Remarkable Criminals* (1735), *The Newgate Calendar* (1774), and even Camden Pelham's *Chronicles of Crime* published as late as 1886, there are no "lady-killers." Highwaymen, pirates, cut-throats, housebreakers galore; but no lady-killers.

The authors go on to observe that the situation changed radically in 1888 when:

> ...the savage and apparently motiveless murders of five London East End prostitutes, by the unknown killer nicknamed Jack the Ripper, signalled the beginning of a new age—the age of sex crime.

As indicated by that last phrase, Colin Wilson was one of the editors of this encyclopedia.

See also Judith Walkowitz, "Jack the Ripper and the Myth of Male Violence," *Feminist Studies*, 8 (1982), 543-574.

[21]See. R. E. L. Masters and Eduard Lea, *Sex Crimes in History* (New York: Julian Press, 1963), pp. 8-55; Raymond T. McNally and Radu Florescu, *In Search of Dracula: A True History of Dracula and Vampire Legends* (New York: Warner Paperbacks, 1973); Rossell Hope Robbins, *The Encyclopedia of Witchcraft and Demonology* (New York: Crown, 1959), pp. 403-7.

[22]See Masters and Lea, pp. 56-78, 95-114; F. E. Frenkel, "Sex-Crime and Its Socio-Historical Background," *Journal of the History of Ideas*, 25 (1964), 333-52.

[23]Masters and Lea, pp. 206-11; Brownmiller, pp. 31-113.

[24]Masters and Lea, pp. 79, 93-4; Alan Barnard, ed., *The Harlot Killer: Jack the Ripper* (New York: Dodd, Mead, and Co., 1953), p. 8. This also discusses other rippers at that time.

[25]Richard von Krafft-Ebing, *Psychopathia Sexualis,* trans. from the twelfth German edition and with an Introd. Franklin S. Klaf (New York: Stein and Day, 1965), pp. 58-9.

[26]Walkowitz, p. 550.

[27]Cullen, p. 14.

[28]Cited in Edmund R. Leach, "Ritual," *International Encyclopedia of the Social Sciences* (New York: MacMillan Co. and the Free Press, 1968), XIII, 520-26.

[29]J.S. LaFontaine, ed., *The Interpretation of Ritual: Essays in Honor of A. I. Richards* (London: Tavistock, 1972), p. xvii.

[30]Kate Millett notes the occurrence of expressions of titillation, amusement, envy and identification which typically accompany the news of such exemplary atrocity as the mass murders committed by Richard Speck. As she writes, "Probably a similar collection *frisson* sweeps through racist society when its more 'logical' members have perpetrated a lynching. Unconsciously, both crimes may serve the larger group as a ritual act, cathartic in effect." *Sexual Politics,* p. 45.

[31]Vietnam Veterans Against the War, *The Winter Soldier Investigation: An Inquiry into American War Crimes* (Boston: Beacon Press, 1972), p. 74.

[32]Compare atrocities reported throughout *The Winter Soldier Investigation.* See also Mark Baker, *Nam: The Vietnam War in the Words of the Men and Women who Fought There* (New York: Morrow and Company, 1982); Arlene Eisen, *Women and Revolution in Vietnam* (London: Zed Books, 1984), pp. 35-56; Brownmiller, *Against Our Will,* pp. 31-113.

[33]Robert R. Hazlewood and John E. Douglas, "The Lust Murderer," *FBI Law Enforcement Bulletin,* 49, No. 4 (1980), pp. 18-22.

[34]Quoted in Ted Schwarz, *The Hillside Strangler: A Murderer's Mind* (Garden City, N.Y.: Doubleday, 1981), pp. 60-61.

[35]Suzanne Lacy, "In Mourning and In Rage (With Analysis Aforethought)," *Ikon,* Fall/Winter 1982-83, pp. 60-67, esp. 63.

[36]Claude Lévi-Strauss, *Structural Anthropology* (New York: Basic Books, 1963), p. 200.

[37]See Robert Graves, *The Greek Myths,* revised ed. (Baltimore: Penguin Books, 1960), I, 56, 74, 93. Graves recounts the multi-rapes of the Goddesses and suggests that these rapes represent the usurpation of shrines as well as the seizure of control of agriculture, fishing, etc.

[38]Adolphe Jensen, *Myth and Cult among Primitive Peoples,* trans. Marianna Tax Cholsin and Wolfgang Weissleder (Chicago: University of Chicago Press, 1963); René Girard, *Violence and the Sacred,* trans. Patrick Gregory (Baltimore: The Johns Hopkins University Press, 1977).

[39]Exemplifying this type of myth is the Babylonian "creation" story in which the boy-god Marduk slays the primordial creator Tiamat, then forms the world from her dismembered body. For a translation of this myth see Charles Long, *Alpha: The Myths of Creation* (New York: Brazillar, 1963), pp. 88-93.

[40]Charles Doria, "The Dolphin Rider," in *Mind in the Water: A Book to Celebrate the Consciousness of Whales and Dolphins,* ed. Joan McIntyre (New York: Scribners, 1974), pp. 33-34.

[41]I first developed these ideas in Jane E. Caputi, " 'Jaws' as Patriarchal Myth," *The Journal of Popular Film,* 6 (1978), pp. 305-26.

[42]See Mary Daly, *Gyn/Ecology: The Metaethics of Radical Feminism* (Boston: Beacon Press, 1978), especially pp. 107-112.

[43]Eliade, p. 254.

[44]Quoted in "The Random Killers," *Newsweek*, 26 Nov. 1984, pp. 100-106D, esp. 104.

[45]Quoted in Baker, p. 152.

[46]Some of these ideas were suggested by Fran Chelland, conversation, Somerville, Mass., July 1986.

[47]Annie McCombs, "A Letter *Ms.* Didn't Print," *Lesbian Ethics*, 1, No. 3 (Fall 1985), 85-88, esp. 86.

[48]"The Whitechapel Murder," The *Times* (London), 27 Sept. 1888, p. 5.

[49]Krafft-Ebing, p. 59.

[50]Lunde states, "Sex and aggression get fused early in life and they [sex killers] can't differentiate them by the time they are adults." Quoted in "The Random Killers," p. 104. Abrahamsen concurs: "In some way, usually in early childhood, the individual [the sex killer] confuses sex with violence." He is quoted in Jon Nordheimer, "All-American Boy on Trial," *New York Times Magazine*, 10 Dec. 1978, pp. 60.

[51]Orne's opinions are given in an interview on "The Mind of a Murderer," prod. and dir. Michael Barnes, *Frontline*, PBS, 27 March 1984.

[52]"Housecall," *Penthouse*, Aug. 1982, p. 6.

[53]For statistics and discussion which might lead to this conclusion see Russell, *Sexual Exploitation*; Wini Breines and Linda Gordon, "The New Scholarship on Family Violence," *Signs: Journal of Women in Culture and Society*, 8 (1983), 490-531; Jane O'Reilly, "Wife Beating: The Silent Crime," *Time*, 5 Sept. 1983, pp. 23-26; "Study Details Family Violence," *New York Times*, 24 April 1984, Sec. A. p. 17, col. 1; Louise Armstrong, *The Home Front: Notes from the Family War Zone* (New York: McGraw-Hill, 1983).

[54]For a flagrant illustration of this see William Broyles Jr., "Why Men Love War," *Esquire*, Nov. 1984, pp. 55-65.

[55]All of Andrea Dworkin's writings are invaluable here. See especially *Pornography: Men Possessing Women* (New York: Perigee, 1981), esp. pp. 129-98; Andrea Dworkin, "Censorship, Pornography, and Equality," *Harvard Women's Law Journal*, 8 (1985), reprinted in *Trivia: A Journal of Ideas*, 7, Summer 1985, 11-32. Other feminist analysts have also contributed measurably to this understanding. Kate Millett has noted that, "Patriarchal force...relies on a form of violence particularly sexual in character and realized most completely in the act of rape." *Sexual Politics*, p. 44. Catharine MacKinnon, co-author with Dworkin of antipornography legislation, has argued that sex and violence are necessarily twinned in patriarchy for that system "creates male supremacy through the eroticization of dominance and submission." Sex and violence become "mutually definitive," resulting in, among other things, those traditional confusions and inabilities to distinguish rape from "normal" intercourse. Catharine A. MacKinnon, "Feminism, Marxism, Method and the State: Toward Feminist Jurisprudence," *Signs: Journal of Women in Culture and Society*, 8 (1983), 635-658. Not surprisingly, researchers have found that a significant proportion of male subjects (30%) become sexually aroused from watching so-called nonsexual violence against women. These studies were conducted by Neil Malamuth; see Daniel Goleman, "Violence Against Women in Films if Found to Alter Attitudes of Men," *New York Times*, 28 Aug. 1984, National ed., p. 19, col. 4.

[56]Two obvious examples of this are the continuing eroticizations of Black slavery in America and of Nazism. Exemplifying the former, is the popular literary genre, the "plantation novel." For commentary on this genre see Christopher D. Geist,

"Violence, Passion, and Sexual Racism: The Plantation Novel in the 1970s," *The Southern Quarterly*, 18 (1980), 60-72; and Christopher D. Geist, "The Sordid South: Racism, Sex and Violence in Recent Popular Novels of the Antebellum South," *The Gamut*, 1 (1980), 16-27. For commentary on the eroticization of Nazism, see Susan Sontag, "Fascinating Fascism," in *Under the Sign of Saturn* (Farrar Straus Giroux, 1980), pp. 73-105.

[57]Two special agents from the FBI Behavioral Science Unit define a "lust-murder" as one which involves "a mutilating attack or displacement of the breasts, rectum or genitals." See Hazlewood and Douglas, p. 18.

[58]See Steven Marcus, *The Other Victorians: A Study of Sexuality and Pornography in Mid-Nineteenth Century England* (New York: Basic Books, 1966), p. 283.

[59]Quoted in Cullen, p. 274.

Chapter 1

[1]Tom A. Cullen *When London Walked in Terror* (Boston: Houghton Mifflin Company, 1965), pp. 3-4.

[2]Judith R. Walkowitz, "Jack the Ripper and the Myth of Male Violence," *Feminist Studies*, 8 (1982), 543-74.

[3]Mark Schechner, "Male Chauvinist Romp," rev. of *Confessions of a Lady-Killer*, by George Stade, *New York Times Book Review*, 18 Nov. 1979, p. 15.

[4]Marvin Kittman, "Jack the Ripper on Television," *Newsday* (Long Island, N.Y.), 18 June 1981.

[5]John O'Connell, rev. of "Prime Suspect," *New York Times*, 20 Jan 1982, Sec. 3, p. 27., col. 1.

[6]Marie Bonaparte, *Female Sexuality* (New York: International Universities Press, 1953; reprint ed., New York: Grove Press, 1965), pp. 79-80.

[7]Cited in Donald Rumbelow, *The Complete Jack the Ripper*, Introd. Colin Wilson (Boston: New York Graphic Society, 1975), p. 204.

[8]Orrin E. Klapp, *Heroes, Villains, and Fools: The Changing American Character* (Englewood Cliffs, N.J.: Prentice-Hall, 1962), p. 59.

[9]Harlan Ellison, Afterword to "The Prowler in the City at the Edge of the World," in *Dangerous Visions*, ed. Harlan Ellison (Garden City, N.Y.: Doubleday, 1967), p. 154.

[10]Personal interview with a junior at Colorado Springs College, 27 March 1982. This student told me of a party game played there called "Jack the Ripper," which some might recognize as a variation of "Killer in the Dark." Cards are passed out; the Ace of Spades designates the "killer" or in this case "Jack the Ripper" who must then "murder" the other players without being caught when the lights are out.

[11]Rumbelow, dedication and acknowledgements in *The Complete Jack the Ripper*.

[12]Robert Bloch, *Out of the Mouth of Graves* (New York: The Mysterious Press, 1979), p. xi.

[13]Frank Donegan, "Are you loveable?" *Penthouse*, Feb. 1980, pp. 155-157.

[14]*San Francisco Chronicle*, 7 Oct. 1971. This was cited in Susan Brownmiller, *Against Our Will* (New York: Simon and Schuster, 1975), p. 294.

[15]Toto, "Stranger in Town," *Isolation*, Columbia, QC 33962, 1984.

[16]Sal Gittelman, *Frank Wedekind* (New York: Twayne Publishing, 1969), pp. 2, 74.

[17]Bob Dylan, "Tombstone Blues," *Highway 61 Revisited*, Columbia, CS9189,

1965.

[18]Robert Bloch, Introd. to "The Prowler in the City at the Edge of the World," a story by Harlan Ellison, in *Dangerous Visions*, ed. Ellison, p. 130.

[19]Alexander Kelly, *Jack the Ripper: A Bibliography and Review of the Literature*, Introd. to the murders and the theories by Colin Wilson (London: Association of Assistant Librarians, 1973), p. 16.

[20]Rumbelow, p. 217.

[21]David Wallechinsky and Irving Wallace, *The People's Almanac* (Garden City, N.Y.: Doubleday, 1975), p. 1225.

[22]Frank Spiering, *Prince Jack: The True Story of Jack the Ripper* (New York: Jove Publications, 1980), is particularly blameworthy. This book alleges that Prince Edward, heir to the throne of England, was the Ripper and tells its story purely through the eyes of "Eddy."

[23]A few examples of these are Alan Hynd, "Murder Unlimited," *Good Housekeeping*, Feb. 1945, pp. 29; Richard G. Hubler, "A Stunning Explanation of the Jack the Ripper Riddle," *Coronet*, Nov. 1956, pp. 101-6; James Stewart-Gordon, "The Enduring Mystery of 'Jack the Ripper,' " *Reader's Digest*, June 1973, pp. 119-23; "Who was 'Jack the Ripper?' " *Time*, 9 Nov. 1970, p. 29.

[24]Wallechinsky and Wallace, pp. 575-6.

[25]Rumbelow, p. 106. This listing is taken from Sir Melville Macnaghten's notes on the case, although I have added some details.

[26]Wallechinsky and Wallace, p. 575.

[27]Kelly, pp. 22-25.

[28]Cullen, unpaged, caption to an illustration.

[29]Walkowitz, p. 546.

[30]Cullen, p. 163.

[31]Cullen, p. 105.

[32]Cullen, pp. 110-11.

[33]Cullen, p. 162.

[34]Cullen, pp. 168-69.

[35]Rumbelow, p. 91. Sir Robert Anderson was an Assistant Commissioner of the Metropolitan Police; it was he who ascribed the letters to an "enterprising journalist" in his memoirs, *The Lighter Side of My Official Life* (London: Hodder and Stoughton, 1910).

[36]Donald McCormick, *The Identity of Jack the Ripper* (London: Arrow Books, 1970), cited in Cullen, pp. 166-69.

[37]McCormick, quoted in Cullen, p. 106.

[38]Paul O'Neil, "Was Clarence the Ripper?" *Life*, 13 Nov. 1970, pp. 85-88.

[39]R.E.L. Masters and Eduard Lea, *Sex Crimes in History* (New York: Julian Press, 1963), p. 87.

[40]*Crimes and Punishment: A Pictorial Encyclopedia of Aberrant Behavior* (England: Phoebus Publishing, 1973), XX, 20.

[41]Cullen, p. 167.

[42]Jonathan Goodman, *Bloody Versicles: The Rhymes of Crime* (New York: St. Martin's Press, 1971), pp. 62, 61.

[43]Colin Wilson, *A Casebook of Murder* (London: Leslie Frewin, 1969), pp. 139-40.

[44]Details about the Ripper suicide theory can be found in Cullen, p. 246. The jump rope rhyme is included in Iona and Peter Opie, *Lore and Language of*

Schoolchildren (Oxford, Clarendon Press, 1959), p. 11.

[45]Alexander Kelly's *Bibliography* contains the most detailed review of the various theories. Several of the key works are Leonard Matters, *The Mystery of Jack the Ripper* (London: Allen, 1929), the Harley Street surgeon theory; Hargrave Lee Adam, *Trial of George Chapman* (London: Hodge, 1930), the hanged poisoner who confessed to being the Ripper as the noose was tightened; Donald McCormick, *The Identity of Jack the Ripper*, 2nd ed. (London: Long, 1970), the Czarist secret agent; Robin Odell, *Jack the Ripper in Fact and Fiction* (London: Harrap, 1965), the Jewish slaughterman theory; William Steward, *Jack the Ripper: A New Theory* (London: Quality Press, 1939), the Ripper as a woman; Daniel Farson, *Jack the Ripper* (London: Michael Joseph, 1972), blames Montague Druitt, a failed barrister; and Tom A. Cullen *When London Walked in Terror* (Boston: Houghton Mifflin, 1965), suggests Druitt, and also, after George Bernard Shaw, considers the Ripper as an overzealous and misguided social reformer. A great deal also has been written suggesting that the Duke of Clarence was the Ripper. The original article that sparked the controversy was by Thomas E.A. Stowell, "Jack the Ripper—a solution?", *The Criminologist*, November 1970. The story was subsequently picked up by the international press, including the *New York Times* throughout November 1970 and made the subject of at least one book, Frank Spiering's *Prince Jack* (New York: Jove, 1978).

[46]Kelly, p. 38.

[47]Walkowitz, p. 546.

[48]This broadside is reproduced in Cullen, *When London Walked in Terror*. The quote from *Punch* is cited in *Crimes and Punishment*, XX. p. 26.

[49]Victor E. Neuburg, *Popular Literature: A History and Guide* (Harmondsworth: Penguin Books, 1977), p. 127.

[50]*Crimes and Punishment*, XX. p. 29.

[51]Neuburg, p. 165.

[52]Cullen, p. 205.

[53] *The New York Review of Books*, 17 Dec. 1970, p. 39; cited in Brownmiller, p. 294.

[54]Cullen, p. 104.

[55]Karl Alexander, *Time After Time* (New York: Delacorte, 1979); Richard Gordon, *Jack the Ripper* (New York: Atheneum, 1980); Robert Tine, *Uneasy Lies the Head* (New York: Viking, 1982).

[56]Gittelman, p. 74. See also Walter H. Sokel, "The Changing Role of Eros in Wedekind's Drama," *German Quarterly*, 39 (1966), pp. 201-7.

[57] *Lulu* was broadcast in its entirety on PBS, 20 Dec. 1980. Wedekind's play was also the basis for the film *Pandora's Box*, dir. by G.W. Pabst in 1929 and starring Louise Brooks.

[58]Cullen, p. 287; Marie Belloc Lowndes, *The Lodger* (London: Methuen, 1913). It has appeared in many editions hence.

[59]Isak Dinesen, "Uncle Seneca," in *Carnival: Entertainments and Posthumous Tales* (Chicago: University of Chicago Press, 1977); Ellery Queen, *A Study in Terror* (New York: Lancet, 1966); Anthony Boucher, "A King of Madness," *Ellery Queen's Mystery Magazine*, August 1972, pp. 36-42; Robert Bloch, "A Toy for Juliette," in *Dangerous Visions*, ed. Harlan Ellison; Harlan Ellison, "The Prowler in the City at the Edge of the World," in *Dangerous Visions*, ed. Ellison; Marcel Carne's film is *Drole de Drame*, 1937; Phyllis Tate turned *The Lodger* into an opera in 1964. For a dated though still extensive listing of Ripper fiction in all genres and media

see Alexander Kelly's bibliography and review of the literature.

[60]Nigel Morland, *An Outline of Sexual Criminology* (New York: Hart, 1966), p. 138.

[61]Cullen, p. 277.

[62]Walkowitz, p. 570.

[63]"A Wolf in the Fold," writ. Robert Bloch, *Star Trek*, created by Gene Roddenberry, NBC, 22 Dec. 1967.

[64]Bloch in *Dangerous Visions*, ed. Ellison, p. 120. The story by Robert Bloch, "Your's Truly Jack the Ripper," first appeared in *Weird Tales*, July 1943. It is reprinted in *The Best of Robert Bloch*, ed. and Introd. Lester del Rey (New York: Ballantine, 1977).

[65]Pete Axthelm et al., "The Sick World of Son of Sam," *Newsweek*, 22 August 1977, pp. 16-21.

[66]"Trash-bag Murders," *Newsweek*, 18 July 1977, p. 22; "Twenty-Eight and Counting...," *Time*, 18 July 1977, p. 49.

[67]In May, 1984, Carlton Gary was indicted as the "Stocking Strangler," *New York Times*, 5 May 1984.

[68]"Suspicious killing of seven black women in New Haven," *New York Times*, 19 October 1978, Sec. 1, p. 19.

[69]"Gacy admits to strangling 32 young boys," *New York Times*, 27 December 1978, Sec. 1, p. 7, col. 5.

[70]"Stalking the Roxbury Killers," *The Boston Phoenix*, 5 June 1979.

[71]Carol Kennedy, "Jack the Ripper's Latest Disciple," *Macleans*, 9 July 1979.

[72]"The Strangler of the Andes," *Time*, 2 June 1980, p. 49.

[73]Jack Levin and James Alan Fox, *Mass Murder: America's Growing Menace* (New York: Plenum, 1985), pp. 65-8.

[74] *New York Times*, 12 January 1981, Sec. 1, p. 14, col. 6.

[75] *New York Times*, 2 March 1982, Sec. A, p. 12.

[76]Mark Starr with Pamela Abramson, "Washington's 'Green River Killer,' " *Newsweek*, 9 January 1984, p. 25. See also "2 More Deaths Laid to Killer in Washington," *Boston Globe*, 4 January 1986, p. 9.

[77] *New York Times*, 14 Nov. 1982, Sec. 1, p. 81, col. 1; *Washington Post*, 26 Oct. 1982, p. Al, col. 1.

[78]Suspect in Trial in Texas Says He Has Murdered 360 People," *New York Times*, 12 April 1984, Sec. 1, p. 19, col. 4.

[79]"Ex-Prosecutor on Trial in Murder by Math, *Newsday*, 22 July 1983, p. 13.

[80]Susan Prentice, "Pattern Suspected: Detectives Compare Girls' Slayings," *Columbus Citizen-Journal*, 12 Aug. 1983, p. 1.

[81]Bob Carlsen, "Alaska's Mass Murderer Stalked Go-Go Dancers," *Front Page Detective* 47, No. 10, October 1984, p. 30.

[82]"Journey of Terror," *People Weekly*, 30 April 1984, pp. 38-43.

[83]Michael Winerip, "Murder Suspect Recalled as Odd By His Friends," *New York Times*, 3 July 1984, Sec. B, p. Bl, col. 6.

[84]"Midwest Fugitive Caught in Illinois," *New York Times* Sec. A, p. 7, col. 6.

[85]"Slayings of Redheaded Victims Baffle Officials," *New York Times*, National edition, 7 May 1985, p. 9, col. 4.

[86]"Bodies Hunted," New York *Daily News*, 10 June 1985, p. 2.

[87]Richard Holguin, "Arrest in Calif. Killings," *Boston Globe*, 1 Sept. 1985, p. 1, col. 5.

[88]"The Monster of Florence," *Time*, 24 March 1986, p. 54.

[89]Scott Harris, "Prostitute Slain; Serial Killer May have Claimed 11th," *Los Angeles Times*, 25 Dec. 1985, Part 2, p. 1. See also, "The L.A. Slayer," *Newsweek*, 9 June 1986, p. 28.

[90]See, for example, an article in *Science News* reporting on the connection between pornography and violence against women. This piece begins with a neat articulation of the myth-mastered mindset: "Sexual attacks against women—our newspapers, magazines, novels, movies and television shows are full of such incidents. Considering the long history and continued prevalence of this kind of violence, it might seem that little can be done to curb it." Of course, common sense would spot the reversal in this logic and suggest that the very fact that "our newspapers" etc. are filled with such depictions, is itself a causal factor for sex crime. See "Sex and Violence: Pornography Hurts," *Science News*, 118 (13 Sept. 1980), 166-72.

[91]Roland Barthes, "Myth Today," in *Mythologies*, trans. Annette Lavers (New York: Hill and Wang, 1972), p. 129.

[92]Basil Thompson, *The Story of Scotland Yard* (New York: Literary Guild, 1936).

[93]Rumbelow, p. 182.

[94]"Ripper's Return," *Time*, 23 April 1979, p. 43.

Chapter II
[1]Virginia Woolf, *Three Guineas* (New York: Harcourt, Brace and World, 1938; Harbinger Books, 1966), p. 66.

[2]Quoted in Tom A. Cullen, *When London Walked in Terror* (Boston: Houghton Mifflin, 1965), p. 105.

[3]Max H. Seigel, "Berkowitz Outbursts Disrupt Court; Sentencing Put Off, Tests Ordered," *New York Times*, 22 May 1977, Sec. 1, p. 1, col. 1.

[4]Quoted in Ted Schwarz with Kelli Boyd, "Inside the Mind of the 'Hillside Strangler'," *Hustler*, Aug, 1981, p. 37.

[5]John Beattie, *The Yorkshire Ripper Story* (London: Quartet Books, 1981), p. 133.

[6]"Serial Murderers," narr. Sylvia Chase, *ABC News 20/20*, 5 July 1984.

[7]Alan Hynd, "Murder Unlimited," *Good Housekeeping*, Feb. 1945, p. 200.

[8]Basil Thompson, *The Story of Scotland Yard* (New York: Literary Guild, 1936), p. 335.

[9]Robert Bloch, "Yours Truly, Jack the Ripper," in *The Best of Robert Bloch*, ed. and introd, Lester del Rey (New York: Ballantine, 1977), pp. 1-20. This story originally appeared in *Weird Tales*, July 1943.

[10]Jack Iams, "The Search for the Strangler," *Saturday Evening Post*, 18 May 1963, pp. 28-37.

[11]" 'Son of Sam'—The Killer Who Terrorized New York," *Reader's Digest*, Nov. 1977, p. 149.

[12]"Spurred by his taunts, police search for Britain's bloodiest ripper since Jack," *People Weekly*, 15 Oct. 1979, pp. 117-18.

[13]See Donald Rumbelow, *The Complete Jack the Ripper* (Boston: New York Graphic Society, 1975), p. 204.

[14]Gerold Frank, *The Boston Strangler* (New York: New American Library, 1967), p. 64.

[15]Pete Axthelm et. al., "The Sick World of Son of Sam," *Newsweek*, 22 August 1977, p. 19.

[16]For information on Gordon Cummins, the "Blackout Ripper," see *Crimes and Punishment: A Pictorial History of Aberrant Behavior* (England: Phoebus Publishing, 1973), XVII, 45-52. For information on the "Düsseldorf Ripper" and "Jack the Stripper," see Rumbelow, pp. 195-202.

[17]"The Killer," *Newsweek*, 21 Dec. 1964, p. 38.

[18]"Ripper's Return," *Time*, 27 April 1979, p. 43.

[19]Frank, p. 64.

[20]Nathan M. Adams, "To Catch a Killer: The Search for Ted Bundy," *Reader's Digest*, March 1981, pp. 210-39.

[21]Harold K. Banks, *The Strangler: The Story of Terror in Boston* (New York: Avon Books, 1967), p. 47.

[22]This is the opinion of Dr. Ames Robey, former medical director of Bridgewater State Hospital who had personally examined Albert DeSalvo; quoted in Edward Keyes, *The Michigan Murders* (New York: Pocket Books, 1976), p. 99.

[23]Ed Blanche, "Hunt for a 20th Century Ripper," *The Toledo Blade, Toledo Magazine*, 9 March 1980, p. 24.

[24]Fred Hauptfuhrer, "Olivia Reivers Has Reason to Wonder: Was She the Yorkshire Ripper's Last Date?," *People Weekly*, 26 Jan. 1981, p. 70.

[25]John Kifner, "DeSalvo, Confessed Boston Strangler, Found Stabbed to Death in Prison Cell," *New York Times*, 27 Nov 1973, Sec. 1, p. 28, col. 3.

[26]"The Mind of a Murderer," prod. and dir. Michael Barnes, *Frontline*, PBS, 20 March 1984 and 27 March 1984.

[27]"Berkowitz Describes a Cult," *Newsday* (Long Island), 20 Jan. 1982, Sec. A, p. 27, col. 1.: David Abrahamsen, "Confessions of 'Son of Sam,' " *Penthouse*, Nov. 1983, pp. 60.

[28]When a Florida police official, Norm Chapman, questioned Ted Bundy about his possible involvement in thirty-six sex murders, Bundy reportedly replied, "Add one digit to that and you'll have it." See Ann Rule, *The Stranger Beside Me* (New York: New American Library, 1980), p. 313: see also Stephen G. Michaud and Hugh Aynesworth, *The Only Living Witness* (New York: Simon and Schuster, 1983) for his third person "speculations."

[29]"Scores of Confessions Of a Killer Called Bogus," *New York Times*, 8 May 1986, Sec. A, p. 18, col. 6.

[30]See "Suspect in Trial in Texas Says He has Murdered 360 People," *New York Times*, 12 April 1984, Sec. A, p. 19, col. 4; Brad Darrach and Joel Norris, "An American Tragedy," *Life*, August 1984, pp. 58; Allan Sonnenschein and Hugh Aynesworth, "Serial Killers: Henry Lee Lucas: 'Killing Every Way Known to Man,' " *Penthouse*, February 1985, pp. 32; "Serial Murderers," narr. Sylvia Chase, *ABC News 20/20*, 5 July 1984.

[31]Two reporters from the *Dallas Times Herald* were the first to argue that Lucas' confessions were an elaborate hoax and that he was not responsible for more than three murders. They suggest that police agencies, anxious to clear up unsolved crimes "ignored or failed to pursue leads that would have proven the deceit of many of his confessions...[and] actually amended information to conform to Lucas' confessions." See Hugh Aynesworth and Jim Henderson, "A Serial Killer or Perpetrator of Hoax?" *Los Angeles Times*, 14 April 1985, Part 1, p. 4.

[32]Michaud and Aynesworth, p. 17.

[33]Film critic Robin Wood has pointed out that since the 1960s, the motif of the monster as human psychotic has been a key one in American horror film. See

Robin Wood, "The Return of the Repressed," *Film Comment*, 14, No. 4 (1978), 23-32.

[34]Blanche, p. 24.

[35]Ted Schwarz, *The Hillside Strangler: A Murderer's Mind* (Garden City, N.Y.: Doubleday, 1981), p. 70.

[36]Quoted in Lawrence D. Klausner, *Son of Sam* (New York: McGraw-Hill, 1981), p. 141.

[37]Klausner, p. 168.

[38]"Talk of the Town," *New Yorker*, 15 Aug. 1977.

[39]Klausner, p. 146.

[40]For an analysis of urban legends see Jan Brunvand, *The Vanishing Hitchhiker: American Urban Legends and Their Meanings* (New York: Norton, 1981). Such legends include the widely circulated stories about rats in buckets of commercially fried chicken, ghost cars and hitchhikers, escaped convicts and stalking sex maniacs. Brunvand stresses that although these must be considered to be objectively "false," they are also "true" in the sense that they unselfconsciously reflect major cultural values, fears, and concerns. Many are cautionary or fear stories for women and communicate the typical messages of women as prey, whether at home, travelling alone, babysitting, etc. Some are aimed at both males and females and implant a general fear of sexuality. One of the most popular of these goes under the general title of "The Hook" and tells of a girl and boy kissing in a car when they hear a radio announcement warning of an escaped maniac "with a hook in place of a hand." The girl gets scared and begs the boy to take her home. Although annoyed, he agrees, but when they get home they find that on the door handle is a bloody hook. The setting and events of many of the "Son of Sam" killings—his nighttime attacks on parking couples— eerily enacted many aspects of this legend. See particularly Klausner's version of the attack on Stacey Moskowitz and Robert Violante in *Son of Sam*, pp, 222-27.

[41]Richard F. Shepard, "About New York: A .44 Caliber Cloud of Fear," *New York Times*, 4 Aug. 1977, Sec. 2, p. 7, col. 1. See also "The David Berkowitz Story," *Commonweal*, 2 Sept. 1977, pp. 547-48.

[42]"Where the 'Son of Sam' struck, young women walk in fear," *New York Times*, 30 June 1977, Sec. 2, p. 1, col. 1.

[43]Shepard, p. 7.

[44]This is reported by Pam MacAllister in "Wolf Whistles and Warnings," *Heresies: A Feminist Publication on Art and Politics*, 6 (Summer 1978), 37-39. She comments:

> In the wake of the Son of Sam's terrorizing, Madison Avenue saw fit to profit on the linking of desirability and vulnerability. 'Warning!...A Pretty Face Isn't Safe In This City!' was the slogan for Max Factor's face mosturizer 'Self-Defense.' In the smaller print it was explained that this was self-defense against the city's dirt and pollution which could ruin a face with skin problems, but the terminology was blatantly based on the fact of crimes against women. The warning was true and Max Factor played on every woman's victim role to sell that moisturizer. It used male predators as the status quo....

[45]The women, variously, had been bound, strapped in a chair, raped, sodomized with various objects, hung from poles, injected with cleaning solutions, gassed, and burned with electric cords. Compare also the murders by Bittaker and Norris as reported in Jack Levin and James Alan Fox, *Mass Murder: America's Growing Menace* (New York: Plenum Press, 1985), pp,. 65-68. Torture also was paramount in the killings

by Christopher Wilder and Leonard Lake and Charles Ng. In the male on male sex killings, torture marked the cases of Dean Corll (Texas, mid-1970s), John Wayne Gacy, and the "Trashbag Murders."

[46]Schwarz, p. 66.

[47]Robert Lindsey, "Judge Refuses to Drop Case Against Suspect in Stranglings on Coast," New York Times, 22 July 1981, Sec. 1, p.12, col. 1.

[48]Frank, pp. 39-40.

[49]Iams, p. 32.

[50]Joseph Collins, "A New Jack The Ripper is terrorizing England," Us, Oct. 1979, p. 31.

[51]Carol Kennedy, "Jack the Ripper's Latest Disciple," Macleans, 9 July 1979; "Striking Again," Time, 17 Sept. 1979, p. 49.

[52]"Striking Again," p. 49.

[53]Kennedy, p. 49.

[54]A photograph of this billboard illustrates an article by Arthur Osman and Richard Ford, "Lost Chances, Bad Luck and Malice of the Tapes foiled untiring Search," The Times (London), 23 May 1981, Sec. 1, p. 5.

[55]Guy Martin, "The Ripper," Esquire, Jan 1981, pp. 58-69.

[56]Osman and Ford, p. 5, col. 1.

[57]Beattie, p. 81.

[58]Personal communication, name withheld, 28 May 1982.

[59]Judith R. Walkowitz, "Jack the Ripper and the Myth of Male Violence," Feminist Studies, 8 (1982), 543-74, esp. 561.

[60]Suzanne Lacy, "In Mourning and in Rage (with Analysis Aforethought)," Ikon, Fall/Winter, 1982-83, pp. 60-67, esp. 61.

[61]Personal communication, name withheld, 10 August 1984.

[62]Kate Millett, Sexual Politics (Garden City, N.Y.: Doubleday, 1970), p. 45.

[63]Barbara Smith, Introd. "Twelve Black Women: Why Did They Die?," by The Combahee River Collective in Fight Back, ed. Frederique Delacoste and Felice Newman (Minneapolis: Cleis Press, 1981), p. 68.

[64]Personal communication, name withheld, 15 March 1982.

[65]Personal communication, name withheld, 12 May 1982.

[66]Trevor Rabin and Smith, "The Ripper," Face to Face, Chrysalis 1221, 1980.

[67]Philip Lynott, "Killer on the Loose," Thin Lizzy, Chinatown, Warner Bros, BSK 3496, 1980.

[68]The Rolling Stones, "The Midnight Rambler," words and music by Mick Jagger and Keith Richard, Gimme Shelter, ABKCO Music, Inc., 1969. Quoted in Brownmiller, p. 296.

[69]Brownmiller, p. 295.

[70]Don Heckman, "As Cynthia Saggitarius says—'Feeling...I mean, isn't this what the Rolling Stones are all about?' " New York Times Magazine, 16 July 1972, p. 38. Quoted in Brownmiller, p. 296.

[71]Brownmiller, p. 296.

[72]Steven Winn and David Merrill, Ted Bundy: The Killer Next Door (New York: Bantam, 1980), p. 217.

[73]Richard Slotkin, Regeneration Through Violence: The Mythology of the American Frontier, 1600-1860 (Middletown, Ct.: Wesleyan University Press, 1973), p. 564.

[74]Brownmiller, p. 294.

[75]Richard W. Larsen, *Bundy: The Deliberate Stranger* (Englewood Cliffs, N.J.: Prentice-Hall, 1980), p. 182.

[76]Rule, p. 255.

[77]Jon Nordheimer, "All-American Boy on Trial," *New York Times Magazine*, 10 Dec. 1978, pp. 46

[78]Larsen, p. 185.

[79]Warren Zevon, "Excitable Boy," *Excitable Boy*, Asylum, 6Ell8, 1978.

[80]Mark Pinsky, "Just an Excitable Boy?," *New Times*, 27 Nov. 1978, pp. 53-65.

[81]Adams, pp. 210-39.

[82]Winn and Merrill, p. 238.

[83]Michael Daly, "Murder! Did Ted Bundy Kill 36 Women and Will He Go Free?," *Rolling Stone*, 14 Dec. 1978, pp. 55; James Horwitz, "Ted Bundy: Portrait of a Compulsive Killer," *Cosmopolitan*, Nov. 1980, pp. 328-336.

[84]"Cameras in the Courtroom," *Time*, 23 July 1979, p. 76.

[85]See Elizabeth Kendall, *The Phantom Prince: My Life with Ted Bundy* (Seattle: Madrona Press, 1981); C. Terry Cline, *Missing Persons* (New York: Arbor House, 1981): also Larsen; Rule; Winn and Merrill; and Michaud and Aynesworth.

[86]"David Berkowitz's Letters Attract Auction Bids," *New York Times*, 29 March 1979, Sec. 3, p. 4, col. 5; "Berkowitz Letter to Brooklyn Woman is Sold for $400," *New York Times*, 4 Dec. 1977, Sec. 1, p. 81, col. 1.

[87]Abrahamsen, p. 190.

[88]Julia Penelope (Stanley), "Prescribed Passivity: The Language of Sexism," in *Views on Language*, eds. Reza Ordoubadian and Walburga von Raffler-Engel, (Murfreesboro, Tennessee: Inter-University Publications, 1975), pp. 96-108.

[89]"Serial Murderers," narr. Sylvia Chase, *ABC News 20/20*, 5 July 1984.

[90]R. E. L. Masters and Eduard Lea, *Sex Crimes in History* (New York: The Julian Press, 1963), p. 81.

[91]Christopher H. Sterling and Timothy R. Haight, *The Mass Media: Aspen Institute Guide to Communication Industry Trends* (New York: Praeger, 1978), p. 346.

[92] *Hustler*, August, 1980, p. 20.

[93]Preying Mantis Women's Brigade, "Actions Against Hustler," in *Fight Back: Feminist Resistance to Male Violence*, ed. Frederique Delacoste and Felice Newman (Minneapolis: Cleis Press, 1981), pp. 264-65.

[94]For an analysis of the collusion between pornography and sex crime see Andrea Dworkin, "Censorship, Pornography, and Equality," *Harvard Women's Law Journal*, 8, 1985; reprinted in *Trivia: A Journal of Ideas*, 7, (Summer 1985), 11-32.

[95] *Hustler*, March 1984, p. 22.

[96]Quoted in Marj Von Beroldingen, "I Was the Hunter and They Were the Victims," *Front Page Detective*, March 1974, pp. 29

[97]Quoted in Michaud and Aynesworth, p. 123.

[98]Letter to Captain Joseph Borelli, April 1977, quoted in Klausner, pp. 141-42.

[99]Slotkin, p. 22.

[100]Slotkin, p. 563, 564.

[101]Ted Schwarz with Kelli Boyd, "Kenneth Bianchi: Inside the Mind of the 'Hillside Strangler,' " *Hustler*, Aug. 1981, pp. 36.

[102]Raymond Williams, *Television: Technology and Cultural Form* (Glasgow: Fontana/Collins, 1974), pp. 78-118.

[103]Richard Milner, "Orgasm of Death," *Hustler*, Aug. 1981, pp. 33-4.

[104]Schwarz with Boyd, p. 36.

[105]Jimmy McDonough, "I Can Teach You How to Read the Book of Life," *Bill Landis' Sleazoid Express*, 3, No. 7 (1984), 3-5.

[106] *Life* magazine reports that an "alarming number of serial murderers (one out of 10) are doctors, dentists, or other health professionals." See Brad Darrach and Dr. Joel Norris, "An American Tragedy," *Life*, August 1984, pp. 58.

[107]I am thinking here particularly of Shel Silverstein's *The Giving Tree* (New York: Harper and Row, 1964). This still popular book is frankly a simple story of sado-masochism and the mutilation and exploitation of both nature and the female by the archetypal "boy." The story is told from the point of view of the tree who accepts and even glories in *her* mutilation.

Chapter III

[1]John G. Cawelti, *Adventure, Mystery, and Romance: Formula Stories as Art and Popular Culture* (Chicago: University of Chicago Press, 1976), p. 34.

[2]Shane Stevens, *By Reason of Insanity* (New York: Dell, 1979), pp. 498-99.

[3]*Gorenography* is a termed coined in the trade for the slasher—violence as sexual titillation—film. To grasp the extent of this genre as well as the fascination it exerts on its fans, one can look at the specialty magazines that track the gore phenomenon. These include *Bill Landis' Sleazoid Express*, *Scarephanalia*, and *Fangoria* (all out of New York), *Gore Gazette* and *Confessions of a Trash Fiend* (New Jersey); *The Splatter Times* (Tennessee); *Chicago Shivers* among others. For commentary see Kurt Loder, "Night Creatures," *Rolling Stone*, 19 July/ 2 August 1984, pp. 91.

[4]Jack Sullivan, "Chopping Up Women," rev. of *By Reason of Insanity*, by Shane Stevens, *New York Times Book Review*, 18 Mar. 1979.

[5]Dan Greenburg, *Love Kills* (New York: Pocket Books, 1978); Steven Whitney, *Singled Out* (New York: William Morrow, 1978; Berkley Books, 1981); Dave Klein, *Blind Side* (New York: Charter Books, 1980); George Stade, *Confessions of a Lady-Killer* (New York: Alpha/Omega, 1979); T. Jeff Williams, *Strangler* (New York: Bantam, 1979); Jonathan Valin, *Final Notice* (New York: Avon, 1980); Stephen King, *The Dead Zone* (New York: Viking Press, 1979).

[6]William Goldman, *No Way to Treat a Lady* (Greenwich, Ct.: Fawcett Publications, 1964).

[7]Quoted in Karl Menninger with the collaboration of Jeanetta Lyle Menninger, *Love Against Hate* (New York: Harcourt, Brace and Company, 1942), p. 33.

[8]Colin Wilson, *A Casebook of Murder* (London: Leslie Frewin, 1969), p. 135.

[9]Quoted in Jon Nordheimer, "All-American Boy on Trial," *New York Times Magazine*, 10 Dec. 1978, pp. 60, esp. p. 124.

[10]Quoted in Ted Schwarz, *The Hillside Strangler: A Murderer's Mind* (Garden City, N.Y.: Doubleday, 1981), p. 149. The psychiatrist is Dr. Ron Markham, brought in by the defense.

[11]See particularly Dorothy Dinnerstein, *The Mermaid and the Minotaur: Sexual Arrangements and Human Malaise* (New York: Harper and Row, 1976); Andrea Dworkin, *Woman Hating* (New York: Dutton, 1974); H.R. Hayes, *The Dangerous Sex: The Myth of Feminine Evil* (New York: G.P. Putnam's Sons, 1964); Wolfgang Lederer, *The Fear of Women* (New York: Harcourt, Brace, Jovanovich, 1968); Erich Neumann, *The Great Mother: An Analysis of the Archetype*, Bollingen Series 47, trans. Ralph Manheim (Princeton, N.J.: Princeton University Press, 1963).

[12]"Eve Cigarettes," ad campaign, late 1970s through early 1980s.

[13]Mary Daly, *Beyond God the Father: Toward a Philosophy of Women's Liberation* (Boston: Beacon Press, 1973), p. 62. See also Karen Horney, "The Distrust Between the Sexes," in her *Feminine Psychology*, ed. Harold Kelman (New York: Norton, 1967), p. 112; Kate Millett, *Sexual Politics* (Garden City, N.Y.: Doubleday, 1970), pp. 52-54.

[14]Gerold Frank, *The Boston Strangler* (New York: New American Library, 1967), pp. 165-72.

[15]Susan Brownmiller, *Against Our Will* (New York: Simon & Schuster, 1975), pp. 203, 204.

[16]Colin Campbell, "Portrait of a Mass Killer," *Psychology Today*, May 1976, pp. 110-11.

[17]Robert Bloch, *Psycho* (Greenwich, Ct.: Fawcett, 1959). Alfred Hitchcock, dir., *Psycho*, Paramount, 1960.

[18]Lederer, p. 7.

[19]Gregory Bateson, *Steps to an Ecology of Mind* (San Francisco: Chandler Publishing Company, 1972), p. 217.

[20]Menninger, pp. 117-18.

[21]David Abrahamsen, "Confessions of Son of Sam," *Penthouse*, Nov. 1983, pp. 60; See also David Abrahamsen, *Confessions of Son of Sam* (New York: Columbia University Press, 1985).

[22]Quoted in Lawrence D. Klausner, *Son of Sam* (New York: McGraw-Hill, 1981), p. 141-42. "Mr. Borrelli" refers to a member of the New York City police department.

[23]Schwarz, p. 239.

[24]"The Mind of a Murderer," prod. and dir. Michael Barnes, *Frontline*, PBS, 20 March and 27 March 1984.

[25]"Murder: No Apparent Motive," prod. and dir. Imre Horvath, Home Box Office Special, broadcast throughout 1984.

[26]Margaret Cheney, *The Coed Killer* (New York: Walker and Company, 1976), pp. 208-9.

[27]"Serial Murderers," narr. Sylvia Chase, *ABC News 20/20*, 5 July 1984.

[28]Joseph Berger, "Traits Shared by Mass Killers Remain Unknown to Experts," *New York Times*, 27 August 1984, p. 1, col. 1.

[29]Daly, *Beyond God the Father*; Mary Daly, *Gyn/Ecology: The Metaethics of Radical Feminism* (Boston: Beacon Press, 1978), p. 8, passim. See also Mary Daly in cahoots with Jane Caputi, *Websters' First New Intergalactic Wickedary of the English Language* (forthcoming, Beacon Press, 1987).

[30]Frank, pp. 178-79.

[31]General beliefs are that the woman provokes the attack through her dress, body movements, or "promiscuity." See Susan Griffin, *Rape: The Power of Consciousness* (San Francisco: Harper and Row, 1979), pp. 86-87. In 1982, a Lancaster, Wisconsin judge ordered a 90 day jail sentence and probation for a man accused of sexually molesting a five-year old girl. The judge, William L. Reinecke, stated, "I am satisfied we have an unusually sexually promiscuous young lady, and he did not know enough to refuse. No way do I believe Mr. Snodgrass [the defendant] initiated sexual contact." The *Daily Sentinel-Tribune*, Bowling Green, Ohio, 10 May 1982, p. 7, col. 1. See also Martha Burt, "Cultural Myths and Supports for Rape," *Journal of Personality and Social Pyschology*, 38, No. 2 (1980), 217-30.

[32]Suzanne Lacy, "In Mourning and In Rage (With Analysis Aforethought)," *Ikon*, Fall/Winter, 1982-83, pp. 60-67, esp. 63.

[33]Mark Schechner, "Male Chauvanist Romp," rev. of *Confessions of a Lady-Killer* by George Stade, *New York Times Book Review*, 18 Nov. 1979, p. 15.

[34]John Leonard, rev. of *Confessions of a Lady-Killer*, by George Stade, *New York Times*, 26 Nov. 1979, Sec. C. p. 18, col. 3.

[35]Martin Washburn, "The Sex Vacuum," rev. of *Confessions of a Lady-Killer*, by George Stade, *Village Voice*, 24 Dec. 1979, p. 46.

[36]Keith Opdahl, "Macho Madness," rev. of *Confessions of a Lady-Killer*, by George Stade, *Nation*, 15 Dec. 1979, p. 631-32.

[37]Millett, *passim*.

[38]*Los Angeles Times*, 18 Dec. 1977, Pt. I, p. 30; cited in Lacy.

[39]Cawelti, p. 18.

[40]*At The Movies*, hosted by Gene Siskel and Roger Ebert, KSAF Santa Fe, 3 Sept. 1984.

[41]Raymond Durgnat, "Inside Norman Bates," in *Great Film Directors: A Critical Anthology*, ed. Leo Braudy and Morris Dickstein (New York: Oxford, 1978), pp. 496-506, originally in R. Durgnat, *Films and Feelings* (Cambridge: MIT Press, 1967). Francois Truffaut, *Hitchcock* (New York: Simon and Schuster, 1971), p. 207.

[42]J. Hoberman, "Double Indemnity," *Village Voice*, 28 August 1984, pp. 45-6.

[43]For an analysis of the sexuality in *Dirty Harry* see Anthony Chase, "The Strange Romance of 'Dirty Harry' Callahan and Ann Mary Deacon," *Velvet Light Trap*, 17, Winter 1977, pp. 13-18.

[44]Robert Mazzocco, "The Supply-Side Star," *New York Review of Books*, 1 April 1982, pp. 29.

[45]For an analysis of the interconnecting male roles of protector and violator, see Susan Griffin, "The Politics of Rape," in *Made From This Earth: An Anthology of Writings* (New York: Harper and Row, 1983), pp. 39-58. This piece was first published in *Ramparts* in 1971.

[46]Herbert Marcuse, *One-Dimensional Man* (Boston: Beacon Press, 1964), pp. 90-94.

[47]Cawelti, p. 34.

[48]Andrea Dworkin, *Pornography: Men Possessing Women* (New York: Perigee, 1981), p. 53.

[49]*At the Movies*, 3 Sept. 1984.

[50]Durgnat, p. 503.

[51]Lunde was interviewed on "Serial Murderers," *ABC News 20/20*, 5 July 1984.

[52]Nordheimer, p. 124.

[53]Orne was interviewed on "The Mind of a Murderer," prod. and dir. Michael Barnes, *Frontline*, PBS, 27 March 1984.

[54]Quoted in Michael Mills, "Brian De Palma," *Moviegoer* 2 (12), December 1983, 8-13. This is a free supplement passed out in movie theaters.

[55]Quoted in Kurt Loder, "Night Creatures," *Rolling Stone*, 19 July/2 Aug. 1984, pp. 91 esp. 121.

[56]Catharine A. MacKinnon, "Feminism, Marxism, Method, and the State: An Agenda for Theory," *Signs: Journal of Women in Culture and Society*, 7 (1982), 515-44, esp. 541.

[57]Ian Cameron and V.F. Perkins, Interview with Alfred Hitchcock, *Movie*, 6, Jan. 1963; reprinted in *Interviews with Film Directors*, ed. Andrew Sarris (Indianapolis: Bobbs-Merrill, 1967), pp. 199-205, esp. 202.

[58]Durgnat, p. 505.

Chapter IV

[1]Mary Daly, *Beyond God the Father: Toward a Philosophy of Women's Liberation* (Boston: Beacon Press, 1973), pp. 62-63.

[2]Donald Rumbelow, *The Complete Jack the Ripper* (Boston: New York Graphic Society, 1975), p. 193.

[3]Arthur Osman and Richard Ford, "Lost Chances, Bad Luck and Malice of the Tapes Foiled Untiring Search," The *Times* (London), 23 May 1981, Sec. 1, p. 5.

[4]Quoted in Joan Smith, "Getting Away With Murder," *New Socialist*, May/June 1982, pp. 10-12.

[5]Quoted in Arthur Osman and Richard Ford, "The Shy Man Who Brought Fear to the North," The *Times* (London), 23 May 1981, Sec. 1, p. 4.

[6]The investigator is Robert Keppel, quoted in "The Random Killers," *Newsweek*, 26 November 1984, pp. 100-106D, esp. 106.

[7]See Joseph Berger, "Traits Shared by Mass Killers Remain Unknown to Experts," *New York Times*, 27 August 1984, Sec. 1, p 1, col. 1.

[8]Researcher Barbara Reskin has found that jurors in rape trials tend to base their verdicts on the victim's demeanor, reputation, social life, and appearance—believing her if she seems to be a virgin, married, etc., and disbelieving her if she seems to be sexually active or knew her assailant. See Nadine Brozan, "Jurors in Rape Trails Studied,"*New York Times*, 17 June 1985, Sec. C, p. 13, col. 2. Such attitudes have been exposed as rooted in the judiciary as well. In a September 1984 installment of *ABC News 20/20*, Geraldo Rivera interviewed judge John L. Angelotta, who told him: "A nice girl who gets raped is different than a bad girl who is raped, the bad girl being one who carries on this course of conduct with men." After the broadcast, Angelotta sued Rivera and Barbara Walters for libel and invasion of privacy. He was, however, reelected after his remarks were broadcast on national television. See *Wall Street Journal*, 13 Dec. 1984, p. 24, col. 3.

[9]For commentary see Angela Y. Davis, *Women, Race, and Class* (New York: Random, 1981). See also Charles Herbert Stember, *Sexual Racism: The Emotional Barrier to an Integrated Society* (New York: Elsevier, 1976). Stember does, however, express some sexist/racist attitudes of his own.

[10]For this tradition in American literature see Leslie Fiedler, *Love and Death in the American Novel* (New York: Stein and Day, 1960, 1966). On p. 296 he writes, "All through the history of the novel, there had appeared side by side with the Fair Maiden, the Dark Lady—sinister embodiment of the sexuality denied the snow maiden." That stereotype continues to pervade every form of popular culture: westerns, soap operas, detective stories etc. For a current example, compare blonde, good, wifely Crystal with dark, evil, sexual Alexis on ABC's top rated nighttime soap, *Dynasty*.

[11]Guy Martin, "The Ripper," *Esquire*, Jan. 1981, pp. 58-69.

[12]Daly, *Beyond God the Father*, pp. 62-63.

[13]Gordon Rattray Taylor, *Sex in History* (New York: Vanguard Press, 1970), p. 216.

[14]Charles Henry Lea, *History of the Inquisition of the Middle Ages*, 3 vols. (New York: Macmillan, 1906), III, 548-49.

[15]Matilda Joslyn Gage, *Woman, Church and State* (c. 1893; New York: Arno, 1972), pp. 218, 291.

[16]Gage writing in 1893 gave a firm estimate of nine million witches executed, p. 247. Andrea Dworkin, in *Woman Hating* (New York: Dutton, 1974), p. 149, repeats this figure. Gordon Rattray Taylor also cites what he calls the "well-known estimate of the total deathtoll, from Roman times onward, of nine millions," although he

says it is probably somewhat too high, p. 127. More conservative estimates are offered by Rossell Hope Robbins, in *The Encyclopedia of Witchcraft and Demonology* (New York: Crown, 1969), p. 180, who gives the oft-quoted and "cautious" estimate of 200,000. Nachman Ben-Yehuda, "The European Witch Craze of the 14th to 17th Centuries: A Sociologist's Perspective," *American Journal of Sociology*, 86 (1980), 1-13, gives the range of 200,000 to 500,000 executed between the early decades of the 14th century and 1650. See also Francis L. K. Hsu, "A Neglected Aspect of Witchcraft Studies," *Journal of American Folklore*, 73 (1960), 35-38. Hsu places the numerical limits between a minimum of 30,000 and a maximum of several million.

[17]Ben-Yehuda, p. 6. He arrives at this percentage after comparing estimates from Lea, E.W. Monter, and H.C. Erik Midelfort.

[18]Joseph Hansen, *Zauberwahn, Inquisition and Hexenprozess in Mitelalter* (Munich: R. Oldenbourg, Verlag, 1900), cited in E.W. Monter, *European Witchcraft* (New York: Wiley, 1969), p. 9.

[19]E.W. Monter, *Witchcraft in France and Switzerland* (Ithica: Cornell University Press, 1976), p. 17.

[20]Hugh Trevor-Roper, *The European Witch-craze of the Sixteenth and Seventeenth Centuries and Other Essays* (New York: Harper and Row, 1967), p. 101.

[21]Hansen, in Monter, p. 9.

[22]Hansen, in Monter, p. 5.

[23]Monter, p. 18.

[24]Innocent VIII, "Summis desiderantes affectibus," in Heinrich Kramer and James Sprenger, *The Malleus Maleficarum*, trans. with Introductions and notes by Montague Summers (c. 1928; New York: Dover, 1971), pp. xliii-xlv.

[25]Ben-Yehuda, p. 11.

[26]Kramer and Sprenger, pp. 43-47.

[27]Kramer and Sprenger, p. 47.

[28]See Robbins, pp. 461-68. This section deals with "Sexual relations with Devils."

[29]See Robbins, pp. 399-401 and 498-510.

[30]See Mary Daly, *Pure Lust: Elemental Feminist Philosophy* (Boston: Beacon Press, 1984), p. 2.

[31]Kramer and Sprenger, p. 58.

[32]H.C. Erik Midelfort, *Witch Hunting in Southwestern Germany 1562-1684: The Social and Intellectual Foundations* (Stanford, Ca.: Stanford University Press, 1972), p. 5.

[33]Kramer and Sprenger, pp. 117-18.

[34]Kramer and Sprenger, pp. 118, 121.

[35]Julio Caro Baroja, *The World of the Witches*, trans, O. N. V. Glendenning (Chicago: University of Chicago Press, 1964), p. 250.

[36]Lea, I, p. 203.

[37]Quoted in Marian Christy, "That Elusive Quality Known as Glamour," *Boston Globe*, 22 Jan. 1979, p. 13, col. 2.

[38]See Jane Caputi, "The Glamour of Grammar," *Chrysalis: A Magazine of Women's Culture*, No. 4 (1977), 35-43.

[39]Carolyn Matalene, "Women as Witches," *International Journal of Women's Studies*, 1 (1978), 573-87. Matalene writes, "Of all the stereotypes of women in Western culture...perhaps none is so clearly defined, so historically tenacious, and so easily envisioned as the witch." A brief, but telling example from popular song is The Eagles, "Witchy Woman," written by Don Henley and Bernie Leadon, *The Eagles*,

Asylum, SD-5054, 1972. The lyrics read in part, "Well I know you want a lover, but let me tell you brother, she's been sleeping in the devil's bed"...Ooh, ooh, witchy woman. See how high she flies. Ooh, ooh, witchy woman, she's got the moon in her eyes."

[40]Trevor-Roper, p. 91. See also Robbins, p. 9. See also Jeffrey Burton Russell, *Witchcraft in the Middle Ages* (Ithaca, N.Y.: Cornell University Press, 1972), p. 234.

[41]Ben-Yehuda, p. 16.

[42]Ben-Yehuda, p. 25.

[43]Mary Daly, *Gyn/Ecology: The Metaethics of Radical Feminism* (Boston: Beacon Press, 1978), p. 184.

[44]Ben-Yehuda, p. 24. See also p. 13.

[45]Ben-Yehuda, pp. 21-22.

[46]See for example Janet Zillinger Giele, *Woman and the Future: Changing Sex Roles in Modern America* (New York: The Free Press, 1978); "Working Women: Joys and Sorrows," *U.S. News and World Report*, 15 Jan 1979. pp. 64-68.

[47]Andrew J. Cherlin, *Marriage, Divorce, Remarriage* (Cambridge, Ma.: Harvard University Press, 1981).

[48]The position of the Catholic Church is that abortion is murder. Both it and contraception are considered sinful. See Richard L. Ganz, ed., *Thou Shalt Not Kill: The Christian Case Against Abortion* (New Rochelle, N.Y.: Arlington House, 1978).

[49]George L. Ginsberg, William A. Frosch, and Theodore Shapiro, "The New Impotence," *Archives of General Psychiatry*, 26 (1972), 218-20; Philip Nobile, "What is the New Impotence and Who's Got it?," *Esquire*, Oct. 1972, pp. 95; See also George Gilder, *Sexual Suicide* (New York: Quadrangle, 1973); Christopher Lasch, *The Culture of Narcissism: American Life in an Age of Diminishing Expectations* (New York: Norton, 1979; rpt. New York: Warner Books, 1979), pp. 319-49.

[50]See for example Orrin E. Klapp, *Collective Search for Identity* (New York: Holt, Rinehart and Winston, 1969); Herbert Marcuse, *One-Dimensional Man* (Boston: Beacon Press, 1964); George Steiner, *In Bluebeard's Castle: Some Notes Toward the Redefinition of Culture* (New Haven, Ct.: Yale University Press, 1974).

[51]Alvin Toffler, *The Third Wave* (New York: William Morrow and Company, 1980), p. 28.

[52]"A Deluge of Disastermania," *Time*, 5 March 1979.

[53]*New York Times*, 6 April 1980, Sec. 7, p. 27. Lindsey's books include, with C.C. Carlson, *The Late Great Planet Earth* (Toronto: Bantam, 1970); Hal Lindsey, *Satan Is Alive & Well on Planet Earth* (New York: Bantam, 1974); Hal Lindsey, *The Nineteen Eighties: Countdown to Armageddon* (New York: Bantam, 1982); Hal Lindsey, *The Rapture* (New York: Bantam, 1983).

[54]Clyde Nunn, "The Rising Credibility of the Devil in America," *Listening*, 9 (1974), 84-98.

[55]Ira Levin, *Rosemary's Baby* (New York: Random, 1967). The *New York Times* used the term "satanophany" in its review of *The Omen*. This is quoted in Marshall W. Fishwick, *Common Culture and the Great Tradition: The Case for Renewal*, Contributions to the Study of Popular Culture, No. 2 (Westport, Ct.: Greenwood Press, 1982), p. 226. See also pp. 115-21 for Fishwick's discussion of the devil as a "super star" in popular culture.

[56]Robin Wood, "The Return of the Repressed," *Film Comment*, 14, No. 4 (1978), 23-32.

[57]The Rolling Stones, *Their Satanic Majesties Request*, London, NPS-2, 1967.

The Rolling Stones, "Sympathy for the Devil," *Beggars Banquet*, London, PS 539, 1968. See also Philip Norman, *Sympathy for the Devil: The Rolling Stones' Story* (New York: Simon and Schuster, 1984; rpt. Dell, 1985).

[58]Iron Maiden, *The Number of the Beast*, EMI Records, St-12202, 1982. Judas Priest, *Defenders of the Faith*, Columbia, FC 39219, 1984.

[59]As friends told the police, Ramirez' favorite song on that album was something called "Night Prowler." Its lyrics go in part: "Was that a noise outside your window, or a shadow on your blind?/ As you lie there naked, like a body in a tomb/suspended animation as I slip into your room." Angus Young, Malcolm Young, Bon Scott, "Night Prowler," AC/DC, *Highway to Hell*, Atlantic, 19244, 1979. These lyrics are reprinted in Ralph Cipriano, "To Fans and Critics 'Night Prowler' Is Supposed To Be Fun," *Los Angeles Times*, 2 Sept. 1985, Part 1, p. 3, col. 1. See also "Night Stalker,"*People Weekly*, 16 Sept. 1985, pp. 43-45. See also, " 'Night Stalker' left devil-worship symbols, reports say," *Albuquerque Tribune*, 2 Sept. 1985, p. A6.

[60]Sandra Salmans, "Man in the Moon loses job at P&G," *New York Times*, 25 April 1985, Sec. D, p. 1.

[61]Ben-Yehuda, p. 24.

[62]Kate Millett, *Sexual Politics* (Garden City, N.Y.: Doubleday, 1970), p. 25.

[63]Daly, *Gyn/Ecology*, pp. 153-77; Dworkin, *Woman Hating*, pp. 118-50; Gage, *Woman, Church, and State*, pp. 217-94.

[64]Millett, p. 43.

[65]James Horwitz, "Ted Bundy—Portrait of a Compulsive Killer," *Cosmopolitan*, Nov. 1980, pp. 328-36.

[66]Thomas Szasz, *The Myth of Mental Illness: Foundations of a Theory of Personal Conduct*, rev. ed. (New York: Harper and Row, 1974).

[67]J.C. Pritchard, *A Treatise on Insanity and Other Disorders Affecting the Mind* (London: Sherwood, Gilbert, and Piper, 1835). For a historical survey of the concept see Richard T. Rada, "Sexual Psychopathology: Historical Survey and Basic Concepts," in *Clinical Aspects of the Rapist*, ed. Richard T. Rada (New York: Grune and Stratton, 1978), pp. 1-19.

[68]Thomas Strentz and Conrad V. Hassel, "The Sociopath—A Criminal Enigma," *Journal of Police Science and Administration*, 6 (1978), 135-40. The psychologist quoted is Robert E. Hardin from his book, *The Rapist and the Victim*.

[69]Robert J. Smith, "The Psychopath as Moral Agent," *Philosophy and Phenomenological Research*, 14, No. 2 (1984), 177-92. Smith notes that his use of the term corresponds with that of Hervey Cleckly in his standard work, *The Mask of Sanity*, 5th ed. (St. Louis: C.V. Mosby, 1976). The list of traits Smith offers is gleaned from "criteria generally agreed upon by clinicians and researchers."

[70]Smith, "The Psychopath as Moral Agent," p. 193.

[71]See, for example, E. Sutherland, "The Sexual Psychopath Laws," *Journal of Criminal Law and Criminology*, 40 (1950), 543-44; Domenico Caporale, "Sexual Psychopathy—A Legal Labyrinth of Medicine, Morals and Morality," *Nebraska Law Review*, 36 (1957), 320-53.

[72]Paul H. Gebhard, John H. Gagnon, Wardell B. Pomeroy, and Cornelia V. Christenson, *Sex Offenders: An Analysis of Types* (New York: Harper and Row, Publishers, and Paul B. Hoeber, 1965), p. 846. See also Andrea Dworkin's critique of this report in *Pornography: Men Possessing Women* (New York: Perigee, 1981), pp. 188-98.

[73]Norman Mailer, "The White Negro," in *Advertisements for Myself* (New York:

Signet, 1959), pp. 302-22; Wayne J. Douglass, "The Criminal Psychopath as Hollywood Hero," *Journal of Popular Film and Television*, 8, No. 4 (1981), 30-40. Douglass also refers to an article by Dr. Michael Glenn, "The Psychopath: Hero of Our Age," in *The Village Voice*, 1968.

[74]Alan Harrington, *Psychopaths* (New York: Simon and Schuster, 1972), p. 33.

[75]This scenario is enacted with utter clarity in the acclaimed film *Prizzi's Honor* (John Huston, 1985)—a snuff movie for intellectuals and film connoisseurs. The milieu is the New York Mafia, the microcosm of patriarchy, with its focus on the old godfather, a.k.a. the fathergod of all patriarchal religions. Jack Nicholson plays the chief hit man for "The Family," who long ago made a literal pact in blood with the godfather to always protect his all-male Family. Nicholson falls genuinely in love with an outsider, a woman who is herself a hired killer. For a while all goes well, but it is clear that she is not properly subordinate and will prove a threat to the solidarity and well-being of the Family. Just as David Berkowitz as the "Son of Sam" heard and followed a command to kill from his father figure, so too is Nicholson ordered by his godfather to kill the woman he loves. Although suffering a few pangs, he nevertheless complies for he knows that he would be utterly alone and vulnerable without his true Family, the brotherhood of Man. In order to make the ending seem more "fair" or less explicitly gynocidal, the script calls for the wife (Kathleen Turner) to realize that her husband is going to kill her. Thus in the last scene, they are in the bedroom, purportedly preparing for sex, but actually for murder. He is in bed waiting with his knife; she comes in with a gun. But of course, the woman never had a chance. Her shot misses its aim, while Nicholson tosses his knife straight through her throat and impales her against the wall. The camera lingers here on the "snuff" scene for the enjoyment, or terrorization, of the male or female viewers.

[76]See Daly, *Gyn/Ecology*, pp. 178-222.

[77]Quoted in Susan Brownmiller, *Against Our Will* (New York: Simon and Schuster, 1975), p. 205.

[78]Quoted in Amanda Spake, "The End of the Ride: Analyzing a Sex Crime," *Mother Jones*, April 1980, pp. 34-43.

[79]Quoted in Wendy Hollway, " 'I just wanted to kill a woman' Why?: The Ripper and Male Sexuality," *Feminist Review*, 9 (Oct. 1981), 33-40, esp. 37.

[80]Quoted in Ann Jones, "A Little Knowledge," in *Take Back the Night: Women on Pornography*, ed. Laura Lederer (New York: Morrow, 1980), pp. 179-84.

[81]See "The Mind of a Murderer," prod. and dir. Michael Barnes, *Frontline*, PBS, 27 March 1984.

[82]Quoted in Stephen G. Michaud and Hugh Aynesworth, "When One Murders: Ted Bundy Talks about the Unthinkable," *Esquire*, March 1983, p. 76.

[83]See "Serial Murderers," narr. Sylvia Chase, *ABC News 20/20*, 5 July 1984.

[84]See Diane Lewis, "Paradiso found guilty of 2nd degree murder," *Boston Globe*, 22 July 1984, Sec. 1, p. 1.

[85]Major Kraske of the Seattle Police, interviewed on "Murder: No Apparent Motive," prod. and dir. Imre Horvath, *Home Box Office Special*, broadcast throughout 1984.

[86]Quoted in John Beattie, *The Yorkshire Ripper Story* (London: Quartet Books, 1981), p. 133.

[87]Quoted in "the Random Killers," *Newsweek*, 26 Nov. 1984, p. 104.

[88]Quoted in "Sam Told Me to do it...Sam is the Devil," *Time*, 22 Aug. 1977,

pp. 22-27; Lawrence D. Klausner, *Son of Sam* (New York: McGraw Hill, 1981), p. 168.

[89]See "The Mind of a Murderer."

[90]Elizabeth Kendall, *The Phantom Prince: My Life with Ted Bundy* (Seattle: Madrona Publishers, 1981).

[91]Indeed, the commonality of this situation may contribute to the popularity of the gothic romance genre among women. See Joanna Russ, " 'Somebody's Trying to Kill Me and I Think It's My Husband': The Modern Gothic," *Journal of Popular Culture*, 6 (Spring 1973), 666-91; see also Andrea Dworkin, "The Root Cause," in *Our Blood: Prophecies and Discourses on Sexual Politics* (New York: Harper and Row, 1976). We might also recall Dan Greenburg's happily sadistic title of his sex crime novel, *Love Kills*.

[92]Allan Griswold Johnson, "The Prevalence of Rape in the United States," *Signs: Journal of Women in Culture and Society*, 6, No. 1 (Autumn 1980), 136-50, esp. 145. Johnson's findings are corroborated by Diana E.H. Russell and Nancy Howell, "The Prevalence of Rape in the United States Revisited," *Signs: Journal of Women in Culture and Society*, 8, No. 4 (Summer 1983), 688-95.

[93]Steven A. Egger, "A Working Definition of Serial Murder and the Reduction of Linkage Blindness," *Journal of Police Science and Administration*, 12, No. 3 (1984), 348-357, esp. 351.

[94]Gage, pp. 242-43.

[95]Smith, "Getting Away with Murder," p. 12.

[96]Midelfort, pp. 195-96.

[97]Roger Langley and Richard C. Levy, *Wife Beating: The Silent Crisis* (New York: Dutton, 1977), p. 3. They write, "No one knows how many American women are being routinely beaten by their husbands, ex-husbands, boy friends, common-law spouses, and dates." See also Vicki McNickle Rose and Susan C. Randall, "Where Have all the Rapists Gone? An Illustration of the Attrition-of-Justice Phenomenon," in *Violent Crime: Historical and Contemporary Issues*, ed. James A. Inciardi and Anne E. Pottieger, Sage Research Progress Series in Criminology, Vol. 5 (Beverly Hills: Sage Publications, 1978), pp. 75-90. Rose and Randall write, "In spite of current interest in the problem, we really know very little about the actual incidence of rape or other sexual assaults in the United States."

[98]Brownmiller, p. 197.

[99]See Robert Lindsey, "Officials cite rise in killers who roam U.S. for victims," *New York Times*, 21 Jan. 1984, Sec. A, p. 1, col. 5. See also Egger, "A Working Definition of Serial Murder," p. 349. Also, it should be noted that the Federal Government has announced that it will initiate the operation of a $5-million computer system which will provide a clearinghouse of information on serial murders across the country. See Peter Johnson, "Computers to help track repeat slayers," *USA Today*, 17 April 1984, p. 3A.

[100]In three recent cases, boyfriends who murdered their lovers were barely punished at all. See Dominick Dunne, "Justice," *Vanity Fair*, March 1984, pp. 86-106; Peter Meyer, *The Yale Murder* (New York: Empire Books, 1982): Carolyn Weaver, "The Killing of Laura," *Mother Jones*, Feb/March 1984, pp. 32-39.

[101]Some 2,000 to 4,000 women are beaten to death annually by their "lovers." Jane O'Reilly, "Wife Beating: The Silent Crime," *Time*, 5 Sept. 1983, pp. 23-26.

[102]During the Witchcraze, perhaps fifteen percent of the victims were male, victimized particularly, as Midelfort notes, toward the end of the craze. Indeed, as

the murderous fury began to spill over and condemn more men, the culture started to come to its "senses" and end the craze. Again, no precise percentage breakdowns are available regarding the sex of those who become victims of sexual murder in this country, but, as with women, most male victims are "marginal"—runaways, missing children, vagrants, homosexuals, etc.

[103]Smith, "Getting Away with Murder."

[104]Egger, p. 348.

[105]Martin, p. 59.

[106]"Serial Murderers."

[107]Brownmiller, p. 15.

[108]Daly, *Gyn/Ecology*, p. 362.

[109]For a most insightful analysis of street harassment of women, see Pam MacAllister, "Wolf Whistles and Warnings" *Heresies: A Feminist Publication on Art and Politics*, 5 (Summer 1978), 37-39.

[110]Derek Morgan, "Absolutely Ripping!" rev. of *When London Walked in Terror*, by Tom A. Cullen, *The Reporter*, 18 Nov. 1965, pp. 54-55.

[111]June Jordan, "Against the Wall" (1978), in *Civil Wars* (Boston: Beacon Press, 1981), pp. 147-49.

[112]"London: Whitechapel Paranoiac's Victims," *New York Times*, 8 Oct. 1888, pp. 4-5.

[113]Daly, *Gyn/Ecology*, p. 39.

[114]The notion of the "sacred of transgression" was first introduced by Roger Caillois. See his *Man and the Sacred*, trans. Meyer Barash (Glencoe, Ill,: The Free Press, 1959), pp. 97-127. For additional commentary see Georges Bataille, *Death and Sensuality: A Study of Eroticism and the Taboo* (New York: Walker and Company, 1962), pp. 63-70; see also Richard Stivers, *Evil in Modern Myth and Ritual* (Athens, Georgia: The University of Georgia Press, 1982), pp. 17-47.

Chapter V

[1]Gregory Zilboorg, *The Medical Man and the Witch During the Renaissance*, The Hideyo Nogushi Lectures (Baltimore: John Hopkins Press, 1935), p. 58; cited in Thomas Szasz, *The Myth of Mental Illness: Foundations of a Theory of Personal Conduct*, rev. ed. (New York: Harper and Row, 1974), p. 183.

[2]Tom A Cullen, *When London Walked in Terror* (Boston: Houghton Mifflin, 1965), pp. 31-32.

[3]Barbara Ehrenreich and Deirdre English, *For Her Own Good: 150 Years of the Experts' Advice to Women* (Garden City, N.Y.: Anchor Press/Doubleday, 1978), pp. 29-35; Barbara Ehrenreich and Deirdre English, *Witches, Midwives and Nurses: A History of Women Healers* (Old Westbury, N.Y.: Feminist Press, 1972); Matilda Joslyn Gage, *Woman, Church, and State* (c. 1893; New York: Arno, 1972) Thomas Szasz, *The Manufacture of Madness* (New York: Dell, 1970); Szasz, *Myth of Mental Illness*.

[4]Ehrenreich and English, *Witches, Midwives and Nurses*, p. 6.

[5]Simone de Beauvoir, *The Second Sex*, trans. H.M. Parshley (c. 1952; New York: Knopf, 1971), p. xvi.

[6]Henry Charles Lea, *Materials Toward a History of Witchcraft*, ed. Arthur C. Howland, 3 Vols. (New York: Thomas Yoseloff, 1957), III, 1079.

[7]Georges Bataille, *Death and Sensuality: A Study of Eroticism and the Taboo* (New York: Walker and Company, 1962), p. 131.

[8]G.J. Barker-Benfield, "Sexual Surgery in Late-Nineteenth Century America," in *Seizing Our Bodies: The Politics of Women's Health*, ed. Claudia Dreifus (New York: Vintage Books, 1977), pp. 13-41.

[9]Barker-Benfield, "Sexual Surgery," p. 21.

[10]Barker-Benfield, "Sexual Surgery," p. 14.

[11]Barker-Benfield, "Sexual Surgery," p. 28.

[12]De Beauvoir, p. xiii.

[13]"The Whitechapel Murder," The *Times* (London), 27 Sept. 1888, Sec. 1, p. 5, col. 4.

[14]Mary Daly, *Gyn/Ecology: The Metaethics of Radical Feminism* (Boston: Beacon Press), pp. 227, 237-38.

[15]Barker-Benfield, "Sexual Surgery," p. 15.

[16]Barker-Benfield, "Sexual Surgery," pp. 28, 38-39.

[17]G.J. Barker-Benfield, *The Horrors of the Half-Known Life: Male Attitudes Toward Women and Sexuality in Nineteenth Century America* (New York: Harper and Row, 1975), p. 250.

[18]Barker-Benfield, "Sexual Surgery," p. 27.

[19]Barker-Benfield, "Sexual Surgery," p. 21.

[20]Daly, p. 237.

[21]*Hustler*, Nov. 1977, p. 6.

[22]Cited in Barker-Benfield, *Horrors of the Half-Known Life*, p. 95.

[23]Gerold Frank, *The Boston Strangler* (New York: New American Library, 1967), p. 62, note.

[24]Ted Schwarz with Kelli Boyd, "Kenneth Bianchi: Inside the Mind of the 'Hillside Strangler,' " *Hustler*, Aug. 1981, pp. 36.

[25]*Hustler* has run an erotic photo series called "A Day in the Life of a Gynecologist," *Hustler*, July 1976, pp. 40-47. This same series then appeared in *The Best of Hustler* 2, 1975-1976.

[26]Jean-Paul Sartre, "The Hole," in *Existentialism and Human Emotions* (New York: The Philosophical Library, 1957), pp. 84-90. See also Peggy Holland, "Jean Paul Sartre as a *No* to Women," *Sinister Wisdom*, 6 (Summer 1978), 72-79.

[27]Harold K. Banks, *The Strangler: The Story of Terror in Boston* (New York: Avon, 1967), p. 75.

[28]Daly, *Gyn/Ecology*, pp. 234, 237.

[29]Richard von Krafft-Ebing, *Psychopathia Sexualis*, trans, from the twelfth German edition and with an introduction by Franklin S. Klaf (New York: Stein and Day, 1965), pp. 58-59.

[30]Barker-Benfield, "Sexual Surgery," p. 24.

[31]Barker-Benfield, "Sexual Surgery," p. 22.

[32]Ben Barker-Benfield, "The Spermatic Economy: A Nineteenth Century View of Sexuality," *Feminist Studies*, 1, No. 1 (1972), 45-74.

[33]Barker-Benfield, "Sexual Surgery," p. 32.

[34]Barker-Benfield, "Sexual Surgery," p. 32.

[35]Barker-Benfield, "Spermatic Economy," p. 60.

[36]Ely Van de Warker, "The Fetich of the Ovary," *American Journal of Obstetrics*, 54 (1906); cited in Barker-Benfield, *Horrors*, pp. 131-32.

[37]Maggie Scarf, rev, of *Medical and Psychological Interfaces Vol. 1: Sexual and Reproductive Aspects of Women's Health Care*, by Malkah Notman and Carol Nadelson, *New York Times*, 12 Dec. 1978, Sec. 7, p. 11.

[38]Deborah Larned, "The Greening of the Womb," *New Times*, Dec. 1974, pp. 35-39; see also Gena Corea, "The Ceasarean Epidemic," *Mother Jones*, July 1980, pp. 28; Mirian F. Hirsch, *Women and Violence* (New York: Van Nostrand, 1981); Jeann Rodgers, "Rush to Surgery," *New York Times Magazine*, 21 Sep. 1975, pp. 34-42.

[39]Larned, pp. 36-37.

[40]Quoted in Larned, p. 37.

[41]Hirsch, pp. 246-53; Rose Kushner, "The Politics of Breast Cancer," in *Seizing Our Bodies*, pp. 186-94.

[42]Cited in Hirsch, p. 249.

[43]Dee Wedemeyer, "After mastectomy: the options for breast reconstructions," *New York Times*, 9 Dec. 1976, Sec. 1, p. 56, col. 1.

[44]Larned, p. 38.

[45]Quoted in Kay Weiss, "What Medical Students Learn About Women," in *Seizing Our Bodies*, pp. 212-22. The text is by J.R. Willson, C.T. Beecham, and E.R. Carrington, *Obstetrics and Gynecology*, 4th ed. (St. Louis, Mo.: C.V. Mosby, 1971).

[46]Matt Clark with Dan Shapiro, "Breast Surgery before Cancer," *Newsweek*, 1 Dec. 1980.

[47]Barbara Ehrenreich and Deirdre English, *Complaints and Disorders: The Sexual Politics of Sickness*, Glass Mountain Pamphlet No. 2 (Old Westbury, N.Y.: The Feminist Press, 1973), p. 43.

[48]Szasz, *Myth of Mental Illness*, pp. 190-91.

[49]Cited in Daly, p. 223. This is taken from Sigmund Freud, *Dora: An Analysis of a Case of Hysteria*, 1905, trans. by Alix and James Strachey, in *The Case of Dora and Other Papers* (New York: Norton, 1952).

[50]Jean Baker Miller, ed., *Psychoanalysis and Women: Contributions to New Theory and Therapy* (New York: Brunner/Mazel, 1973), p. vii.

[51]Ehrenreich and English, *Complaints and Disorders*, p. 43.

[52]Phyllis Chesler, *Women and Madness* (Garden City, N.Y.: Doubleday, 1972); Shulamith Firestone, *The Dialectic of Sex* (New York: Bantam, 1970); Kate Millett, *Sexual Politics* (Garden City, N.Y: Doubleday, 1970). For a more sympathetic treatment see Juliet Mitchell, *Psychoanalysis and Feminism* (New York: Pantheon Books, Random House, 1974).

[53]L. D. Klausner, *Son of Sam* (New York: McGraw Hill, 1981), p. 60.

[54]Quoted in Ellis E. Conklin, "Killer's Violence Left No Pattern," *Boston Globe*, 1 Sept. 1985, p. 12, col. 6.

[55]Klausner, p. 140.

[56]Sigmund Freud, "Some Psychological Consequences of the Anatomical Distinction Between the Sexes" (1925), *The Standard Edition of the Complete Psychological Works of Sigmund Freud*, XIX (London: Hogarth, 1953), p. 252.

[57]Freud, "An Outline of Psychoanalysis," *Standard Edition*, XXIII, pp. 202-03.

[58]Angela Carter, *The Sadeian Woman and the Ideology of Pornography* (New York: Pantheon Books, 1978), p. 23.

[59]Phyllis Greenacre, "Certain Relationships between Fetishism and Faulty Development of the Body Image," *Psychoanalytic Study of the Child*, 8 (1953), p. 93.

[60]Leonard R. Sillman, "Femininity and Paranoidism," *Journal of Nervous and Mental Disease*, 143 (1966), 163-70.

[61]See Diana E.H. Russell, *Rape in Marriage* (New York: Macmillan, 1982), especially pp. 17-24, 227-236.

[62]Freud, "Dreams," *Standard Edition*, XV, p. 154.

[63] *Hetero-relations* is a word invented by Janice G. Raymond to express "the wide range of affective, social, political, and economic relations that are ordained between men and women by men." See Janice G. Raymond, *A Passion for Friends: Toward a Philosophy of Female Affection* (Boston: Beacon Press 1985), p. 7.

[64]Richard A. Spears, *Slang and Euphemism* (Middle Village, N.Y.: Jonathan David Publishers, 1981).

[65]John Rockwell, "The Sex Pistols: A Fired-Up Rock Band," *New York Times*, 7 Aug. 1977, Sec. 2, p. 16, col. 1.

[66]D.H. Lawrence, *Studies in Classic American Literature* (New York: Penguin Books, 1977), p. 68.

[67]Mickey Spillane, *I, The Jury* (c. 1947; New York: New American Library, 1973), pp. 173-4.

[68]Helen Caldicott, *Missile Envy: The Arms Race and Nuclear War* (New York: Morrow, 1984), p. 297.

[69]See Steven Heller, *War Heads: Cartoonists Draw the Line* (New York: Penguin Books, 1983), p. 66.

[70] *Public Illumination Magazine*, 21 June 1982, p. 14.

[71]Quoted in Bob Bach, Letter, *New York Times*, 2 February 1984, Sec. A, p. 18, col. 5.

[72] *New York Times*, 24 March 1983, Sec. I, p. 20, col. 1.

[73]Quoted in Philip M. Boffey, "Dark Side of 'Star Wars': System Could Also Attack," *New York Times*, 7 March 1984, National ed., p. 1, col. 3.

[74]Sartre, p. 86.

[75]Daly, *Gyn/Ecology*, p. 244.

[76]Peter Gay, *The Bourgeois Experience: Victoria to Freud* (New York: Oxford, 1984), p. 207.

[77]For a discussion of these motifs in contemporary literature see Gershon Legman, *Love and Death* (New York: Hacker Art Books, (1949, 1963); Leslie Fiedler, *Love and Death in the American Novel* (New York: Stein and Day, 1966).

[78]Annie Goldson, "Three-Minute Heroes," *Heresies: A Feminist Publication on Art and Politics*, 16, No. 4 (1983), 6-10.

[79] *Doubledream* from Daly, *Gyn/Ecology*, p. 333.

[80]Daryl Hall and John Oates, "Maneater," *Rock 'n Soul Part 1*, RCA, CPL1-4858, 1983.

[81]Van Stevenson, "Modern Day Delilah," *Righteous Anger*, MCA Records, MCA-5482, 1984.

[82]Wendy Hollway, " 'I just wanted to kill a woman' " Why?: The Ripper and Male Sexuality, *Feminist Review*, 9, Oct. 1981, 33-40, esp. 37. The quote from the *Observer* is from 7 May 1981.

[83]Christopher Lasch, *The Culture of Narcissism: American Life in an Age of Diminishing Expectations* (New York: Norton, 1979: rpt. New York: Warner Books, 1979), p. 203. See also Wolfgang Lederer, *The Fear of Women* (New York: Harcourt Brace Jovanovich, 1968), pp. 35-43.

[84]Jane E. Caputi, " 'Jaws' as Patriarchal Myth," *Journal of Popular Film*, 6 (1978), 305-25.

[85]For a comprehensive account of the "Terrible Mother" see Erich Neumann, *The Great Mother: An Analysis of the Archetype*, trans. Ralph Manheim, 2nd ed., Bollingen Series 47 (Princeton: Princeton University Press, 1963; rpt. Bollingen

paperback, 1973); for a concise explication of the *vagina dentata* motif see Maria Leach, ed., *Standard Dictionary of Folklore, Mythology and Legend* (New York: Funk and Wagnalls, 1949-50), s.v. *"vagina dentata."*

[86]"The Terror that Stalks Black Women," The *Boston Globe*, 14 June 1979, p. 73.

[87]Amanda Spake, "The End of the Ride: Analyzing a Sex Crime," *Mother Jones*, April 1980, pp. 34-43.

[88]Beth Day, *Sexual Life Between Blacks and Whites: The Roots of Racism* (New York: Thomas Y. Crowell, 1974), p. 69.

[89]Ironically, the popular image of "Bluebeard" is of a wife-killer, but the persona was actually based upon a purported killer of boys, Gilles de Rais. As Susan Brownmiller writes:

> The Gilles de Rais story...has metamorphosed from a terrifying account of a sex-murderer of small boys to a glorified fantasy of a devilish rake who killed seven wives for their "curiosity." It is almost as if the *truth* of Bluebeard's atrocities was too frightening to men to survive in the popular imagination—but turned about so that Bluebeard's victims were acceptably female, the horror was sufficiently diminished (but not, of course, to women).

See Brownmiller, *Against Our Will: Men, Women and Rape* (New York: Simon and Schuster, 1975), p. 292.

[90]Andrea Dworkin, "Why So-Called Radical Men Love and Need Pornography," *in Take Back the Night: Women on Pornography*, ed. Laura Lederer (New York: Morrow, 1980), pp. 148-154, esp. 152.

[91]Richard Meryman, "Marilyn Lets Her Hair Down About Being Famous," *Life*, 3 Aug. 1962, p. 36.

[92]Margaret Cheney, *The Coed Killer* (New York: Walker and Company, 1976), p. 208.

[93]Vietnam Veterans Against the War, *The Winter Soldier Investigation: An Inquiry into American War Crimes* (Boston: Beacon Press, 1972), p. 74.

[94]de Beauvoir, p. 261.

[95]James Laver, *Taste and Fashion* (London: Harrap, 1938), p. 98.

[96]"The New American Woman," *Esquire*, February 1967, pp. 30.

[97]Robert R. Hazlewood and John E. Douglas, "The Lust Murderer," *FBI Law Enforcement Bulletin*, 49, No. 4 (1980), 18-22. This article is illustrated with rough sketches of a sex murderer dumping women's bodies into garbage cans. In a recent article in *Life*, the authors tell us that the "The recreational killer...kills with total ferocity, sometimes discarding bodies like garbage, sometimes painstakingly arranging them as though for a pornographic photo." Brad Darrach and Joel Norris, "An American Tragedy," *Life*, August 1984, pp. 58-74.

[98]See John G. Cawelti, *Adventure, Mystery and Romance: Formula Stories as Art and Popular Culture* (Chicago: University of Chicago Press, 1976), pp. 148-61; E. Ann Kaplan, *Women in Film Noir* (London: British Film Institute, 1978).

[99]Michael Wood, *America in the Movies* (New York: Dell, 1975), p. 51.

[100]Ernest Becker, *Escape From Evil* (New York: The Free Press, 1975), pp. 146-70.

[101]Cheney, p. 208.

[102]In September, 1985, the catholic evangelical movement staged a daylong rally in the Boston Garden, attended by an estimated 13,000 believers (many bussed in

from other parts of the country). The *Boston Globe* reports that Ralph Martin, first of a team of four speakers, told the crowd: " 'What we know as Western civilization...had its roots in Christianity.... The triumph of Christianity lifted up the level of life in the West, but today our generation is living on borrowed capital.... The church is divided. There is skepticism about the authority of scripture and the church. Are we not in danger of slipping back into our barbaric tribes?' He said there was a growth in 'pagan practices,' citing witchcraft, superstition, fear of having children and 'a general diminution of the value of human life.' " See James L. Franklin, "13,000 Catholics rally at Garden," *Boston Globe*, 22 Sept. 1985, pp. 29, 45.

[103]George Stade, *Confessions of a Lady-Killer* (New York: Alpha/Omega, 1979), p. 41.

Chapter VI

[1]Andrea Dworkin, "The Root Cause," in *Our Blood: Prophecies and Discourses on Sexual Politics* (New York: Harper and Row, 1976), 96-111, esp. 100.

[2]Michelle Citron and Ellen Seiter, "Teaching: The Woman with the Movie Camera," *Jump Cut*, No. 26 (Dec. 1981), pp. 61-62.

[3]Notorious here is photographer Les Krims, who produced a series of pictures entitled "The Incredible Case of the Stack 'o' Wheats Murders." This series is often described by its defenders as a humorous treatment of the phenomenon of serial "signature" murder, i.e. those in which the killer subjects the victim to a characteristic mutilation or in which a particular fetish/object is left at the scene of each crime. All of the photographs show a women, either entirely nude or stripped from the waist down, and lying in what appears to be her own blood. She is often gagged and bound and her head is sometimes covered with a bag or cloth. In some of the prints, her body shows realistic looking knife wounds. Frequently her legs are spread; in one photograph an upright Coke bottle stands between her thighs—a clear allusion to the common device of rape with an object. Each picture also contains a stack of whole wheat pancakes. The "blood" in each picture is actually Hershey's syrup and Krims promises one can of syrup and enough pancake mix to make one Stack o' Wheats to anyone who purchases the series.

On March 31, 1980, anti-rape activist Deborah Spray checked out a set of the photographic prints from the Universtiy of Santa Cruz Library, tore them up, and poured Hershey's syrup over the remains; a photographer recorded the scene. Spray called her action, "The Incredible Case of the Stack o' Prints Mutilations." As D.A. Clarke further reports: "The day after Deborah Spray saw the Stack o' Wheats prints for the first time, the murder of Barbara Schwartz made the front page of the San Francisco Chronicle; she was stabbed to death while jogging in broad daylight, on Mount Tamalpais, her screams overheard by golfers who did not respond. Two USC women had been murdered in the summer and fall of 1979—Jennifer McDowell and Diane Steffy. Residents of Santa Cruz remember well the time of the Kemper murders, when woman after woman was found dead and mutilated. Some of us will never forget Larry Singleton, who raped fifteen-year-old Mary Vincent and then hacked off both her arms, any more than we will forget the Boston Strangler, the Hillside Strangler, or 'Stinky,' the rapist. Every month or so there is something new to remember," D.A. Clarke, "The Incredible Case of *The Stack o' Prints Mutilations*," *Quest: A Feminist Quarterly*, 5, No. 3 (1981), 81-91.

[4]Michael Arlen, *The Camera Age: Essays on Television* (New York: Farrar Straus

Giroux, 1981); Susan Sontag, *On Photography* (New York: Delta, 1977), p. 24.

[5]See Harold Lasswell, "The Structure and Function of Communication in Society," in *The Communication of Ideas*, ed. L. Bryson (New York: Harper and Row, 1948), pp. 37-51; Marshall McLuhan and Carpenter, *Explorations in Communications* (Boston: Beacon Press, 1960); Edmund Carpenter, *Oh, What a Blow that Phantom Gave Me!* (New York: Holt, Rinehart and Winston, 1972, 1973); Tony Schwartz, *Media: The Second God* (New York: Random, 1981); George Gerbner, "The Dynamics of Cultural Resistance," in *Hearth and Home: Images of Women in the Media*, ed. Gaye Tuchman. Arlene K. Daniels, and James Benet (New York: Oxford, 1978), pp. 46-50; Gregor T. Goethals, *The TV Ritual: Worship at the Video Altar* (Boston: Beacon Press, 1981).

[6]Lasswell, "The Structure and Function of Communication."

[7]Gerbner, "The Dynamics of Cultural Resistance," p. 47.

[8]For an analysis of the role of religion in the social construction of reality see Peter Berger, *The Sacred Canopy: Elements of a Sociological Theory of Religion* (New York: Doubleday, 1967).

[9]Gaye Tuchman, "Introduction: The Symbolic Annihilation of Women by the Mass Media," in *Hearth and Home*, pp. 2-28.

[10]George Gerbner and Larry Gross write, "Among females, more vulnerable than men in most categories, both young and old women as well as unmarried, lower class, foreign, and nonwhite women bore especially heavy burdens of relative victimization. Old, poor, and black women were shown only as killed and never as killers. Interestingly, "good" women, unlike "good" men, had no lethal power, but "bad" women were even more lethal than "bad" men." See George Gerbner and Larry Gross, "Living with Television: The Violence Profile," *Journal of Communication*, 26, No. 2 (Spring 1976), reprinted in *Television: The Critical View*, ed. Horace Newcomb, 2nd ed. (New York: Oxford, 1979), pp. 363-402.

[11]Richard Meryman, "Marilyn Lets Her Hair Down About Being Famous,"*Life*, 3 Aug. 1962, pp. 31-34.

[12]Andrea Dworkin, *Right-wing Women* (New York: Perigee, 1983), p. 21.

[13]"The Night That 38 Stood By as a Life Was Lost," *New York Times*, 12 March, 1984, Sec. B, p. 1, col. 2.

[14]See Marcia Pally, "Double Trouble," *Film Comment*, 20, No. 5 (Oct. 1984), 12-17, esp. 17.

[15]Daniel Goleman, "Violence Against Women in Films is Found to Alter Attitudes of Men," *New York Times*, 28 Aug. 1984, Sec. C, p. 1, col. 3.

[16]For reports on these see Karen Durbin, "Pretty Poison: The Selling of Sexual Warfare, *Village Voice*, 9 May 1977, pp. 18-23; "Really Socking It to Women," *Time*, 7 Feb. 1977, p. 58; Suzanne Lacy, "Learning to Look: The Relationship Between Art and Popular Culture Images," *Exposure*, 18, No. 3 (1981), 8-15; Gerbner and Gross, "Living with Television"; Sally Bedell Smith, "Why TV Won't Let Up on Violence," *New York Times*, 13 Jan. 1985, Sec. 2, p. 1, col. 2. See also the regular *Newsreport* of Women Against Pornography, 358 West 47th St, New York, N.Y. 10036; *News Page*, from Women Against Violence in Pornography and Media, P.O. Box 14635, San Francisco, CA 94114; *The Backlash Times*, from Feminists Fighting Pornography, P.O. Box 6731, Yorkville Sta., New York, NY 10123. See also the regular reports of the National Coalition on Television Violence (NCTV), P.O. Box 2157, Champaign, IL 61820.

[17]A few examples of these include a Guy Bourdin photograph in an ad for

"Wedgies," a type of shoe (French *Vogue*, Spring/Summer 1975). This photo depicts the scene of a fatal car crash. A chalk outline and bloody puddle indicate where a woman's body lay. Her wedgies remain. Another from Bourdin appeared in *Harper's Bazaar* in 1977. Again for shoes, the picture showed a seemingly dead woman lying in a gift box. In *Vogue* (Oct. 1978) an unsigned photograph ad for Maud Frizon shoes showed a woman wearing glamorous boots, but suffocated under a plastic bag. An ad for Bloomingdale's perfume (*Harper's Bazaar*, 1978) depicted a nude woman who had just been shot with a gun. And, for the more mundane, *Woman's Day* (April 1981) displayed an ad for "Round the Clock" stockings which showed a woman's lower half wearing the stockings; her top half was buried under sand. For commentary see "Fashion's Kinky Look," *Newsweek*, 4 Oct. 1976, pp. 98-99.

[18]The 1970s were first marked by an increase in "kinky" and violent imagery in pornography—"advances" which were facilitated by the findings of a 1970 National Commission on Obscenity and Pornography which concluded that pornography was largely harmless. For information concerning pornographic content in the 1970s, see Neil M. Malamuth and B. Spinner, "A Longitudinal Content Analysis of Sexual Violence in the Best-Selling Erotic Magazines," *The Journal of Sex Research*, 16, No. 3 (1980), 226-37.

For a content analysis of conventional use of force and increasing depiction of rape in hard-core paperbacks see D.G. Smith, "Sexual Aggression in American Pornography: The Stereotype of Rape," presented at the annual meetings of the American Sociological Association, New York, 1976 and D.G. Smith, "The Social Content of Pornography," *Journal of Communication*, 26, (1976), 16-33. Two other researchers found a marked increase of bondage and domination imagery in hard-core heterosexual magazines. See Park E. Dietz and Barbara Evans, "Pornographic Imagery and Prevalence of Paraphilia," *American Journal of Psychiatry*, 139, No. 11 (Nov. 1982), 1493-95.

[19]See Kathleen Barry, *Female Sexual Slavery* (Englewood Cliffs, N.J.: Prentice-Hall, 1979), esp. pp. 174-214: Andrea Dworkin, *Pornography: Men Possessing Women* (New York: Perigee, 1981); Susan Griffin, *Pornography and Silence: Culture's Revenge Against Nature* (New York: Harper and Row, 1981); Laura Lederer, ed. *Take Back the Night: Women On Pornography* (New York: William Morrow, 1980). In this work, see especially articles by Florence Rush, Irene Diamond, Pauline Bart and Margaret Jozsa, and Diana E.H. Russell. See also Diana E.H. Russell, *Sexual Exploitation: Rape, Child Sexual Abuse, and Workplace Harassment*, Sage library of social research, Vol. 155 (Beverly Hills, Calif.: Sage Publications, 1984), esp. pp. 123-32. For a concise statement of Andrea Dworkin's analysis of pornography, see Andrea Dworkin, "Censorship, Pornography, and Equality," *Harvard Women's Law Journal*, 8 (1985), reprinted in *Trivia: A Journal of Ideas*, 7 (Summer 1985), pp. 11-32.

[20]Dworkin, "Censorship, Pornography, and Equality," p. 19.

[21]*Ibid.*

[22]A 1980s National Institute of Justice study on sexual murder in which 36 serial murderers were interviewed by FBI agents, revealed that the murderers, in categorizing their highest sexual interest, ranked pornography as number one. See U.S. Congress, Senate, Subcommittee on Juvenile Justice of the Committee on the Judiciary, *Effect of Pornography on Women and Children*, 98th Congress, 2nd sess., 1984, pp. 123-24, 131. For other sources in which police agents as well as psychologists link the use of pornography to serial sex killers see, Robert Lindsey, "Officials Cite a Rise

in Killers Who Roam U.S. for Victims, *New York Times*, 21 Jan. 1984, Sec. A, p. 1., col. 5. See also Robert H. Morneau and Robert R. Rockwell, *Sex, Motivation and the Criminal Offender* (Springfield, Ill.: Charles Thomas, 1980); Robert R. Hazelwood and John E. Douglas, "The Lust Murderer," *FBI Law Enforcement Bulletin*, 49, No. 4 (April 1980), 18-22; Bruce Porter, "Mind Hunters," *Psychology Today*, April 1983, pp. 44.

²³See Jay Robert Nash, *Bloodletters and Bad Men*, abridged ed., 3 Vols. (New York: Warner Books, 1973, 1975), III, 138-43.

²⁴See Darcy O'Brien, *Two of a Kind: The Hillside Stranglers* (New York: New American Library, 1985). O'Brien claims that he has "reconstructed several of the stranglings and their accompanying brutalities in precise detail" so that the reader can understand the legal and psychiatric melodrama which followed upon them. But these "reconstructions" are definitively pornographic in tone, grotesquely taking the reader "inside" the experiences of Bianchi and Buono.

²⁵On July 4, 1985 Nikki Craft and Melissa Farley, co-founders of Citizens for Media Responsibility, were arrested for tearing up copies of *Penthouse* in several Provincetown stores. They and others have ripped up copies of *Penthouse* in nineteen communities, mostly in the Midwest, in retaliation for the December 1984 issue which featured the Asian women in bondage. Craft connects that issue with the murder of the Chinese girl in North Carolina. See *Sojurner*, (Boston) Oct. 1985, p. 12. See also an interview with Craft in *off our backs*, (Washington, D.C.) July 1985.

²⁶"The Random Killers," *Newsweek*, 26 Nov. 1984, p. 105.

²⁷ *New York Daily News*, 7 Aug. 1983, cited in *Newsreport* (Women Against Pornography), 5, No. 2 (Fall/Winter 1983), 5.

²⁸See "Journey of Terror," *People Weekly*, 30 April 1984, pp. 38-43.

²⁹"Two Ex-Convicts Facing Charges in California in Slayings of Five Girls," *New York Times*, 16 Feb. 1980, Sec. 1, p. 8, col. 5; for more detail see Jack Levin and James Alan Fox, *Mass Murder: America's Growing Menace* (New York: Plenum Press, 1985), pp. 65-68.

³⁰"List of possible California murder victims grows," *Boston Globe*, 12 June 1985, p. 10, col. 3; the statement about the horror film is from Sheriff Claude Ballard and is cited in the *New York Daily News*, 10 June 1985, p. 2, col. 1. See also Wallace Turner, "Torture Site May Yield Just 4 Dead, Officials Say," *New York Times*, Sec. A, p. 12, col. 4. This article reveals that Lake's former wife returned to the cabin after his death in order to obtain some videotapes which, police said, showed her and Lake when they were still married. We might assume that Lake's interest in making and acting out pornography pre-dated his actual torture and murder of strangers.

³¹Stephen G. Michaud and Hugh Aynesworth, *The Only Living Witness* (New York: Linden Press, Simon and Schuster, 1983), p. 117.

³²See the proceedings of the hearings on the effects of pornography conducted in Minneapolis, 1983, reported on in *Women Against Pornography Newsreport*, 6, No. 1 (Spring/Summer 1984). See also Linda Marchiano's (formerly Linda Lovelace) account of her years of coercion in the pornography industry, Linda Lovelace, with Mike McGrady, *Ordeal* (Secaucus, N.J.: Citadel Press, 1980). In *Female Sexual Slavery*, pp. 84-5, Kathleen Barry reports that the California Attorney General's Advisory Committee on Obscenity and Pornography determined that some producers of child pornography are actually child molesters who make photographs of their victims and sell and distribute them. Andrea Dworkin (speech, Harvard University, Oct. 29,

1985) reported that rape crisis centers report an increased use of cameras during rape. As she put it, there is now a "profit motive for rape." Clearly the information is only just beginning to be gathered on how much of pornography is a *record* of real, not simulated, acts of physical abuse, rape, and even murder as in the snuff film. The conventional degradation of women in pornography is, of course, always real.

[33]Barry, p. 175.

[34]Montague Summers, Introd., *The Malleus Maleficarum*, by Heinrich Kramer and James Sprenger (c. 1928; New York: Dover, 1971), p. xix, note. This passage is cited by Mary Daly in *Gyn/Ecology*: The Metaethics of Radical feminism (Boston: Beacon Press, 1978), p. 193, note, where she states that such destruction by imagery is what is done to women by men through the mass production of "pin-up girls," *Playboy* centerfolds, et cetera, ad nauseum. These mutilate and destroy women's image, and the *intent* of this technological voodoo is to effect the *death* of the female-identified Self."

[35]This characteristic conundrum was epitomized in the controversy surrounding the 1975 film *Snuff*. The film was advertised as depicting the actual death of a woman— "Made in South America Where Life Is Cheap!" Later, the murder in that particular film was shown to have been simulated. For feminist commentary on that film see Beverly Labelle, "*Snuff*—the *Ultimate* in Woman-Hating," in *Take Back the Night: Women on Pornography*, ed. Laura Lederer (New York: Morrow, 1980); Dorchen Leidholdt, "Coalition Stops 'Snuff'," *Newsreport* (Women Against Pornography), 5, No. 2 (Fall/Winter 1983), 1, and in that same issue Lesley Rimmel, "Seeing 'Snuff.' " For a rundown on the snuff-type film in contemporary slasher/horror films see Don Howland, "The Great Snuff Movie Hoax," *Fear of Darkness*, Summer 1982, pp. 31-34. Howland is loudly antifeminist, claiming that anyone would know the murder in *Snuff* was faked, and deploring all the controversy that film raised.

[36]Morneau and Rockwell, p. 213.

[37]Walter Benjamin, "The Work of Art in the Age of Mechanical Reproduction," in *Illuminations*, ed. and with an Introd. by Hannah Arendt, trans. Harry Zohn (New York: Schocken, 1969), pp. 219-53, esp. 224.

[38]Marshall McLuhan, *Understanding Media: The Extensions of Man* (New York: McGraw-Hill, 1964).

[39]Sontag, pp. 14-15, 24.

[40]The Vapors, "Turning Japanese," *New Clear Days*, UAR, LT-1049, 1980.

[41]David Thompson, "The Director as Raging Bull," *Film Comment*, Jan./Feb. 1978, pp. 9-15.

[42]For a New definition of *eyeballer* see Mary Daly in Cahoots with Jane Caputi, *Websters' First New Intergalactic Wickedary of the English Language*, forthcoming, Beacon Press, 1987.

[43]Bert Stern, "The Last Sitting," *Vogue*, Sept. 1982, pp. 512-25, 578-83.

[44]For video visions of Marilyn Monroe as photograph see the music video which has consistently been voted the most popular ever on MTV, Def Leppard's "Photograph" (David Mallet, 1983). The words to this song, and the images in the video, are not necessarily logical, but are purely evocative. The boys wail that they can't really *have* their fantasy, Monroe, in the flesh, but only in a photograph. A woman dressed up as Monroe is shown being strangled to death; newspaper headlines flash out the news of a "Passion Killer." A refrain whines, "I want to touch you." On the word *touch*, we see a switchblade knife opening. Women in cages look on

as the boys stroke their guitars and sing. The pseudo-Monroe seems to return from her strangling death to suggest a *vagina dentata*-like threat, but the last image of the video shows her in black lingerie, bound and lashed with barbed wire.

For commentary on the abuse of Marilyn Monroe in image, see Susan Griffin, *Pornography and Silence*, pp. 204-17. See also David Thompson, "Baby Go Boom," *Film Comment*, 18 (Sept./Oct. 1982), 34-41.

[45]This is quoted in a brochure publicizing *Peeping Tom* which is issued by the film's distributor, Corinth Films of New York, c. 1979.

[46]The quote from Powell is cited by Elliot Stein, "'A Very Nice Film, A Very Tender One,' " printed in the brochure issued by Corinth films, c. 1979.

[47]See Francois Truffaut, *Hitchcock* (New York: Simon and Schuster, 1971), p. 204.

[48]Raymond Durgnat, "Inside Norman Bates," in *Great Film Directors: A Critical Anthology*, ed. Leo Braudy and Morris Dickstein (New York: Oxford, 1978), pp. 496-506, esp. 499. This essay appeared originally in Raymond Durgnat, *Films and Feelings* (Cambridge, Mass.: MIT Press, 1967).

[49]One of the most outrageous examples of this convention is a scene in *The Toolbox Murders* (Dennis Donnely, 1978). In this scene, a naked woman sits in a bathtub and slowly masturbates. Just as she reaches orgasm, the masked killer enters the room. He chases her around the apartment and finally kills her.

[50]See, for example, the criticism of William Rothman, *Hitchcock: the Murderous Gaze* (Cambridge, Mass.: Harvard University Press, 1982).

[51]Truffaut, p. 211.

[52]Simone de Beauvoir, *The Second Sex* (c. 1952: New York: Knopf, 1971), cited in Catharine A. MacKinnon, "Feminism, Marxism, Method, and the State: An Agenda for Theory," *Signs: Journal of Women in Culture and Society*, 7, No. 3 (Spring 1982), 515-44, esp. 537-38.

[53]Sontag, p. 14.

[54]Michaud and Aynesworth, p. 123.

[55]Quoted in Marj Von Beroldingen, "I Was the Hunter and They Were the Victims," *Front Page Detective*, March 1974, pp. 29-55, esp. 30.

[56]John Berger, *Ways of Seeing* (London: The BBC and Penguin Books, 1972), pp. 46-47.

[57]Laura Mulvey, "Visual Pleasure and Narrative Cinema," *Screen*, 16, No. 3 (1975), 6-18. This article is reprinted in Gerald Mast and Marshall Cohen, eds., *Film Theory and Criticism*, 3rd ed (New York: Oxford University Press, 1985), pp. 801-16.

[58]Susan Gubar, " 'The Blank Page' and the Issues of Female Creativity," *Critical Inquiry*, 8, No. 2 (Winter 1981), 243-63.

[59]Benjamin, p. 223.

[60]Marshall McLuhan, *The Mechanical Bride: Folklore of Industrial Man* (Boston: Beacon Press 1951). See particularly pp. 93-101.

[61]Michaud and Aynesworth, p. 130.

[62]As Andrea Dworkin analyzes the classic fairy tale: "Snow-white was already dead when the heroic prince fell in love with her. 'I beseech you,' he pleaded with the 7 dwarfs, 'to give it to me, for I cannot live without looking upon Snow-white.' It awake was not readily distinguishable from it asleep." Andrea Dworkin, *Woman Hating* (New York: Dutton, 1974), p. 42.

[63]Irving Berlin, "The Girl on the Magazine Cover," from the film *Easter Parade* (Charles Walters, 1948).

[64]Van Halen, "I'll Wait," *1984*, Warner Bros., 23985-1, 1984.

[65]Quoted in Donald T. Lunde, *Murder and Madness* (Stanford, Calif.: Stanford Alumni Association, 1975), p. 55.

[66]The Mills Brothers, "Paper Doll," *Mills Brothers Greatest Hits*, Dot, DLP25257, 1943.

[67]de Beauvoir, p. 267.

[68]For commentary on the myth of Pandora see Jane Ellen Harrison, *Mythology* (London: Longmans Green, 1924), pp. 50-51. For commentary on "Barbie," see Marilyn Ferris Motz, " 'I Want to be A Barbie Doll When I Grow Up': The Cultural Significance of the Barbie Doll," in *The Popular Culture Reader*, 3rd edition, ed. Christopher D. Geist and Jack Nachbar (Bowling Green, Ohio: Bowling Green University Popular Press, 1983), pp. 122-36.

[69]Griffin, p. 40.

[70]Villiers de l'Isle Adam, *The Future Eve*, 1887. Although I have not been able to get this book, it is referred to and quoted from in Edmund Bergler, *Fashion and the Unconscious* (New York: Robert Brunner, 1953), pp. 271-72.

[71]Ira Levin, *The Stepford Wives* (New York: Random House, 1972). See also the film directed by Bryan Forbes, 1974.

[72]See Phyllis and Eberhard Kronhausen, *Erotic Fantasies: A Study of the Sexual Imagination* (New York: Grove Press, 1969). *La Femme Endormie* is by "Madame B——————, Avocat" (Paris [?]: J. Renold, 1899), and is excepted on pp. 362-84. The advertisement for the "Female Belly" is on p. 387. See also Griffin's discussion in *Pornography and Silence*, pp. 42-45.

[73]A terrible story is told by Lady Aberconway, daughter of Melville McNaughten, one of the police investigators of the original Jack the Ripper case. She says that when she was a child, her father took her to Scotland Yard one Sunday after church. "Suddenly all hell broke loose as she was discovered looking through some photographs [of Ripper victims] which had been left unlocked and were snatched away. 'But to me,' she said, 'the mutilated bodies looked just like broken dolls.' " See Daniel Farsen, *Jack the Ripper* (London: Michael Joseph, 1972), p. 49.

[74]R. Donovan, "That friend of your wife called Dior," *Colliers*, 10 June 1955, pp. 34-9.

[75]Andrea Dworkin writes: "Women are reared, and often forced, to conform to the specific requirements of ideal beauty, whatever they are at any given time. From foot-binding to waist binding, ideal beauty often requires deforming of the natural body. From clitoridectomy to breast enlargement or reduction to surgically altered noses, ideal beauty often requires mutilation of the natural body." See *Pornography, Men Possessing Women*, pp. 116-17.

[76]For information see Nancy Hall-Duncan, *The History of Fashion Photography* (New York: Alpine, 1979); Rose De Neve, "The Fashion Photo: From Cool to Kinky and How it Got There," *Print*, July/August, 1976, pp. 24-32; "Fashion's Kinky Look," *Newsweek*, 4 Oct. 1976, pp. 98-99.

[77]Edward Behr, Introd. to Helmut Newton,*Sleepless Nights* (New York: Congreve, 1978), unpaged.

[78]We need not look only to the signatured *avant-garde* to observe these motifs. They also appear in the most seemingly innocuous of ads. One for Rutledge nightgowns *(Mademoiselle)*, March 1975 groups five women in a store window. A man roams among the motionless women, arranging their gowns. The copy reads: "If you happen to wake up one morning in the window of your favorite story, don't

worry, you'll look terrific." That advice, again, sounds something like, "If you're raped, lie back and enjoy it" and like that phrase, it is also a veiled threat. See also the pictorial campaign for Dior eyeglasses (late 1970s). In one ad, seven heads are grouped around in a clock-like circle. At least one of the figures is a real woman; the rest range from obvious mannequins to one ambiguous figure (*Vogue*, July 1977). For other illustrations of Newton's deliberate mixture of living women and artificial dummies see his *White Women* (New York: Congreve, 1976), as well as a fashion spread for "Saint Laurent—*rive gauche*" in *Vogue*, Sept. 1982. Another celebrated fashion photographer, Guy Bourdin does much the same in his photo essay, "Woman Now," *Vogue*, August 1979, pp. 109-13.

[79]See "A Living Mannequin Startling Shoppers," *New York Times*, 13 Dec. 1977.

[80]This is the opinion of Robert Benzio of Saks Fifth Avenue, New York. See "They Find Right Face—Then Create a Mannequin to Resemble It," *New York Times*, 28 Nov. 1977, Sec. A, p. 38, col. 1.

[81]Lunde, p. 61.

[82]Irving Berlin, "The Girl that I Marry,"from the film *Annie Get Your Gun* (dir. George Sidney, 1950).

[83]"Girl Machine," written by Warner (Alfred) Weidler, sung by Johnny Walsh, Warner Brothers 5196 (DX11, 762), 1961.

[84]This ad appeared in *Nuclear News Buyer's Guide*, Mid-February, 1976, a trade magazine for the nuclear industry.

[85]Laurie Anderson, "It Tango," *Big Science*, Warner Bros., BSK 3674, 1981.

[86]McLuhan, *Mechanical Bride*, p. 101.

[87]*Ibid.*

[88]"Tame," *Glamour*, Sept. 1979; Almay, *Vogue*, Sept. 1981; Yves Saint Laurent, *Vogue*, Feb. 1980; Bourdin, *Vogue*, Oct. 1979.

[89]These are the words of James Lawson, convicted with James Russell Odom, for a lust murder in Columbia, S.C., 1975. Quoted in Hazelwood and Douglas, p. 21.

[90]See Hazelwood and Douglas, p. 18.

[91]*Fembot* is a word coined on the show, *The Bionic Woman* (ABC, 1976) to name some female robots created by a mad scientist, robots who were indistinguishable replicas of our heroine's best friends (a heroine, who was herself part artificial). Mary Daly initiated use of this word to designate the patriarchal ideal of the numbed and dumbed woman. For a definition of *fembot* see Daly and Caputi, *Websters' First New Intergalactic Wickedary of the English Language*.

[92]William J. Broad, "The Young Physicists: Atoms and Patriotism among the Coke Bottles," *New York Times*, 31 January 1984, National ed. p. 17, col. 2.

[93]The most prominent of these five fathers is Glenn Seaborg who is wont to describe plutonium as a "bad child."

[94]See James Agee's discussion of Chaplin in his article, "Comedy's Greatest Era," in *Agee on Film: Reviews and Comments by James Agee* (London: Peter Owen Limited, 1963), pp. 2-19, as well as his analysis of *Monsieur Verdoux*, pp. 252-62.

[95]Stephen King, *The Dead Zone* (New York: Viking Press, 1979). See also the film by David Cronnenberg, 1983.

[96]The Eurythmics, "Love is a Stranger," words and music by A. Lennox and D. Stewart, *Sweet Dreams are Made of This*, RCA AFL1-4681, 1983.

[97]A picture of a woman wearing a T-shirt with this slogan illustrated by linked male and female symbols, appeared in Ann McMullen, "American Women Back the

Atom," *Electrical Review* 201, No. 19 (11 Nov., 1977).

[98]Benjamin, p. 244.

[99]Robert Jay Lifton and Richard Falk, *Indefensible Weapons: The Political and Psychological Case Against Nuclearism* (New York: Basic Books, 1982), pp. 76-78.

[100]William L. Laurence, "Atomic Bombing of Nagasaki Told By Flight Member," *New York Times*, 9 Sept. 1945, Sec. 1, p. 1, col. 4.

[101]See for example, Arthur Clarke's classic science fiction story, *Childhood's End* (New York: Ballantine, 1953). This posits a human evolution which results in all children under the age of eleven or so merging into a collective mind and emigrating from the Earth. Then, the planet—along with all the obsolete adults and every other living being on it—blows up. This is, according to the logic of the story, a happy ending. Most exemplary in popular religion is the Hal Lindsay phenomenon, epitomized by the title of his first best seller (with C.C. Carlson), *The Late Great Planet Earth* (Toronto: Bantam, 1970), in which the coming Armageddon and destruction of the Earth is rapturously prophesied.

[102]Carolyn Merchant, *The Death of Nature: Women, Ecology and the Scientific Revolution* (San Francisco: Harper and Row, 1980), pp. 164-72.

Epilogue

[1]Annie McCombs, "A Letter *Ms.* Didn't Print," *Lesbian Ethics*, 1, No. 3 (1985), 85-88, esp. 87.

[2]Ntozake Shange, "otherwise i would think it odd to have rape prevention month (2)," *The Black Scholar*, 10, No. 8-9 (May-June 1979), 29-30, esp. 30.

[3]See Robert Jay Lifton, *Death in Life: Survivors of Hiroshima* (New York: Simon and Schuster, Touchstone Books, 1967). See also Robert Jay Lifton and Richard Falk, *Indefensible Weapons: The Political and Psychological Case Against Nuclearism* (New York: Basic Books, 1982).

[4]Mary Daly, *Gyn/Ecology: The Metaethics of Radical Feminism* (Boston: Beacon Press, 1978), pp. 107-112, 130-33.

[5]For an extraordinarily blatant rendition of this motif see Will Haygood, "A devil brings fear to the City of Angels," *Boston Globe*, 15 June 1986, Sec. A, p. 1, col. 2.

[6]"Sex and Violence: Pornography Hurts," *Science News*, 118 (13 Sept. 1980), 166-72.

[7]See Steven Egger, "A Working Definition of Serial Murder and the Reduction of Linkage Blindness," *Journal of Police Science and Administration*, 12, No. 3 (1984), 348-357, esp. 351.

[8]Jack Levin and James Alan Fox, *Mass Murder: America's Growing Menace* (New York: Plenum Press, 1985), p. 53.

[9]*Nemesis*, name of the Goddess of Divine Retribution, is invoked by Mary Daly to name a Virtue which is beyond patriarchal "justice." The word *be-ing* also figures prominently in her philosophy and is a verb signifying participation in Ultimate/Intimate Reality. See Mary Daly, *Pure Lust: Elemental Feminist Philosophy* (Boston: Beacon Press, 1984), esp. pp. 2n, 221, 275-80. See also Mary Daly with Jane Caputi, *Websters' First New Intergalactic Wickedary of the English Language* (forthcoming, Beacon Press, 1987).

Index